THE ALTAR CALL

Its Origins and Present Usage

David Bennett

University Press of America,® Inc.
Lanham · New York · Oxford

Copyright © 2000 by
University Press of America,® Inc.
4720 Boston Way
Lanham, Maryland 20706

12 Hid's Copse Rd.
Cumnor Hill, Oxford OX2 9JJ

Library of Congress Cataloging-in-Publication Data

Bennett, David.
The altar call : its origins and present usage / David Bennett.
p.   cm.
Includes bibliographical references and index.
1. Evangelistic invitations—History of doctrines. I. Title.
BV3793.B42   2000   265'.9—dc21   00-062916 CIP

ISBN 0-7618-1839-1 (cloth: alk. ppr.)

㊛™The paper used in this publication meets the minimum
requirements of American National Standard for Information
Sciences—Permanence of Paper for Printed Library Materials,
ANSI Z39.48—1984

Contents

Part Two

Foreword

David Bennett's history of the altar call is the best sort of engaged history. Many historians have commented on the practice of inviting serious inquirers to the front after a service of Christian proclamation as a part of making a decision for Christ. Until this time, however, no one has worked out the history of the practice so well, and only a few have evaluated its theological significance as carefully as it is evaluated here.

Because Bennett's research has been thorough, his historical sleuthing should be of interest to anyone with the least interest for whatever reason in the antecedents, development, and current use of the altar call. Of special importance is his exhaustive pursuit of this most interesting question: if John Wesley, George Whitefield, and Jonathan Edwards are regarded as the great figures of modern evangelicalism, why did none of these important leaders practice the invitation system that became so important in so many later evangelical groups?

Bennett's historical discussion is especially striking because it is so fair. Historical work driven by theological concerns (as this one clearly is) is often tendentious and selective in use of sources. This book, by contrast, works doubly hard at reading sources as charitably as possible. That feature allows readers to get much closer to what the historical actors may have been trying to do than does historical work where the theological conclusions control what counts as evidence.

A particular strength of this book's history is that its careful work extends to three continents. I especially appreciated the material on early Australian church history, since that subject remains (alas) mostly terra incognita to myself and other North Americans. The judicious use of contemporary surveys adds considerable contemporary value to the book's solid historical basis.

As history written by someone with definite opinions about the subject under consideration, this volume's value goes well beyond the merely historical. Bennett is a sympathetic historian, yet it is also clear that he has his doubts about the invitation system, either because of abuses from which it has suffered or because of the theology implied in its use. Because, however, Bennett sets out his theological reasoning clearly and tries to present alternative interpretations fairly, the book should be as stimulating for those who fully embrace use of the altar call as for those (like Bennett) who see real problems in its use. Regardless of personal theological conclusions about the wisdom of the invitation system, much of what Bennett has to say about it should provoke deeper reflection. His analysis in chapter 15, for example, of the altar call as a kind of evangelical sacrament is only one of the many telling insights that should make all readers pause for careful thought.

In sum, the combination of historical and practical reasoning found in this one volume makes for unusually stimulating reading. For me the history was most compelling, but I suspect others may resonate more with the author's own survey research, his canvassing of pertinent biblical matters, and his discussions of practicalities with respect to worship services. From whichever angle one approaches the book, rewards are there for the taking. It would be a cheap trick to ask readers to "come forward" for the enjoyment of this volume, but they may be urged to do so nonetheless.

Mark Noll
McManis Professor of Christian Thought
Wheaton College

June 2000

Preface

The Altar Call: Its Origins and Present Usage is a revision of my 1997 M.Th. thesis, through the Australian College of Theology, Sydney, entitled *The Public Invitation System in Evangelism*. The idea for this work grew out of a host of experiences gained from attending and working in evangelical churches, and assisting in various evangelistic endeavors, both those based in the local church and those with a larger scope.

The first such experience was the confusion I often felt in my teenage years in England when public invitations were given both in the Methodist church in which I grew up and also in larger denominational and inter-denominational meetings. The practice did not seem to match the doctrine I was being taught. The teaching was that we are saved by grace through faith, not by works. The practice was, upon invitation, to move forward and receive Christ. I responded to these events by asking myself some questions, which I then endeavored to answer. The first one was, "Did this moving forward save?" "No!" came my silent reply, "For one is saved by grace through faith, not works." Yet the wording of some of these invitations gave the impression that it did save. Then came the second question: "What was the point of going forward if it didn't save?" I could not think of a satisfactory answer to that question. The practice then seemed at variance with the doctrine, and to some degree still does.

Over the years I noticed that many who responded to public invitations showed little, and sometimes no, overt evidence of a genuine work of grace. Some did not seem to even begin the Christian life, others made, what appeared, a half-hearted attempt and then fell away. Once more I found the situation rather confusing, and began to wonder if there was something wrong with this method of evangelism.

vii

I also noticed that prolonged and, at times, very emotional appeals were not uncommon. There were even some invitations that did not seem honest. In addition at the first counselor training classes I ever attended (in 1961), counselors were clearly told to move forward immediately the invitation was given, to encourage seekers to do the same. This struck me as being rather devious. These things caused me to question the method more and more.

In my reading over the years I noticed that John Wesley, whose life stretched throughout most of the eighteenth century, did not seem to use the public invitation system. Yet William Booth, who was rooted in the Wesleyan tradition, quite clearly did by the middle of the next century. Once more questions arose: "When did this practice begin? Who began it, and how, and why?" None of the books I read ever seemed to answer these questions properly, and though a couple named Charles Finney as the originator, they gave little information. So the origins of the method remained clouded in mystery. It seemed to me that researching this matter, about which so little seemed to be known, would be a valuable project. This book is the result.

It is disturbing to note that when I told the members of the home group to which I then belonged about my intention to research this topic, nearly every member of this evangelical group began to complain about what they considered abuses of the system. The major reported abuses were: prolonged invitations, and those that seemed dishonest. The system they accepted, but the abuses they did not. This confirmed that this subject did need researching, and that some time should also be spent in looking at its use today.

Acknowledgments

No work of this nature is done without the help of many people, and to all those who rendered assistance, however small, I am most appreciative. First I would like to acknowledge my debt to my predecessors in research into this subject. Though few books seem to have been written about the altar call, and none specifically about its origins, there have been four dissertations that have investigated the subject generally. Though these are varied in quality and coverage, they have all been helpful in providing a foundation upon which to build. My thanks go first, then, to H.R. McLendon, H.G. Olive, W.O. Thompson Jr., and R. Alan Streett.

Secondly, my thanks go to my friends in my old home group, who, without knowing it at the time, assured that this thesis would have a wider scope than first intended.

I would also like to acknowledge the help of the staff of the following libraries and archives: the libraries of the Baptist College of Ministries, the Bible College of Queensland, Kenmore Christian College, Trinity College and the University of Queensland, and the Baptist Archives, Queensland, all in Brisbane; and the Mitchell Library and the Uniting Church in Australia Church Records & Historical Society, in Sydney. Libraries overseas have also been of assistance, most notably the Evangelical Library in London. Others to assist have been the B.L. Fisher Library of Asbury Theological Seminary, the California Graduate School of Theology, the library of Southern Baptist Theological Seminary, and the A. Webb Roberts Library of Southwestern Baptist Theological Seminary, all in America. St. Stephen's Anglican Church, Coorparoo also loaned me a video, and the Billy Graham Evangelistic Association of Minneapolis were very helpful in supplying statistics and other information.

Many individuals have also helped in a variety of ways. First, are

ix

the hundreds of ministers, pastors and church officials who responded to my surveys. The response far exceeded my expectations. Cameron Beahan, Bob Evans, Ken Newton, Stuart Piggin, John Thallon and Preston Walker have all loaned me books or other materials. Douglas Anderson, Frank Baker, John Blanchard, Jim Bramlett, Larry Eskridge, Austin Hukins, Erroll Hulse, Margaret Lamb, Iain Murray, H.G. Olive, Walter Phillips, Judson Polling, Don Prout, David L. Russell, Richard Saxby, J. Clifford Tharp Jr, John A. Vickers, Sir Alan Walker, Rowland Ward, and Graham Warne have all responded to my requests for information. Thanks also go to Ray Bickerstaff, "Bill" (who wished to remain anonymous), Eric Clancy and Jim Rawson who were interviewed or cooperated in more informal conversations.

Acknowledgement should also be given to Jeanette Lewis, who photocopied a mountain of material for me, Bryan Stone, who advertised on my behalf on his Christian Theology Page on the Internet, David McDougall and Robin McNicol who both assisted in a number of ways, and Darryl Stringer who read the manuscript. My thanks also go to the readers of my original thesis Ken Manley and Mark Noll. They made some helpful suggestions, a number of which have been incorporated into this book. I also thank Professor Noll for writing the foreword. My thanks also go to my thesis supervisor, Mark Hutchinson, whose criticisms, encouragement and guidance have all been very helpful

I would also like to thank my fellow booksellers, some of whom have been extraordinarily helpful. They include Archives, Keswick and Koorong in Australia and Dove, Kregel and Stroud in America.

I have also greatly appreciated the help of the staff of the University Press of America, expecially Diana Lavery and Helen Hudson.

Last, but most certainly not least, I am delighted to acknowledge the patience, support and encouragement of my family who have been a marvelous help while I have been working on this project, so my loving thanks go to Claire, Keith and Lynne. I dedicate this book to them, with the prayer that it will be of great use in the proclamation of the good news of Jesus Christ.

David Bennett,
Brisbane
     July 2000

Extracts from "Queensland Baptists in the Nineteenth Century" by Les Ball and "The Light Beneath the Cross Grew Dim", by Rev. John E. Mavor are reprinted with the permission of the authors. Extracts from "The Mourner's Bench" by H.R. McLendon and "The Development of the Evangelistic Invitation" by Howard G. Olive are quoted by permission of the Southern Baptist Theological Seminary. Quotations from the book *The Effective Invitation* by R. Alan Streett are used by permission of Kregel Publications.

The comments of Jim Bramlett on pages 218-19, Erroll Hulse on pages 198 and 223, David McDougall on pages 221-22, John Vickers on pages 3-4,.are reprinted with their permission.

Background material on "Festival '96 with Franklin Graham" and other observations on mass evangelism given by Jim Rawson are quoted with his permission.

The extracts from the Broadcasts of "Festival '96 with Franklin Graham" on pages 169-172 and 201 are printed with the permission of Family Radio.

Statistics from *Reaching People: A Study of Witnessers and NonWitnessers: Pilot Study Phase* on pages by H. Joe Denney are used by permission of the Southern Baptist Convention.

Scriptures are taken from the Holy Bible, New International Version; Copyright 1973, 1978, and 1984, International Bible Society. Used by permission of Zondervan Bible Publishers.

Introduction

The figure of Billy Graham stands on a platform in the enormous stadium. In one part of the arena is an enlarged projection of him on a massive screen. There is a strange hush and an air of expectancy as Graham concludes his sermon and the meeting reaches its climax. "I want you to move from where you are standing and walk to the front of the stadium..." he challenges, his voice echoing around the stands. Then, as music is played, people begin to move forward. There are few at first, but the movement begins to increase and spread until seemingly hundreds of men, women and children are walking forward from all parts of the arena.

This scene, or similar ones on a smaller scale, perhaps at a local church, is very familiar to anyone who has moved regularly in evangelical Christian circles. The request to make "A public confession for Christ", by moving to the front of the scene of evangelism or by indicating in some other visible or audible way, frequently concludes a church service or meeting in an evangelistic crusade. Variously described as the "appeal", the "invitation", or the "altar call", it has become systematized and is regarded by many as a vital part of evangelism, and in some churches is even an integral part of regular worship.

How did this practice of inviting people forward to receive Christ start? Is it of ancient vintage, perhaps with biblical example and support, or are its origins more recent, perhaps with no, or little, biblical warrant? Is it essential to evangelism, a useful addition to it, or could it be a hindrance in the task of winning people to Christ? *The Altar Call: Its Origins and Present Usage* will seek to answer these questions and many others that stem from them.

The book is in two parts. The first examines what appear to be the origins of the altar call, its early history and development into a system in America, Britain and Australia up until the death of one of its major practitioners, D.L. Moody, at the end of the nineteenth century. From that time the method was set firm in the evangelical mind, and from then the questioning of its validity was often viewed with suspicion. The second part looks at how the altar call is used as an evangelistic tool today, examines the rationale for its usage, investigates the counseling methods used in connection with it, and, more briefly, follow up. It also examines the claimed results of this form of evangelism, assesses some criticisms of it, and makes some recommendations. As conversion to Christ is at the hub of the practice, indeed, the primary reason for its existence, this also is examined.

Even in what appear to be its early days the altar call was used for reasons other than the need for, or witness to, conversion. It was often used, for example, for those who desired a specific experience of holiness or for some form of rededication. In our time, this has extended to inviting people forward for such matters as healing and the need of counseling for all sorts of problems such as marriage breakup. This book will look primarily at the altar call as a method of evangelism, though some observations will be made about its wider usage.

Though one cannot discount the possibility of isolated uses of the public invitation in the first sixteen hundred years of church history, there appears to be no justification for believing that the practice was common during those centuries, and may never have been used at all. Certainly, for most of that period the bulk of the church was either calvinistic or sacramentalist, and it would seem unlikely that this form of evangelism would have found favor with either party. Calvinists strongly emphasized the role of God, rather than the convert in Christian conversion, and one would not expect to find them using a form of evangelism which so strongly emphasized human response. In the case of sacramentalists, if grace conveyed through baptism marks the entry into the church, then there is little room left for a distinct conversion experience. Thus it would seem unlikely that this method of evangelism was used prior to the eighteenth century, at least not in a regular or systematic way. Some research was done into the practices of the Anabaptists (sixteenth century) and the early Baptists (seventeenth century), on the grounds that something akin to the altar call might have been used by them in their efforts to identify suitable candidates for baptism, but nothing was found to indicate such a practice. Neither

xiv

has any other solid evidence of it being used by anybody else prior to the eighteenth century been discovered.

Yet, the altar call was in regular usage well before the middle of the nineteenth century for it had passed into folklore by that time. As early as 1845 American humorist, Johnson J. Hooper parodied the evangelistic invitation in a secular Alabamian newspaper. Hooper tells in a short story of personal workers scattered around a Christian camp-meeting waiting to go to work on potential converts and their half leading, half dragging the hero to "the mourner's bench". It is clear that the writer expects his readers to be familiar with the practice, indeed, to be able to empathize with the "victim".[1]

The origins of the altar call, at least its usage in a systematic fashion, are often laid at the door of nineteenth century American evangelist, Charles Grandison Finney.[2] It shall be seen, however, that though he was the first to give an articulate rationale for the practice and was an impetus to its wide acceptance, appeals, even regular ones, for the public confession of Christ had been going on for some time before his ministry, on both sides of the Atlantic. Some go further back and say that the practice began with, or was popularized by, John Wesley, the founder of the Methodist Church, in Britain in the eighteenth century.[3] Yet, as will be shown in chapter one, this is not based on any sound evidence.

It seems most apt to begin this investigation by studying the Wesleyan Revival in Britain and the Great Awakening in America during the eighteenth century. As part of this the evangelistic practices of John Wesley, George Whitefield and Jonathan Edwards, three of the great evangelists of that era, will be examined. A good case can be made for adopting their practices today. True we live in very different times, and some adaptions are necessary, but humanity's fundamental condition has not altered nor has God changed. After the specific examination of Wesley, Whitefield and Edwards, a more general look will be taken at what was happening during those great eighteenth century revivals.

Definitions

It is necessary at this point to establish what is meant in this book by the terms "altar call", "public invitation" and "public appeal", these three phrases being here regarded as synonyms. The systematic use of the altar call is defined as:

A method of evangelism, within which a regular or frequent, planned invitation is given to "unbelievers" to respond to Jesus Christ publicly at the conclusion of a sermon or other gospel presentation, in such ways as: calling out a response, raising a hand, standing, or walking to a designated spot in the evangelistic setting. A response to such an invitation would normally be followed by immediate counseling and later by some form of follow up. It often incorporates an appeal to Christians for such issues as rededication and call to mission. It is not a theology, though it does reflect and support particular theologies.

As noted in that definition the field of reference is wider than just the method of inviting people forward, and includes invitations where people might be requested to just raise a hand or make some other identifiable public response. The key issues are that there must be an invitation for a public response, and that any response to that invitation must, indeed, be public.

Chapter thirteen discusses the subject of Christian conversion, and as conversion is so crucial to the subject of the altar call it is also necessary to define conversion here.

Christian conversion is the life changing experience of a person turning from sin and self to Christ in repentance and faith. This is only made possible by the prior gracious activity of God in regeneration.

Notes

[1] Frank Muir (ed), *The Oxford Book of Humorous Prose* (Oxford: OUP, 1992), 220-26. This story is one of a series by Johnson J. Hooper which appeared in the *East Alabamian*, under the title "Some Adventures of Captain Simon Suggs, Late of the Tallapoosa Volunteers", 1845.

[2] D. Martyn Lloyd-Jones, *Preaching and Preachers* (London: Hodder, 1971), 270; J.I. Packer, *Among God's Giants* (Eastbourne: Kingsway, 1991), 385.

[3] C. E. Autrey, *Basic Evangelism* (Grand Rapids: Zondervan, 1959), 130; R. Alan Streett, *The Effective Invitation* (Grand Rapids: Kregel, [1984] 1995), 91-92. Streett's book is based on his Ph.D. thesis: "The Public Invitation: Its Nature, Biblical Validity and Practicability" (California Graduate School of Theology, 1982). The differences between the two are not major, though they are sometimes significant. The book also has an extra chapter: "Inviting Children to Christ".

Part One

Chapter 1

Wesley, Whitefield and Edwards[1]

If one accepts that the altar call was not used prior to the eighteenth century, and, as has already been stated, it does not seem to have been, with the possible exceptions of isolated incidents, it becomes necessary to ask, did the great evangelists of the seventeen hundreds use it? To answer that question the evangelistic practices of three major evangelists, John Wesley, George Whitefield and Jonathan Edwards will be examined. They will be considered at length for three reasons: first, to determine whether they used the altar call or not; secondly, to discover what methods they did use; and, thirdly, that their methods might be considered as a guide for our evangelism.

In chapter five the theology of these three men will also be investigated, and the relevant theological changes which have occurred since their time will be traced. At this point it is sufficient to note that Wesley and Whitefield were Englishmen, clergy of the Church of England, whilst Edwards was an American Congregationalist. In addition, Whitefield and Edwards were calvinists, while Wesley was an arminian, but, as shall be detailed later, the relevant theology of all three was remarkably similar.

John Wesley (1703-1791)

John Wesley was the son of Samuel Wesley, the Anglican rector of Epworth in Lincolnshire, and his wife, Susanna. He too became a clergyman and went on a mission to Georgia in America, from which he returned in February 1738, regarding himself as a failure and not even a Christian. After contact with some Moravian Christians, most notably Peter Bohler, he had a conversion experience on 24 May 1738. He began outdoor preaching the next year at the suggestion of his friend George Whitefield, and burst upon the scene "like a whirlwind sent by God".[2] For the next fifty years he toured the British Isles preaching the gospel, seeing tens of thousands come to Christ, and founding the Methodist Church, though, even up until the day of his death, he thought of Methodism as still part of the Church of England. It is said that there were over 70 000 Methodists in Britain at the time of his death.

Wesley claimed that on occasions he preached to ten thousand, twenty thousand, and even over thirty thousand people, often for an hour or more. On 22 August 1773, at Gwenap Pit in Cornwall, the far western coastal county of England, he preached to a massive crowd which was by his calculation 32 000.[3] His estimates have often been regarded as exaggerations, and it is probably not unfair to think of him as a better preacher and organizer than he was mathematician, yet some of the crowds that heard him preach must have been very large indeed. Whitefield, as will be seen, also claimed enormous attendances at some of his outdoor preaching, indeed, even larger figures than Wesley. But the same doubts hang over his estimates. Yet even independent witnesses claimed very large crowds at Whitefield's meetings. The *Gentleman's Magazine* of 1739 "computed" a crowd of 20 000 at Kingswood, near Bristol, and in America Benjamin Franklin estimated that Whitefield's voice could be heard by over 30 000. Less precise, but none-the-less noteworthy, are such observations from eyewitnesses as "vast multitudes", "a prodigious concourse", and "a most numerous congregation" being present to hear him.[4] Throughout his long career the numbers John Wesley preached to must have totaled hundreds of thousands, perhaps even more, and this without the modern aids of gigantic halls, sports stadiums and microphones, and with a smaller population than exists today.

Claims about Wesley

Did John Wesley use the altar call, or anything similar to it? There are certainly those who claim that he did. For example, Dr. R. Alan Streett says a loud "Yes" to that question in his book *The Effective Invitation.* He says that Wesley used no less than four forms of "the public invitation". They are, first, that he "employed exhorters or personal workers to be on the look out for anxious souls". These exhorters would then approach the prospective convert and urge "him to make a decision immediately".[5] Secondly, seekers were invited "to attend the mid-week service where they were to join in the public prayers as an indication of their faith". Thirdly, that he invited "the seeker to step forward publicly and present himself for church membership". Lastly, that Wesley "reserved a pew" (sometimes called "the mourner's bench") at the front of each meeting house, which those anxious about their souls could move forward to occupy, that they might be counseled. Streett says, "it seems likely" that Wesley "was the first to practice the use of a mourner's bench".[6]

But is Streett right? Ironically, the source he quotes as indicating that Wesley used four methods of public invitation, pages 16 and 24 of a thesis by American pastor H. G. Olive, not only fails to give even one method Wesley used, but actually seems to conclude that Wesley did not use any form of the public invitation.[7]

Before we look further at Streett's claims, it is necessary to delete the second method he quotes, because it is outside this field of inquiry: inviting people to a mid week meeting where they could join in public prayer cannot fairly be considered a public invitation.

With regard to the idea of Wesley using exhorters to look out for those who needed spiritual counsel, Streett appears to be entirely wrong. He quotes Olive once more as the source for this,[8] but seems to completely misunderstand him. Olive is not talking about the practices of Wesley, but of some other Methodists in America.[9] In addition, a reading of Wesley's *Journal* from 1738 until his final entry in 1790 uncovers no example of such a practice. British Wesleyan authority, Dr. John A Vickers, when shown Streett's claim responded that he knows of no evidence contemporary with Wesley "to justify [this] picture of 'exhorters' waiting to pounce on any 'prospective' convert".[10] Similarly, Dr. Frank Baker, American-based Wesleyan scholar, stated that it is not true "that [Wesley] routinely seeded his gatherings with exhorters".[11] It would seem that on point one Dr. Streett is mistaken.

The third method Streett claims Wesley used was to invite people to step forward to present themselves for "church membership". Once more, here, Streett quotes Olive, and once again he seems to misread him. Olive is quoting from a letter written by a minister called William Burke, in which Burke claims that as a young man, in February 1791, he "went forward" at a Methodist meeting in America, when the preacher "opened the door to receive members".[12] Precisely what Burke meant by that will be discussed later, but for now it is enough to

note that it has nothing directly to do with Wesley. John Telford
records that on 25 February 1791, John Wesley "Returned to City Road
[London] to die", which he did a few days later.[13] Wesley had not put
foot on American soil since the 1730s.

    With Streett's final claim, Wesley's supposed use of the mourner's
bench, there once more seems no evidence to support it, and certainly
Streett quotes no source contemporary with Wesley. Instead he cites
C.E. Autrey's 1959 book *Basic Evangelism*. Autrey states that "we
know John Wesley used the 'mourner's bench'". Indeed, says Autrey,
his "'altar call' was an extended invitation to respond by coming
forward and kneeling at the altar..."[14] But, like Streett, Autrey is not
using an eighteenth century source for his information, but a 1957 book
by C.B. Templeton, titled *Evangelism for Tomorrow*. In turn,
Templeton states that "There are two basic approaches to the invitation
... the John Wesley method and the Charles G. Finney method". He
continues, "John Wesley and the early Methodists popularized what has
come to be called 'the altar call'".[15] Templeton gives no sources at all
to support his claim. However, as shall be seen, some Methodists were,
indeed, using the altar call in the last few years of Wesley's life, but
Wesley does not appear to have been one of them. These preachers
were probably based entirely in America, so it is most likely that
Wesley did not even know about it.

    Baker and Vickers both concede that the word "mourners" was a
common part of Wesley's vocabulary, but this is a long way from
indicating that he used the mourner's bench. Vickers noted that
Wesley's 1780 hymn book had section headings: "For mourners
convinced of sin" and "For mourners brought to birth", while Baker
stated that he was aware of dozens of usages of the word "mourners"
by Wesley, but not the term "mourner's bench".

    But when all these claims that Wesley used the altar call are
assessed, it has to be noted that none of them are made by his
contemporaries. The earliest date for any of these claims is 1957! In
addition, British Wesleyan scholar, A. Skevington Wood, states that the
closest Wesley came to "making a call for decision" was on occasions
holding post-service meetings for those concerned about their souls,
and also "asking those who were interested in joining the Methodist
society to tell him so the next morning".[16] It is also not without
significance that when the altar call did begin to emerge in British
Methodism early in the nineteenth century it was dubbed "the
American custom".[17] Thus it was perceived as an import, rather than a
home bred practice, and was certainly not seen as a strategy used by the
English founder of Methodism.

Not only is there no evidence to support the claims these writers make, but as we now proceed to examine the evangelistic methods Wesley did use, the only conclusion it seems possible to come to is that he did not use the altar call.

Wesley's Preaching

Early in 1739 Wesley, banned from preaching in many churches through unjust accusations concerning his orthodoxy and the fear and jealousy of some clergy, followed his friend George Whitefield's example and commenced preaching in the fields and streets. He frequently preached as often as three times a day in field, street or market place, and, when the Methodist work had become established, in the new meeting houses.

╱ Using the observations of Wesley's contemporaries, Telford says that Wesley's preaching "was remarkable for simplicity of style and force of argument". Whereas "Whitefield was an impassioned orator", and Charles Wesley spoke with "deep emotion" and "forcible application; John Wesley appealed to the reason with irresistible power",\Henry Moore, a contemporary biographer of Wesley, wondered how a man who spoke so simply could "have made so much noise in the world",[18] but that was probably one of the reasons for his success.⟩

⟨If his manner was less dramatic than Whitefield, his style still contained enough drama to be offensive to some. The writer, Horace Walpole, described him as "evidently an actor as Garrick", and complained that towards the end of a sermon he "exalted his voice, and acted very ugly enthusiasm".[19]

He preached biblically, logically and to a distinct plan. To him the ideal sermon had four purposes: "1/ To invite. 2/ To convince. 3/ To offer Christ. 4/ To build up", and these he felt should appear "in some measure in every sermon".[20] Yet it was not inconsistent for him to say to his preachers, "You have nothing to do but to save souls",[21] for the four purposes were all part of that one aim. He also desired to preach to "all who were willing to hear the glad tidings of salvation".[22]

Essential to Wesley's preaching method was his emphasis on the law of God, that is, the moral instruction of the Bible, not just the Old Testament law.[23] He insisted that before one proclaimed the gospel, one must preach the law that God may first "convict sinners". Unless the conscience was first awakened by the law, preaching the gospel as such was usually useless.[24] But he did not normally build a wall between the two, and his sermons commonly contained both elements, cleverly interwoven. He was cynical about those hailed as "gospel preachers", who preached the good news without the contrasting judgment.[25] To Wesley the law convicts of sin through the ministry of the Holy Spirit, though this is done with the help of human "means" such as preaching, though he concedes that occasionally one might be convicted "without any means at all".[26]

A distinction must be drawn, however, between his printed sermons and those he actually preached. After 1735 Wesley normally did not use a manuscript when preaching, be he indoors or out. His printed sermons, by contrast, were carefully prepared as a standard for Methodist belief between 1746 and 1760, to be placed beside his *Notes on the New Testament*.[27] The written form often appeared after the oral, on occasions months, or even years later.[28] It is clear, therefore, that there must have been at the very least differences in wording between the two forms. Certainly, his contemporaries described his spoken sermons as colloquial,[29] a description that could hardly be applied to the more formalized contents of his Standard Sermons.[30] Yet, even though the style was different, there does not seem to be any good reason to suppose that the differences in content and emphasis were great. Certainly, Wesley did not think so.[31]

He was always ready to match his sermons to the specific situation of his hearers, and was even prepared to change mid-stream, if he felt so led. On one occasion some of his congregation had just come from a feast, so he felt it appropriate to "add a few words about intemperance".[32] If he felt his listeners were flippant or drowsy, then he was not afraid to preach on such texts as "Awake thou that sleepest", "Where their worm dieth not", or "I saw the dead small and great, stand before God", three sermons he preached on one day in Perth in 1774.[33] Yet he was not all thunder. On another occasion he recorded: "My design was to have preached seriously [on] 'The harvest is past, the summer is ended, and we are not saved'; but I was turned, I know not how, quite the other way, and could preach scarce anything but consolation".[34]

But, to Wesley, a sermon was of little value unless it was applied to the hearers. On one visit to Scotland he complained, "This very day I heard many excellent truths delivered in the kirk; but as there was no application, it was likely to do as much good as the singing of the lark ... No sinners are convinced of sin, none converted to God, by this way of preaching".[35] When he preached on "How long halt ye between two opinions?" he applied his message "to the conscience of each person rich and poor".[36] As was seen above, his preaching took the needs of the respective congregations into consideration, and he endeavored to speak relevantly to his hearers. His orations were not just intended as teaching; they were expected to achieve something. But sometimes there were no apparent results even with an application.[37]

Though it was his common practice to apply his sermons to his hearers, nowhere in his *Journal* or in his published sermons is there evidence that his applications included the type of invitation claimed by Dr. Streett, with one possible exception. This instance took place at a meeting in Ireland in 1749. Wesley records in his *Journal*:

> Toward the close of the sermon, I asked, "Which of you will give yourself, soul and body, to God?" One cried out, "Oh, I will, I will." And as soon as she could stand, she came forth in the midst, to witness it before all the congregation ... Presently another witnessed the same resolution. And not long after [another] lifted up her head with joy, and continued singing and praising God.[38]

At first this sounds not unlike the conclusion of a modern evangelistic rally, but on further consideration the likeness vanishes.

First, it is not clear whether Wesley expected a verbal response to his question. Certainly, it is not uncommon for preachers or other public speakers to ask their hearers certain questions, without expecting an audible response. This is a common strategy in oratory. A response would be expected, but only an internalized one. Secondly, there is not the slightest indication that Wesley made any invitation for individuals to come forward. That one "came forth" seems to have been entirely upon that woman's own initiative. This appears to have been the only time that this occurred in Wesley's ministry; at least it is the only time that he recorded such in his *Journal*.[39]

When one comes to examine Wesley's sermons, though the sermon applications are evident, there is no indication whatsoever of a public appeal. What is, perhaps, even more significant is that in his instructions to his preachers there is none relating to the altar call, or anything like it. In Wesley's the *Minutes of Several Conversations* (which reached its final form as late as 1789) Methodist preachers are instructed on such diverse subjects as beginning and ending punctually, being "solemn", not rambling, and taking care of their horses, but there is not the slightest hint about anything even resembling public appeals.[40]

However, there were at times most dramatic public responses to Wesley's preaching. On quite a number of occasions people screamed out, fell down, wept loudly, or combined two or even three of these manifestations as the result, presumably, of a spiritual struggle. These incidents occurred mainly in the earlier part of his ministry, but they were not unknown towards the end.[41] If these paroxysms originally took Wesley by surprise (the day after the first such incident he thought it necessary to interview the woman concerned),[42] they did not seem to disturb him greatly. Indeed, he saw them as evidence of a spiritual conflict over the destiny of the soul, which if God won, all was well. After one early incident, he could write to George Whitefield rejoicing that God had won one such battle in a woman.[43]

According to John Cennick, an early Methodist who later became a Moravian, Wesley did deliberately encourage such activity in his early ministry. Cennick records that if there were no outward manifestations of spiritual struggle during a meeting, Wesley would pray to God for his "tokens and signs", and this would often be followed by dramatic outbursts.[44] If this was so, Wesley certainly took a different view in later life. In a sermon preached on 15 August 1789, less than two years before his death, he described "loud shouting, horrid, unnatural screaming ... and throwing about the arms and the legs" as "shocking not only to religion, but to common decency".[45] But even if Wesley did pray in the manner Cennick claimed, there is still no suggestion that he specifically invited people to conduct themselves in this manner.

His understanding of the response to his own preaching is illuminating. Wesley records:

> At first curiosity brings many hearers; at the same time God draws many by his preventing grace to hear His word ... One then tells another. By this means, on the one hand, curiosity spreads and increases, and on the other drawings of God's Spirit touch more hearts ... He now offers grace to all that hear, most of whom are in some measure affected. [Some reject the gospel, while others show a passing interest but] the drawings of God are not followed, and thereby the Spirit of God is grieved. The consequence is, he strives with this and this man no more, and so His drawings end.[46]

Wesley clearly did not use the altar call.

Wesley's Counseling

In a later chapter modern counseling techniques will be compared with those of Wesley, Whitefield and Edwards, so in this chapter each man's counseling methods will be examined in detail. Wesley had personal contact with many seeking Christ, both immediately after his preaching and at other times. How did he operate in such situations? In the cases of the paroxysms just related, his, seemingly, consistent response was prayer.[47] Reasoning was not usually a considered option in such instances, or at least not until the furor had subsided. He did, however, often continue preaching after one of these outbursts, though this was presumably for the benefit of the remainder of the congregation, not those so afflicted. Not all that had these extreme experiences were necessarily converted. After speaking to 26 people who had been so affected at one meeting, Wesley soberly recorded that "some had gone home to their house justified", while the remainder "seemed to be waiting patiently for it". A week later he interviewed a similar group, some of whom "had indeed found rest to their souls", while others were still under conviction.[48] After spending some time with one who had two such outbursts, he did not seem to be concerned about leaving her to go on to his next port of call, apparently reasoning that if God was really working in the woman's life He could bring it to fruition without Wesley's further assistance.[49] Wesley did not appear to apply persuasion to an inquirer to make a "decision", as might occur in post-response counseling today.

These extreme reactions did not only occur during Wesley's actual preaching. One woman approached Wesley and asked him to pray for her. This he did, and almost at once the woman began to scream "as in the pangs of death". But within fifteen minutes "she was full of the peace that passeth all understanding".[50] A similar encounter two weeks later saw a woman racked by "sorrow and fear" approach him. She was in great "agony". He and his associates prayed and the "mourner" saw the Savior "crucified before her eyes" and "then laid hold on Him by faith".[51]

Upon interview Wesley found that such people were usually in good health, that the attacks generally came suddenly, that both their bodies and minds were affected, and that for many during the paroxysm they became strongly aware of their sin and the judgment of God.[52]

The reaction of many people after his preaching was more rational: a strong awareness of sin and a desire for salvation, but without the extravagant behavior.[53] But after speaking to those who desired him to, Wesley also felt free to leave them and go home or on to other places, if their deliverance was not speedy.[54] He did not feel it necessary to press the issue to a definite conclusion as a modern crusade counselor often would. On one occasion a drunkard followed Wesley to a class meeting after a sermon and was "cut ... to the heart", but did not find peace quickly. Wesley once more pushed on to the next town, but this man followed him and was later converted there.[55] Wesley's normal response to the needs of seekers was his prayer for them, plus some counsel.[56] He did not try to get the inquirer to utter a formula prayer on his or her own behalf.

In addition, those who approached him personally also usually reacted rationally. One such man poured out his heart to Wesley, mourning his sins and relating his attempts to get right with God. Wesley's response was, once more, counsel and prayer. And after a little while, the man was able to proclaim that "Christ hath set me free".[57] Wesley visited a sick man who was afraid of dying without God. Wesley and his companions prayed for him "in full confidence", and "the next day God gave him life from the dead".[58] With one woman seeking salvation he just records that he "spent a little time in advice, exhortation and prayer".[59] Towards the end of his life he records how he spent two hours with one seeker " and answered all her questions".[60]

It was not the case that all he counseled came to believe. But with those who resisted the Gospel, though he had no qualms about making his presentation bold, there seems to have been no undue pressure, nor any attempts to place words in the individual's mouth.[61] For example, on one occasion he could speak of some being "deeply convinced", yet, not only were "none delivered from that conviction", he did not seem to regard forcing the issue as his task.[62] He left them in the hands of God. At another time a group of forty or fifty "who were seeking salvation" decided to spend the night together in prayer. Wesley felt quite comfortable leaving them to it, retiring himself at 10 p.m. But early in the morning the noise they made in their desperation awoke him, and he rejoined them. Fortunately, "God heard from his holy place" and gave release to some.[63] Even with those awaiting execution, after a presentation of the gospel and prayer, he did not force the issue. It was left between God and the sinner.[64] He was certainly wary of giving a false peace, and warned against healing "the wound" of those under conviction in a superficial manner.[65] He could, however, say "we claimed and received the promise for several who were 'weary and heavy laden'."[66] But this may well not mean more than prayer and its answer. Skevington Wood says that Wesley's "only concern was with a genuine work of grace; and for this he was ready to bide God's time".[67]

Summary

From the available evidence, and there is much, it seems that John Wesley was always prepared to present the Gospel in clear, bold terms to his hearers, and to counsel and pray with prospective converts. There is, however, no evidence that he used the altar call, indeed his practice declares that he did not. Neither does it appear in counseling that he regarded himself as having the right to press the issue of an individual's conversion to a definite conclusion. John Wesley was responsible for thousands becoming Christians, and with his Methodist associates did much to change the social fabric of England.

Did Whitefield and Edwards use the Altar Call?

If there is debate over whether Wesley used the public invitation or not, there would appear to be none concerning George Whitefield and Jonathan Edwards. Arnold Dallimore, a leading authority on Whitefield, says that Whitefield "made no appeal for people to make a public profession of salvation at his services",[68] and in the course of this study no example of him using it has been found. Nor has any hint been found of Edwards using it. As the practice is usually understood and has been defined in the introduction, these two men did not use the altar call. There would appear to be no dissenting voices with regard to that. It is true that Harry Stout calls Whitefield "the prototype for future mass evangelists", yet by this he seems to be referring to the way in which Whitefield crossed denominational boundaries and attracted vast numbers, rather than the particular methods he used. Indeed, on one occasion Whitefield said, "If the Pope himself would lend me his pulpit, I would gladly proclaim the righteousness of Christ therein".[69]

But it shall still be most instructive to examine the preaching and counseling methods of these two great evangelists, so that we might understand their practice and note the results achieved through them. We will first look at Whitefield.

George Whitefield (1714-1770)[70]

Whitefield's Preaching

George Whitefield came from a quite different background from John Wesley. He was born in his parents' inn in Gloucester. But he too went on to study for Holy Orders, was converted in 1735, and soon after his ordination found himself in trouble with his bishop, when it was claimed that one of his sermons had sent fifteen people mad. As John Wesley was returning from America, Whitefield embarked for that destination for the first of his many trips to that land. Whitefield returned to England at the end of 1738, and like Wesley, was banned from preaching in many churches of his own denomination. He made what was then the controversial move of preaching in the streets and fields. The results were dramatic. In churches he had been limited to hundreds or at best 1000 or so auditors, but in the open air the only limiting factor was the distance his mighty voice could travel. Five thousand, 10 000, 20 000, 50 000, and even 80 000, are the estimates of some of the crowds that heard him. The probable exaggeration in such figures has already been considered, but it cannot be doubted that he struck Britain, and America, like a bombshell. He appears to have been more aware than Wesley of the possibilities of publicity, and seems to have used what he called a "print and preach" strategy, using the press, to some degree at least, to publicize his travels and preaching.[71]

If Walpole thought Wesley as "evidently an actor as Garrick", one can only wonder how he viewed Whitefield. Whitefield was by natural ability and childhood experience a talented actor.[72] Indeed, after hearing him preach Garrick himself said, "I'd give a hundred guineas to be able to say 'Oh!' like Whitefield".[73] But Whitefield dedicated that talent, when called to serve Christ, to the great work of preaching the Gospel. For example, when preaching on the story of Zacchaeus, Whitefield would not just tell the story, he would play the various parts to make the story live, and use appropriate gestures and body movement.[74] Tears, too, frequently flowed from the preacher's eyes as he spoke, and many of his listeners responded in the same manner. Not that his crying was manufactured, produced just to make an impact. Rather it was the outpouring of a compassionate heart. Cornelius Winter, his companion in the last few years of his life, stated, "I truly believe his tears were the tears of sincerity".[75] His natural gifts included a "strong musical voice", with excellent articulation. On one occasion he was said to have been understandable from a distance of two miles.[76]

How was he viewed by his contemporaries? Whitefield made an impact upon all classes. His field preaching was normally attended by the poor, some of whom walked many miles to hear him, but also the rich, who came in their carriages. As noted a figure as Benjamin Franklin had enormous respect for Whitefield and his ability, while not sharing his theology. Franklin spoke of "the extraordinary Influence of his Oratory on his hearers", and stated that even "without being interested in the subject", one could not help "being pleased with his discourse".[77] Ebenezer Pemberton, an American Presbyterian minister regarded his preaching gift as unique, and after Whitefield's death, John Wesley described his preaching as manifesting a "torrent of eloquence" and "an astonishing force of persuasion".[78]

But his preaching was not all drama and eloquence. There was content too, even though, as Sarah Edwards (Jonathan's wife) said, "He makes less of the doctrines than our American preachers".[79] To

Whitefield himself what he preached was "the simple gospel".[80] As with Wesley, for most of his career he preached without nótes, so that one must allow that the printed sermons were to some degree different from his spoken sermons. Yet there seems to be no good reason to believe that those differences were significant. His sermon subjects included: the New Birth (frequently), the imputation of Christ's righteousness to repentant sinners, and the origin of sin and God's method of dealing with it.[81] These are topics that he dealt with thoroughly, not in a light, anecdotal fashion. If the gospel he proclaimed was "simple", it was certainly not simplistic. Stout says that he was more likely to preach theological sermons, if his hearers were assumed to be theologically aware. Like Wesley, he was prepared to adapt his content to match circumstances and the assumed understanding of his congregation, and on occasions he could speak of changing his preaching intentions mid-sermon.[82]

Again like Wesley, he was not afraid to preach on hell. Though his emphasis on God's judgment does not appear to have been excessive in terms of space devoted to it, there can be little doubt that he dealt with the subject in living color. If descriptions of his preaching are accurate, when he spoke of sinners "trembling before the judgment seat", then he trembled, as did his hearers. When he warned of being "tormented with the devil" in hell,[83] no doubt his hearers could feel the flames. Whitefield was not afraid to warn his listeners of God's wrath.

Though there is no evidence to indicate that Whitefield used the altar call, indeed, the evidence points in the other direction, there is an interesting incident in a revival in Scotland in 1741. John Parker, a convert, testified that at the end of one of Whitefield's sermons the evangelist began exhorting listeners to "cast themselves at" Christ's feet. Parker says that "During prayer after [that] sermon, I stood up and felt as if my condition had been much altered". The precise circumstances of his standing up are not related. After going home he says that he was "enabled to close with Christ".[84]

There were many, many individual responses to Whitefield's preaching, which must have totaled many thousands in Britain and America. These responses did not often manifest themselves in the paroxysms witnessed by Wesley. Indeed, Dallimore says that they never occurred when Whitefield was preaching in "virgin" territory. Whitefield only experienced them when preaching in a district where he had been preceded by one such as Wesley, who had, apparently, been the catalyst for these wild manifestations. If Whitefield's preaching frequently began in silence, it often was not long before many in his congregation dissolved into tears,[85] and with these tears

many experienced the working of God's Holy Spirit, and eventually the
new birth. George Whitefield was an extraordinarily effective preacher.

Whitefield's Counseling

Early in his ministry Whitefield frequently had large numbers come
to him seeking spiritual counsel, and he was prepared to spend time
with them in private. "Multitudes after sermon", he recorded on one
occasion, "followed me home, weeping, and the next day I was
employed from seven in the morning till midnight in giving spiritual
advice to awakened souls."[86] At one stage in 1739 he set aside one day
a week to those concerned about their spiritual welfare, often spending
from 7 a.m. to 3 p.m. in that pursuit, yet sometimes even that was
insufficient and he had to set aside further times for it. Later in his
ministry, for the most part, he was forced to give up this practice
because of ill health.[87]

As has just been noted, Whitefield generally dealt with individuals
privately, however, people seeking him out often did so very publicly,
though there is no indication that this was in response to a Whitefield
appeal for public confession. The initiative always seems to have been
on the part of the seeker. Dallimore states that, "Whitefield gave no
seeker reason to believe that such an interview was essential to, or
necessarily productive of, salvation ... and many left his presence [as
with Wesley] to continue to seek ... and to entreat God to make them
objects of his mercy".[88] There is not a lot of detail about Whitefield's
methods with individuals, but what there is seems to confirm
Dallimore's comments.

One encounter outlined in his *Journals*, however, was with a Mr.
B....ll, who had "dropped down as though shot", while Whitefield was
praying. When the preacher visited him and some others the next day
the man was on his bed in agony of mind and "crying out for an interest
in Jesus". But Whitefield offered no shortcuts. He recorded, "After half
an hour's conversation on the nature of the new birth, and the necessity
of closing with Christ, I kneeled down and prayed with them and took
my leave, hoping the Lord would pluck them as brands from the
burning".[89] In spite of the prospective convert's obvious desire for
Christ, Whitefield was not prepared to conclude the issue unnaturally.
He did not perceive conviction of sin and even a desire for the Christian
state, as something that would automatically and immediately result in
conversion.

Some of the meetings he had with individuals were triggered by an unusual method, though on the listener's initiative, not the preacher's. Often during his sermons people gave him notes asking him to pray for their spiritual need, and this at times led to subsequent meetings. Though he was delighted with this, for it showed that the Holy Spirit was working, there is no evidence to suggest he encouraged it.

A little, too, can be learned from his dealings with his friend Benjamin Franklin. Franklin was a Deist, yet the two enjoyed a close friendship. In both conversation and letter Whitefield was able to challenge his friend with his understanding of the faith. After becoming aware of Franklin's experiments with electricity, Whitefield said to him, "As you have made a pretty considerable progress in the mysteries of electricity, I would now humbly recommend to your diligent unprejudiced pursuit and study the mystery of the new birth".[90] On one occasion when Franklin (a printer, in addition to everything else) likened his life to a book which he hoped would be restored through death "in a new and more perfect Edition, corrected and amended by the Author", Whitefield responded, "Believe in Jesus ... and you cannot possibly be disappointed of your expected second edition, finely corrected, and infinitely amended".[91]

Summary

Even in his personal dealings with the great, Whitefield was direct, but knew that in the final analysis God alone could save, and that applied to whether the individual was a great statesman, or at the other end of the social scale. His job was to present the gospel, be it in sermon, letter or personal word; it was God's job to convert. There is no evidence that he ever used the public invitation, and his known methods seem to indicate that he did not.

Jonathan Edwards (1703-1758)

Edwards' Preaching

Jonathan Edwards served as a Congregational minister, first in Northampton, Massachusetts, and later in Stockbridge. His father and grandfather had followed the same calling before him, indeed, grandfather Solomon Stoddard was his predecessor at the Northampton church. Edwards was a man of remarkable intellect and many gifts; he was renowned as theologian, philosopher, pastor and evangelist. As has been previously mentioned there are no claims that Jonathan Edwards used the altar call, but his methods of evangelism are instructive to note.

Though Edwards shared with Wesley and Whitefield a concern for the salvation of men and women, his career followed a very different path. If Wesley's parish was theoretically the world (more literally the whole of the British Isles), Whitefield's area of service was Britain and America, and their ministry was to countless thousands, Edwards' work took place mainly in two small parishes in north America, and his hearers were usually in the hundreds or even less. His usual congregation in Northampton would have been around 600, which increased during times of revival, but it was far less in Stockbridge. He did, however, have a considerable influence over a substantial part of New England through the Northampton Church. But if his immediate impact was limited mainly to a particular area, his vision was wide and embraced the world.

Edwards' sermons have been called "dry and lengthy disquisitions", and as being academic and delivered in "a rigorously unornamented prose".[92] Yet these observations are not entirely true, for as John E. Smith points out, Edwards did not just express ideas but clothed them with "images",[93] as is evidenced by some of his colorful and quite frightening phrasing in his famous sermon *Sinners in the Hands of an Angry God*.[94] No wonder O.E. Winslow observed that Edwards made hell "real enough to be found in the atlas".[95] Yet his logical, well-reasoned sermons were not the dynamic addresses, full of color and drama in the Whitefield mold, nor the type of oration that one might expect to be the catalyst to the revivals which at times certainly accompanied his preaching. His delivery was with a "low and moderate voice ... without any agitation of the body, or anything else in the manner to excite attention, except his habitual and great solemnity, looking and speaking as in the presence of God".[96] One of his hearers said that, "He used no gestures", but just "looked straight forward" as he preached.[97] In some respects his manner appears to have been the opposite of Whitefield.

In his early days he took a full manuscript into the pulpit and read from it, pretty well, word for word, but from around 1742 he just used an outline upon which he elaborated while preaching. Smith points out, and it appears to be supported by the evidence, that he was a less effective preacher after 1742,[98] though it would be hasty to say that this was because of his change of method. Though his sermons were less philosophical than his writings, much of his content must still have floated over the heads of at least some of his hearers. But one elderly man could recall in his own childhood one particular occasion when "the attention of [Edwards'] audience was fixed and motionless until [the sermon's] close, when they seemed disappointed that it should terminate so soon. There was such a bearing down of truth upon the mind ... that there was no resisting it". Another hearer stated that at the end of one of Edwards' sermons "he fully supposed ... the judges would descend and the final separation take place" there and then.[99] It would probably be a mistake to suppose, however, that all his hearers were always so captivated.

His sermons were aimed at the intellect and the heart, though it may be truer to say they were aimed at the heart through the intellect. Indeed, he stated that the greatest need of his hearers was not "to have their heads stored", but "to have their hearts touched", so in his view a preacher should adopt preaching methods that would raise the "affections" of his listeners, but only through the preaching of "nothing but truth". These methods included a careful selection of appropriate texts and an earnest manner of delivery.[100]

Edwards accepted that it was "God's manner to make use of means in carrying on his work". To lead people to salvation, God could use methods as varied as preaching, example, reason, the use of scriptures, or the use of sacred music.[101] But to Edwards human means, of themselves, were of no value in bringing people to Christ. As Jenson puts it, even preaching and prayer were "occasional means only and not causes" of spiritual illumination leading to salvation,[102] for it is God who does the enlightening and saving, not the methods, however valid they be. It was the grace of God through the Holy Spirit that alone could convert a soul. It is important to keep these matters in mind, particularly when the views and practices of Charles Finney are examined in chapter six, for he presents a very different understanding.

Edwards also prepared his sermons with his hearers' needs in mind. For example, a sermon preached in his home church would often be altered or even recast before being delivered to another congregation. Extant manuscripts of his sermons indicate that he selected his words carefully, making frequent changes where he considered it necessary.[103] In Stockbridge part of his ministry was to Mohawk Indians, and he usually adapted his sermons to suit their understanding.[104]

Like Wesley, Edwards insisted that before preaching the Gospel it was necessary to preach the law to awaken sinners. But it could be said that on occasions, in his attempts to preach the law and God's judgment, that he laid too great a stress on hell and its horrors. Indeed, if the American's preaching manner was undramatic, his content was at times decidedly hot. He once said that preachers should not be "mild and gentle" but "sons of thunder".[105] It was, after all, the preacher's first task to bring his unconverted hearers under conviction of sin, then offer gospel grace. In his sermon *Sinners in the Hands of an Angry God* he thundered long and loud, and created a storm that still reverberates. Even as great an admirer of Edwards as Martyn Lloyd-Jones could say of him that with regard to hell he "went at times well beyond what he was warranted to do and say by Holy Scripture".[106] "The God that holds you over the pit of hell ... abhors you", proclaimed Edwards. "He will crush you under his feet without mercy; he will crush out your blood and make it fly..."[107]

However, it must be noted, that though when Edwards did preach on hell it was graphic and fearful, he did not preach on that subject often. At other times he could preach most tenderly and compassionately.[108] It would be to give a false picture to regard him as focusing on just one subject. That was far from the truth.

Yet his preaching during the revival of 1735 was frequently on texts focusing on God's judgment. However, as Murray says, it was not just one doctrine that characterized that awakening.[109] In that great outpouring of God's Spirit, in about six months around 300 people professed conversion in Northampton out of a population of around 1300, and, partly through visits by people from neighboring towns to hear Edwards, the revival spread throughout the region.[110] He was very aware that such movements were totally dependent upon the power of God.[111]

His preaching did not neglect his calvinistic beliefs. According to Jenson, his response to his hearers' question, "How then shall I be saved?" was by God's free choice alone. But that produced positive results rather than negative ones, for it was the desperation resulting from that answer which "produced the weeping" evident in many of his hearers. Conviction of sin might commence on the natural plane, and as such was worthless, but it could then proceed under the convicting power of God's Spirit, and then God would grant saving faith.[112]

Though he knew nothing of the modern altar call, he still pleaded for his listeners to respond to God. In his sermons he invited sinners to Christ. "I invite you now to a better portion", he urged his listeners. "Turn your feet into the way of peace, forsake the foolish and live ... seek after the excellent peace and rest of Jesus Christ ... Taste and see".[113] Indeed, he could say that sinners "should be earnestly invited to come and accept of a Savior, and yield their hearts unto him, with all the encouraging arguments for them ... that the Gospel affords".[114] He was keen to encourage those under conviction of sin "*immediately* to go to God through Christ for mercy" and "to come to Christ".[115] Yet, as John and Jonathan Gerstner point out, in his sermon on the Philippian jailer, whereas Paul instructed the man to "believe", Edwards urged his hearers to "escape", "strive to enter" and "seek",[116] which could be considered a fault in his preaching method.

Many people responded to Edwards' preaching in dramatic and violent ways, similar to those Wesley witnessed. Some of these people were previously outside organized religion, while others already professed Christianity.[117] When he preached *Sinners in the Hands of an Angry God* in July 1741 he had to stop because the outcry in the congregation was so great. An eyewitness named Stephen Williams told the story this way:

> before sermon was done there was a great moaning & crying out through ye whole House What shall I do to be savd oh I am going to Hell ... So yt ye minister was obliged to desist ... yt a prayer was made by Mr. W, & after that we descend from the pulpitt and discoursd with the people Some in one place and Some in another ... & Several Souls were hopefully wrought upon yt night ... we sung a hymn and prayd & dismiss ye Assembly (sic).[118]

This was probably a unique, or at least rare, experience in Edwards' ministry, in that he and others were counseling members of the congregation before the sermon had officially ended. Yet, though there was a most public outburst from members of the congregation, it is clear that this was not in any way due to some form of public invitation.

Charles Chauncy, a critic of the New England revivals, stated that such disorder could not be credited (or debited) to the Holy Spirit, for God was a God of order. That a very high proportion of those so affected were children, teenagers and women suggested to Chauncy that the cause was psychological rather than spiritual. He reasoned that they were "more easily thrown into a commotion" than adult males.[119] Edwards did not dispute that many having these dramatic experiences were in the categories indicated by Chauncy, indeed, it would appear that he knew that some were even illiterate, but he saw those facts in a different light. Though he recognized that the revival had not been without its abuses and he did not actually encourage the extravagant manifestations, he felt that in the high ratio of young being converted God was making use of the "weak and the foolish ... mere babes in age and understanding" to "chastise the deadness of the ministers".[120]

Also, though it seems that more women than men were having these dramatic experiences, there were still many men being added to the church through the revivals. Indeed, it seems that about half of the conversions were male, and they covered a wide age range.[121] As did Wesley, Edwards interviewed those who had been violently affected.

Their response was similar to those spoken to by the Englishman. Many expressed that they, too, had experienced an overwhelming awareness of sin or judgment, or both, later to find release through various thoughts of Christ and an awareness of His presence, at times through the reading of Scripture.[122]

To Chauncy conversion was a rational experience and the revivals just emotionalism. While Edwards, far from seeing conversion as irrational, firmly believed that the emotions would be touched in a genuine work of God.[123] Indeed, as Perry Miller observed, "Edwards wove the supernatural into the natural, the rational into the emotional".[124]

Some periods of Edwards' ministry saw great revival and many coming to Christ, particularly during his time in Northampton. At other times he was not very successful as far as conversions were concerned.

Edwards' Counseling

Edwards did not usually spend much time visiting his parishioners, be they converted or otherwise, and most commonly only did so when someone was sick or sent for him. He did not regard himself as having the gifts that make this kind of ministry effective. Indeed, some of his congregation found him "stiff and unsociable".[125] His preference was to spend the bulk of his time, often thirteen hours a day, in study and the preparation of sermons.[126]

He certainly, however, made himself available for counsel to those in spiritual distress, and sometimes the number of these was considerable. His *Narrative of Conversions* makes it clear that he spent a great deal of time questioning those who sought his help, that he might verify and understand the work of God in the life of these individuals, as well as encourage their search. His detailed accounts of the spiritual quests of various individuals indicate the enormous amount of time he was prepared to spend with each person when he considered it necessary.[127]

He recognized that the emotional outbursts of some of his hearers were at times little, if anything, more than that. Yet with others they were somehow connected with a genuine work of God. Skill was needed in the pastor to distinguish between the true and the false.[128] Edwards did not, as far as can be determined from his writings, believe in "leading people to the Lord" in the common, modern use of that term, but he did his utmost to help people apply scriptural teaching and principles to their own situation.

His *Religious Affections* indicates that he very carefully analyzed the spiritual condition of those he counseled. Do an individual's affections promote "a spirit of love ... and mercy as appeared in Christ?" Have they softened the heart? Do they lead to Christian fruit and a stronger desire for "spiritual attainments"?[129] None Edwards counseled could expect a quick stamp of approval on their confession from him. He was reluctant to declare people "converted" to their faces, seemingly leaving the Holy Spirit to assure those who were His, and whilst recognizing the value in knowing about people's conversions, he would still prefer to speak of them in such phrases as "hopefully converted", rather than something more definite.[130]

As with Wesley and Whitefield, Edwards did not seem to practice leading those under conviction of sin to a definite conclusion to their spiritual struggle. Murray tells of one instance when Edwards spoke to a group of younger teenagers, all of who seemed moved by Edwards' message. No undue pressure was applied to transform that struggle into conversion, and some of them were still crying, the issue unresolved, on their way home.[131]

Even closer to home, in 1755 Edwards wrote to his son Jonathan advising him that a young friend of the boy's had died in Stockbridge. Edwards senior expressed uncertainty about the deceased lad's eternal destiny and urged his son to never give himself rest until he had "good evidence that [he was] converted and become a new creature".[132] Even, perhaps especially, with one so close to him he was not prepared to cut corners for an apparent quick, cheap ride to heaven.

Conclusions

When conclusions are drawn over whether John Wesley, George Whitefield and Jonathan Edwards used the altar call, it is clear that they did not. Though some have argued that Wesley did use it, they provide no evidence contemporary with him to support their position. Indeed, his evangelistic practice and the advice he gave to his preachers seem incompatible with it. It is generally accepted that Whitefield and Edwards did not use it. Yet they were all highly successful evangelists and greatly used of God.

The evangelistic practices of these three evangelists are remarkably similar, even though two were calvinists and one an arminian, and much can be learned from them. Their main method of evangelism was the formal preaching of the Scriptures, which was done frequently and boldly, and usually included both the proclamation of the law of God and the presentation of the gospel. All selected and molded their sermons to match their hearers, though not in a way that compromised

their message. All were prepared to counsel those who were concerned about their spiritual welfare, but none of the three seemed to practice the modern method of pressing the counselee to make a "decision".
Were their methods successful? They were extremely successful. But was this because these men were extraordinarily gifted, or can such methods also be successful when used by those with lesser ability? All three were extremely gifted, but this is far from being the only reason for their success. Their success resulted primarily from the Spirit of God working through them, which is why their work was not uniformly blessed throughout their lives, but had highs and lows.

As the story of the development of the public invitation unfolds, it will be noted that many other preachers, far less gifted than these three, also had great evangelistic successes without the use of the altar call. If God be the same today, as He surely is, then the non-public-invitational methods of Wesley, Whitefield and Edwards and others, adapted to the age in which we live, can be expected to be successful in our time too.

Notes

[1]   The material in chapter one and that on Wesley, Whitefield and Edwards in chapter five can be found in a different form and in slightly more detail in my article on their evangelistic methods in *Lucas* 25 & 26 (1999).

[2]   Stanley Ayling, *John Wesley* (London: Collins, 1979), 110.

[3]   John Wesley, *The Journal of the Rev. John Wesley* (8 vols; ed. Nehemiah Curnock, London: Epworth, 1938), 5:524.

[4]   Arnold Dallimore, *George Whitefield* (2 vols; Edinburgh, Banner of Truth, 1970), 1:295-96; Frank Lambert, *"Pedlar in Divinity" George Whitefield and the Transatlantic Revivals* (Princeton: Princeton Uni., 1994), 113.

[5]   Exhorters were used in Methodism and seem to have had varied functions. The practice of exhorters being on the look out for prospective converts, however, belongs to a later period, see chapter 4.

[6]   Streett, *Effective*, 91-92 (99-101); page numbers in brackets throughout this book are from Streett's thesis. Streett's two accounts of Wesley's methods have only minor variations, though in the thesis, on the fourth point he does use the weaker "Wesley *may have been* the first to use the mourner's bench", (101), (emphasis added).

[7]   Howard G. Olive, "The Development of the Evangelistic Invitation" (M.Th., Southern Baptist Theological Seminary, 1958). There seems to be some confusion with the footnotes in Streett's book and thesis at this point (for example, the same references are used to support different points in the two documents), but nowhere does Olive state what Streett claims.

---

[8] In his book Streett does not cite anyone at this point, but in his thesis he mentions Olive as his source.

[9] Olive, "Evangelistic Invitation", 24-25. Streett quotes page 24, but it is the following page that gives the type of material he quotes. Wesley is not mentioned on either page.

[10] This and later comments by Dr. Vickers of the Wesley Historical Society, England, are from a letter to the author, dated 7 July 1994.

[11] This and later comments by Dr. Baker are from a letter to the author, dated 3 August 1994. Dr. Baker is the Textual Editor of the Bicentennial Edition of the Works of John Wesley.

[12] Olive, "Evangelistic Invitation", 25, quoting from James B. Finley, *Sketches of Western Methodism* (ed W.P. Strickland, Cincinnati: Methodist Book, 1857), 72.

[13] John Telford, *The Life of John Wesley* (London: Epworth, 1947), 382.

[14] Autrey, *Evangelism*, 130.

[15] Charles B. Templeton, *Evangelism for Tomorrow* (NY: Harper, 1957), 166.

[16] A. Skevington Wood, *The Burning Heart* (Exeter: Paternoster, 1967), 166.

[17] Richard Carwardine, *Transatlantic Revivalism* (Wesport: Greenwood, 1978), 120.

[18] Telford, *Wesley*, 315.

[19] R.A. Knox, *Enthusiasm* (London: Oxford, 1950), 513. Knox is quoting from a letter from Walpole to John Chute.

[20] John Wesley, *Minutes of Several Conversations*, in *The Works of John Wesley* (14 vols; 3rd ed. Thomas Jackson, Grand Rapids: Baker, [1831] 1991), 8:317; see also Wood, *Burning Heart*, 157.

[21] Telford, *Wesley*, 229; see also Wood, *Burning Heart*, 159.

[22] John Wesley, *The Letters of John Wesley* (8 vols; ed. John Telford, London: Epworth, 1931), 1:284-87; Wesley, *Journal*, 2:216-18.

[23] John Wesley, *Forty-Four Sermons* (London: Epworth, 1944), 381-95, especially 381-82.

[24] Williams, Colin W. *John Wesley's Theology Today* (London: Epworth, 1960), 58; see Wesley's sermon on Mt. 5:1-4, in Wesley, *44 Sermons*, 185-200, and on Rom. 3:31, Wesley, *44 Sermons*, 395-406, and Wesley, *Journal*, 4:201.

[25] Wesley, *Journal*, 6:131; W.L. Doughty, *John Wesley: Preacher* (London: Epworth, 1955), 173-75; Wood, *Burning Heart*, 150-51.

[26] Wesley, *44 Sermons*, 390.

[27] Telford, *Wesley*, 316, 324.

[28] Wesley, *Journal*, 8:19, 54; Doughty, *Wesley*, 143, 160-61.

[29] Nehemiah Curnock, in Wesley, *Journal*, 6:248.

[30] For a discussion on the possible stylistic differences between Wesley's spoken and written sermons see Doughty, *Wesley*, 144-45.

[31] Doughty, *Wesley*, 143, quoting Wesley.

[32] Wesley, *Journal*, 2:506. See also Telford, *Wesley*, 319-20.

[33] Wesley, *Journal*, 6:20. See also 5:316, 392, 474, and 6:141.

[34] Wesley, *Journal*, 7:412. See also Telford, *Wesley*, 319.

[35] Wesley, *Journal*, 6:239; Wood, *Burning Heart*, 158.

[36] Wesley, *Journal*, 7:93.

[37] Wesley, *Journal*, 6:264; 7:34, 237, 342.

[38] Wesley, *Journal*, 3:405-6.

[39] A search of Wesley's *Journal* from 1738 to the final entry reveals only this one occurrence of this practice.

[40] Wesley, *Works*, 8:299, 317-18.

[41] See, for example, Wesley, *Journal*, 7:18, 139; and Richard Green, *John Wesley: Evangelist* (London: Religious Tract Soc., 1905) 248-260. Nor were such phenomena exclusive to Wesley; Knox lists a number of other eighteenth century preachers who saw similar occurrences, including Whitefield and Howell Harris, Knox, *Enthusiasm*, 525-28.

[42] Wesley, *Journal*, 2:132; Telford, *Wesley*, 121-22.

[43] Wesley, *Journal*, 2:145.

[44] John White, *The Spirit Comes With Power* (Sevenoaks: Hodder, 1992), 128, quoting Cennick.

[45] Wesley, *Works*, 7:295.

[46] Wesley, *Journal*, 4:174.

[47] Wesley, *Journal*, 2:145, 152-53, 180, 184, 187, 189, 204, 221-22, 230, 247-48, 291, 324; 3:89, 468; 4:229, 350; 5:108, 372; Green, *Wesley*, 279; John S. Simon, *John Wesley and the Religious Societies* (London: Epworth, 1955), 285-86; Wood, *Burning Heart*, 164.

[48] Wesley, *Journal*, 2:203, 221-22, 226-27; Green, *Wesley*, 268.

[49] Wesley, *Journal*, 2:376-77; see also 3:468.

[50] Wesley, *Journal*, 2:271.

[51] Wesley, *Journal*, 2:279.

[52] Wesley, *Journal*, 3:69-70; Green, *Wesley*, 258-59; Telford, *Wesley*, 121-25.

[53] Wesley, *Journal*, 2:246; Doughty, *Wesley*, 109, 115-16, 133.

[54] Wesley, *Journal*, 2:246, 256, 259; 4:33.

[55] Wesley, *Journal*, 3:398.

[56] Wesley, *Journal*, 2:79-80, 253; 3:405-6, 432.

[57] Wesley, *Journal*, 2:79-80; see also 2:289, 346; 5:341; 6:524.

[58] Wesley, *Journal*, 3:149; see also 3:242, 452; 5:318; 6:252.

[59] Wesley, *Journal*, 6:105.

[60] Wesley, *Journal*, 8:48.

[61] Wesley, *Journal*, 2:391-92; 3:443-44; 5:127, 237.

[62] Wesley, *Journal*, 2:246; see also 2:247-48, 253, 256, 376-77; 3:52; 6:524; 8:48; Wood, *Burning Heart*, 163-65.

[63] Wesley, *Journal*, 2:375-76; Green, *Wesley*, 313.

[64] Wesley, *Journal*, 4:478.

[65] Wesley, *Journal*, 5:204; 6:66.

[66] Wesley, *Journal*, 2:292.

[67] Wood, *Burning Heart*, 163.

[68] Dallimore, *Whitefield*, 1:137.

[69] Harry S. Stout. *The Divine Dramatist* (Grand Rapids: Eerdmans, 1991), xiv, xviii, 138.

[70] It needs to be noted that many of Whitefield's papers (journals, sermons, etc.) dealing with the later part of his life have been lost, Dallimore, *Whitefield*, 1:8-9, so most of the material used in this section is from his early ministry.

[71] Frank Lambert, "The Great Awakening as Artifact: George Whitefield and the Construction of Intercolonial Revival 1739-1745", *Church History* 60 (June, 1991, No 2), 223-24; Lambert, *Pedlar*, 75-76.

[72] Stout, *Dramatist*, 7-8, 10.

[73] Dallimore, *Whitefield*, 2:530.

[74] Stout, *Dramatist*, 105; see also Stout, 40-41, 83, 95.

[75] Dallimore, *Whitefield*, 2:483.

[76] Dallimore, *Whitefield*, 1:439, 480; Stout, *Dramatist*, 286.

[77] Dallimore, *Whitefield*, 1:116, quoting from the *Memoirs of the Life and Writings of Benjamin Franklin*; Stout, *Dramatist*, 90.

[78] Stout, *Dramatist*, 95; Dallimore, *Whitefield*, 2:512.

[79] Dallimore, *Whitefield*, 1:539.

[80] Stout, *Dramatist*, 138.

[81] Stout, *Dramatist*, xx-xxi, 120; Peter Toon, *Born Again*, (Grand Rapids: Baker, 1987), 159-161; George Whitefield and J.C. Ryle, *Select Sermons of George Whitefield. With an account of his life* (Edinburgh: Banner of Truth, 1958), 116-161. For more details of his sermon topics see Richard Owen Roberts, *Whitefield in Print*, (Wheaton: Roberts, 1988), 18-55.

[82] George Whitefield, *George Whitefield's Journals* (London: Banner of Truth, 1960), 467.

[83] Whitefield, *Sermons*, 94.

[84] D. MacFarlan, *The Revivals of the Eighteenth Century, Particularly at Cambuslang* (Wheaton: R.O. Roberts [1847], 1980), 178-79. See also Arthur Fawcett, *The Cambuslang Revival: The Scottish Evangelical Revival of the Eighteenth Century* (Edinburgh: Banner of Truth, 1971), 160.

[85] Whitefield, *Journals*, 272, 285, 290, 295, 311, 343, 345, 354.

[86] Whitefield, *Journals*, 84-85; see also *Journals*, 264, 290. "Awakened souls" was a common expression referring to those who were undergoing a spiritual experience prior to conversion, such as conviction of sin, Dallimore, *Whitefield*, 1:137.

[87] Whitefield, *Journals*, 196; Dallimore, *Whitefield*, 1:225; 2:478.

[88] Dallimore, *Whitefield*, 1:137.

[89] Whitefield, *Journals*, 448.

[90] Stout, *Dramatist*, 228.

[91] Lambert, *Pedlar*, 129-130; Stout, *Dramatist*, 233.

[92] Robert W. Jenson, *America's Theologian: A Recommendation of Jonathan Edwards* (New York: Oxford, 1988), 57; Perry Miller, *Jonathan Edwards* (New York: Meridian, 1959), 48.

[93] John E. Smith, *Jonathan Edwards* (Notre Dame: Uni. of Notre Dame Press, 1992), 30, 139.

[94] Jonathan Edwards, *The Works of Jonathan Edwards* (ed. Edward Hickman, 2 vols; Edinburgh: Banner of Truth, [1834] 1974), 2:7-12.

[95] O.E. Winslow, *Jonathan Edwards* (NY: Collier, 1961), 193.

[96] Iain H. Murray, *Jonathan Edwards* (Edinburgh: Banner of Truth, 1987), 175, quoting Gillies.

[97] Miller, *Edwards*, 51.

[98] Murray, *Edwards*, 188-89; Smith, *Edwards*, 139.

[99] Murray, *Edwards*, 392, quoting the words of a Dr. West, recorded by Sereno Dwight, Edwards great-grand-son, and Keith J. Hardman, *Seasons of Refreshing: Evangelism and Revivals in America* (Grand Rapids: Baker, 1994), 72.

[100] Edwards, *Thoughts on Revival*, in the *Works*, 1:391. It should be noted that Edwards did not regard the "affections" as something only to do with the emotions. He described them as "the more vigorous and sensible exercises of the inclination and the will of the soul", thus they have much to do with intelligent response, see Jonathan Edwards, *Religious Affections* (ed. John E. Smith, Works of Jonathan Edwards; New Haven: Yale UP, 1959, vol. 2), 96-8.

[101] Edwards, *Memoirs*, in the *Works*, 1:cxxxviii; *Distinguishing Marks*, in the *Works*, 2:263-64.

[102] Jenson, *Edwards*, 72.

[103] Murray, *Edwards*, 137-38.

[104] Miller, *Edwards*, 232-33; Murray, *Edwards*, 392.

[105] Edwards, *Thoughts on Revival*, in the *Works*, 1:401.

[106] D. Martyn Lloyd-Jones, *Conversions Psychological and Spiritual* (London: IVP, 1959), 33.

[107] Edwards, *Works*, 2:7-12. See also other sermons on hell in Edwards, *Works*, 2:78-89, and Miller, *Edwards*, 160-1.

[108] See his sermons in Edwards, *Works*, 2:89-93, 110-13.

[109] Murray, *Edwards*, 130, 170, 173.

[110] Edwards, *Memoirs*, in the *Works*, 1:xliii; Edwards, *Narrative of Conversions*, in the *Works*, 1:349-350; Murray, *Edwards*, 85, 89; Harry S. Stout, *The New England Soul* (New York: Oxford, 1986), 188.

[111] Edwards, *Memoirs*, in the *Works*, 1:cxxxi.

[112] Jenson, *Edwards*, 62-63, 75.

[113] Edwards, sermon in the *Works*, 2:92-93.

[114] John Piper, *The Supremacy of God in Preaching* (Grand Rapids: Baker, 1990), 93, quoting Edwards, *Thoughts on Revival.*
[115] Edwards, sermon in the *Works*, 2:112-13; emphasis added.
[116] John H. Gerstner & Jonathan Neil Gerstner, "Edwardsean Preparation for Salvation", *Westminster Theological Journal*, 42 (Fall 1979), 37; Edwards, sermon in the *Works*, 2:825-29.
[117] Edwards, *Memoirs*, 1:lviii, lix.
[118] Winslow, *Edwards*, 180, quoting from a manuscript of Stephen Williams' diary in the Richard Salter Storr Library, Longmeadow, Mass (spelling etc. as in the original).
[119] Nathan O. Hatch & Harry S. Stout (eds), *Jonathan Edwards and the American Experience* (NY: Oxford, 1988), 169.
[120] Edwards, *Thoughts on Revival*, in the *Works*, 1:366, 371-74, 423; Edwards, *Distinguishing Marks*, in the *Works*, 2:271; Hatch, *American*, 169; Murray, *Edwards*, 218-19.
[121] Edwards, *Narrative of Conversions*, in the *Works*, 1:350; Hatch, *American*, 170.
[122] Edwards, *Narrative of Conversions*, in the *Works*, 1:350-59; Edwards, *Distinguishing Marks*, in the *Works*, 2:270-71.
[123] Edwards, *Narrative of Conversions*, in the *Works*, 1:352; Edwards, *Religious Affections* (Yale), 95; Stout, *New England*, 203, 206.
[124] Miller, *Edwards*, 186.
[125] Miller, *Edwards*, 211.
[126] Edwards, *Memoirs*, in the *Works*, 1:xxxviii-xxxix; Murray, *Edwards*, 137-147.
[127] Edwards, *Narrative of Conversions*, in the *Works*, 1:350-361; Edwards, *Thoughts on Revival*, in the *Works*, 1:376-78.
[128] Edwards, *Thoughts on Revival*, in the *Works*, 1:367.
[129] Edwards, *Religious Affections* (Yale), 344-364, 376-407.
[130] Edwards, *Narrative of Conversions*, in the *Works*, 1:349, 355, 361.
[131] Murray, *Edwards*, 165.
[132] Murray, *Edwards*, 394-95.

Chapter 2

The Early Period of the Altar Call

Its Likely Origins

If Wesley, Whitefield or Edwards were neither the founders nor even users of the altar call system, with whom did it start and when?

The public invitation would appear to have first been used sometime in the eighteenth century, yet does not appear to have become systematized until early in the next. As early as 1810, Francis Asbury, the American Methodist leader, was trying to ensure that new Methodist meeting houses included "as much as one seat space left before the pulpit for mourners",[1] clearly indicating that the public invitation was a common part of American Methodist worship by that time.

In 1812 in Missouri, the Baptist preacher, Wilson Thompson, ended his sermon in "solemn stillness". Later he recalled, that at first there "was not a motion nor a sound ... until simultaneously, some twenty or more persons arose from their seats and came forward."[2] There had been no invitation for public response, but it would seem that these new settlers from the east (Missouri had only just been declared a territory, and most of the population were recent arrivals) had been so used to that practice that when they became religiously aroused through Thompson's preaching, they adopted the practice with which they were familiar.

It is probably impossible to pinpoint with certainty the precise beginnings of the public invitation system. However, it most likely came into being through various incidents, most of which were spontaneous rather than planned, which, in some cases at least, were noticed, adopted and adapted, and slowly developed into a system. (To qualify as a "system" the public invitation would need to be conducted regularly, or at least frequently, and there would need to be at least some measure of prior intent to use it.) Its history will here be examined from the Great Awakening in America and the Evangelical Revival in the British Isles, for as has been suggested in the introduction its origins are unlikely to predate that.

The Pietists in America

An argument can be made for regarding the commencement of the American Great Awakening as being in the mid-1720s. Certainly the American colonies experienced revivals before the coming of George Whitefield, and the most significant of these revivals were amongst the Dutch Reformed pietists in New Jersey in the 1720s.[3] Whilst revival should not be equated with the altar call, is it possible that the pietists, with their intensely personal religion, first used the public invitation, or set in place the foundation for its use? Pietism was born in seventeenth century Germany, and subsequent German immigration to America was considerable; according to W.W. Sweet, 70 000 Germans came to America between 1727 and 1765,[4] plus many Dutch. So if, as seems probable, the public appeal was born in America, some pietistic influence in its birth is possible.

The key figure in the New Jersey revival of the 1720s was T.J. Frelinghuysen, who enthusiastically preached a clear gospel of personal conversion.[5] There are echoes in his sermons of many modern day evangelistic addresses. In one he encourages his listeners to forsake everything, and to give themselves "over completely and for all time - not just for once - to God", and to "daily renew the surrender".[6]

W.O. Thompson says, with justification, that it is difficult "To determine the full significance of Frelinghuysen upon the emergence of the invitation",[7] and what is said of the one man, might be said also of the pietistic movement as a whole. Its ministers preached a religion stressing an individual and personal relationship with God, and in the case of Frelinghuysen some of his phrases fit perfectly with the theology behind the public invitation. (The theological backdrop to the altar call will be examined in chapter five). It is probably best, however, to think of pietism, and Frelinghuysen in particular, as one of several foundation stones upon which the system was built. That Frelinghuysen may have also had a small impact upon the introduction of the public invitation through his pronouncements about the Lord's Supper will be looked at later in this chapter.

Two Suitable Seed Beds

It had become increasingly common in the eighteenth century on both sides of the Atlantic for ministers to pray with and counsel those concerned about their spiritual well being, either immediately after sermon or sometime during the following week, as has been noted with Wesley, Whitefield and Edwards.[8] It would seem highly probable that the seed beds of British and American evangelistic counseling were sources from which the public invitation grew. Sometimes the preacher met with individuals, at other times with groups. But in the early part of the eighteenth century the initiative to hold such an encounter was most often with the subject, and it was never in response to a public invitation.

In the early 1740s a revival broke out in Cambuslang near Glasgow and spread to adjoining districts and other parts of Scotland.[9] On 16 May 1742 in Kilsyth (a nearby town), James Robe recorded that after he had officially dismissed his congregation he attempted to get a number of spiritually "distressed" people into his barn, so that he might speak to them about their spiritual condition, but there were too many to fit there, so they had to be taken back into the kirk. Speaking proved more difficult than Robe expected because he was unable to make himself heard above their "cries and groans". He then gave his helpers instructions to bring those under conviction to his office one at a time, whilst advising his elders to pray with those that remained in the church. He also sent for another minister to assist him in the demanding task of counseling dozens of inquirers.[10] In that same revival an unnamed person wrote that one minister had to preach almost daily because of the demands of his parishioners, and after he had preached he "usually" spent time "in exhortation, prayer and singing psalms" with those who needed help.[11] On another occasion one young lady, so overcome by spiritual concern that she cried out during a service, was led by an elder from the church into an adjoining room used for counseling, but though this may have been public, there is not even a hint in the account that this might have been the result of a public invitation.[12]

In the 1750s Thomas Walsh, one of Wesley's preachers in England, at times "endeavoured to have as many private interviews" with seekers as possible. On one occasion he was said to have met "the penitents" after an evening service,[13] but no mention is made of how the penitents were assembled.

In America, James Davenport, a member of an important New England Christian family (and apparently at times mentally unbalanced),[14] was noted for using extravagant methods. Joshua Hempstead recorded that on 18 July 1741 in New London, Connecticut, at the end of a service Davenport

> went into the broad alley (aisle), which was much crowded, and there screamed out, "Come to Christ! Come to Christ! Come away!" Then he went into the third pew on the women's side and kept there, sometimes singing, sometimes praying; he and his companions all taking their turns, and the women fainting in hysterics.[15]

Pastor Joseph Fish, whose ministry Davenport disrupted for a time, recalled that he gave "unrestrained liberty to noise and outcry", and those of his listeners who groaned in remorse one moment and then cried out in joy the next were "instantly proclaimed converts".[16]

The Public Invitation

Once counseling after sermon had become common it was probably inevitable that some preachers would look for quick and efficient methods to get those showing spiritual concern into a counseling situation. But the earliest occurrences of the public invitation in the period under discussion appear to have been incidental rather than planned.

Perhaps the first incident identifiable as a public invitation was in the ministry of Eleazer Wheelock, a relative of James Davenport.[17] Whilst visiting Taunton in Massachusetts on 1 November 1741, Wheelock concluded one sermon, but the people would not go home, so, after a short break, he preached again, this time on Hos. 13:13 ("The sorrows of a travailing woman shall come upon him"). The minister of the Taunton church, Josiah Crocker, reported that Wheelock spoke about the matters which hinder a "person's convictions from issuing in conversion". Crocker's account continues:

> He was delivering his discourse very pleasantly and moderately ... By and by, some began to cry out, both above and below, in awful distress and anguish of soul, upon which he raised his voice, that he might be heard above their outcries; but the distress and outcry spreading and increasing, his voice was at length so drowned that he could not be heard. Wherefore, not being able to finish his sermon ... he called to the distressed [after

consultation with Crocker], and desired them to gather themselves together in the body of the seats below. This he did, that he might the more conveniently converse with them, counsel, direct, exhort them, &c.[18]

If Crocker's account is accurate, and there seems to be no good reason to believe otherwise, it is clear that Wheelock's act was not premeditated, but, seemingly, a desperate solution to a particular set of circumstances. But it is clearly a public invitation as has earlier been defined: at the conclusion of a presentation of the gospel (a forced conclusion it is true), people were invited to make an observable, public response by gathering in a specific part of the building, and this was followed by counseling.

Joseph Tracy, who included this account in his study of the Great Awakening, said that Wheelock "ought not to have done it ... He should have sent his hearers home, to engage in solitary, serious thought, in reading the Bible and in prayer." Tracy goes on, though, to state that it was not long before others followed Wheelock's example. He says that, "from about this time, and in the mode here exemplified, false conversions were fearfully multiplied",[19] but he gives no details. As Tracy was writing a century after the actual event, this comment cannot be taken as proving that soon after Wheelock's impromptu venture others were using the public invitation ("the mode here exemplified"), without other evidence. None has so far been found.

Another invitation, though one that probably does not quite fit our definition (there are insufficient details given), was made two months later when Crocker was a guest preacher in Middleborough, Massachusetts. During one sermon there was no audible distress from anyone in the congregation, but after the people had been dismissed about 100 remained outside the church crying out in despair. Crocker and his host, Peter Thacher, then invited them back into the meeting house to be counseled.[20]

Early Development of the Public Invitation in America

The Presbyterian Church in America experienced a temporary division into two factions during the Great Awakening, forming the "New Sides" and the "Old Sides". There were several reasons for the split. Amongst them were differences over the revival and itinerancy. The "New Sides" were very evangelistic and strongly favored the revival, and also approved the right to itinerate, whereas the "Old Sides" rejected what they perceived

as the Awakening's excesses and the idea of one minister working in
another's territory uninvited. The Presbyterians divided in 1741, but
reunited in 1758.[21]

In February 1744 (or 5), Parson Henry, a Church of England minister
from Virginia, accused the New Side Presbyterian preachers of using a
very dramatic and even aggressive pulpit manner to raise "conviction" in
their congregations,

> until the weaker sort of [their] hearers being scar'd, cry out, fall down &
> work like people in convulsion fits... and if only a few are thus brought
> down, the Preacher gets into a violent passion again, Calling out Will no
> more of you come to Christ? ..and they who thus cry out and fall down are
> caress'd and commended as the only penitent Souls who come to Christ,
> whilst they who don't are often condemn'd by the lump as hardened
> wretches almost beyond the reach of mercy (sic).

If this is an accurate presentation of "New Side" Presbyterian methods,
then here is an early example of pressure being brought to bear on a
congregation to respond in some observable form, though the details are
not quite sufficient to determine whether it fits within our definition. It
must be remembered, however, that Henry and other Anglican clergy had
been strongly attacked by the "New Sides", and the comments above were
part of Henry's response to that criticism.[22] These words may, therefore,
be well laced with hyperbole. No other evidence has been found to suggest
that any section of the Presbyterian Church in America was using the
public invitation as early as the mid-eighteenth century.

The Great Awakening also caused division in the Congregational
Church in New England. In 1743 its annual meeting in Massachusetts
passed, against considerable opposition, a declaration condemning many
revival practices, such as itinerancy and lay exhorting. Those favoring the
revival were dubbed the "New Lights", their opponents the "Old Lights".
The eventual result was a three-way split. The "Old Lights" formed one
group, the "New Lights" two. One of the "New Light" groups, which
included Jonathan Edwards and Wheelock, strongly favored the revival,
though they had some reservations about certain aspects of it. The third
group was made up of out and out revivalists, dubbed "Separates",[23] who
in some instances at least, were influenced by James Davenport.[24] Both
"New Light" groups had strong objections to the "Halfway Covenant",
that symbol of a sleeping church, which allowed adults who had been
baptized as infants to be considered in some sense part of the church and
to take communion, even though they had shown no evidence of

conversion.[25] The Separates also encouraged the use of lay exhorters to supplement the work of the ordained ministers.[26]

The Separates desired a pure church, which contained only those who had been born again, and often excommunicated those who did not measure up. Also, they frequently quoted "Wherefore come out from among them, and be ye separate, saith the Lord" (2 Cor. 6:17).[27] Is it possible that in this Separatist climate the desire for a clear distinction between the converted and the unconverted led to a method to distinguish between the two? It is, indeed, possible that an early system of public invitation developed in this environment on the basis of coming "out from among them". Many of the Separates eventually became Baptists,[28] and these Separate Baptists definitely were amongst the first to use the public invitation, and may have been the first to systematize it.

In his *History of Grassy Creek Baptist Church,* R.I. Devin records a practice which appears to have occurred some time towards the end of the eighteenth century in that North Carolina Separate Baptist church. He says,

> At the close of the sermon, the minister would come down from the pulpit and while singing a suitable hymn would go around among the brethren shaking hands. The hymn being sung, he would then extend an invitation to such persons as felt themselves to be poor guilty sinners, and were anxiously inquiring the way of salvation, to come forward and kneel near the stand, or ... kneel at their seats, proffering to unite with them in prayer for their conversion.[29]

Howard Olive dates this method as being used from the 1750s right through to the 1780s; W.O. Thompson regards it as common practice by the Separate Baptists of North Carolina by 1771, though he concedes that Devin's dating is unclear. William Lumpkin does not venture a date, but includes it with other material dated in the 1770s and Steve O'Kelly regards this as their practice by 1770.[30] If these datings are close to being correct, then some of the Separate Baptists regularly used a specific form of the public invitation with some frequency and prior consideration, and thus by the 1770s had systematized it.

But there are doubts about this early dating of the practice, nor is it really certain how frequently or widely it was used at first. Devin's *History,* which appears to be the only source of this information, does not date it clearly. Devin states that coming forward to sit on an "anxious seat" was not used at Grassy Creek until "about 1825 or '30", and seems to indicate that the "anxious seat" replaced the method mentioned above.

He also said, writing in 1880, that he had searched the church's records "running back more than *a hundred and ten years*", thus to 1770. Devin also says that the coming forward to kneel and the methods related to it were the measures "then employed", "then" seemingly referring to the period prior to the introduction of the "anxious seat" in 1825.[31] So it becomes a question of how far back Devin's "then" goes. It could be to the 1770s, but may be one, two or even three decades later.

It may be significant that one of the nine Christian rites practiced by the Separate Baptists of Sandy Creek in North Carolina[32] (and some other Separate Baptist churches), from their early days in 1755 was giving the "right hand of fellowship", though the circumstances in which that hand was extended are not stated.[33] This method of Baptist preachers descending from the pulpit and walking around the congregation, shaking hands and exhorting individuals to repent, is also mentioned as happening at the commencement of the next century.[34] It is possible, then, that some Separate Baptist churches were regularly using a form of the altar call by the 1770s, but it is, perhaps, more likely that at that time their usage of the public invitation was occasional rather than frequent and they probably did not use it regularly until the end of that century or the beginning of the next.

O'Kelly regards the public invitation as one of nine practices related to evangelism and worship "perpetuated" by the Separate Baptists, though he does not elaborate. Strangely, he describes it as a practice that they "reinstituted", it having not been used "for many centuries", but he gives no evidence to support this[35]

The Sandy Creek Separate Baptists did not adopt their first full confession of faith until 1816, and then they revised it along less calvinistic lines in 1845.[36] McBeth suggests that their "evangelistic practices tended to determine their theology", rather than the other way round,[37] so this change in theology may have been moved by a change in evangelistic method. The geographically well-situated Sandy Creek church, under the leadership of the energetic Shubal Stearns, was very influential and spawned many other churches.[38] Morgan Edwards has called it "the mother of all the Separate Baptists."[39]

In the Canterbury Separate Church it would seem possible that going forward was used in another way too, if the following reference is to be taken literally. In the church's minutes it is recorded that the church voted to

give Br Cleaveland fellowship in his gifts and Calling and Desier that he

Improve as god Shall give him grase and opertunity and allso that Every
member of this Church *Cum forward* to Improve the giftes god hath given
for the Edifycation of the body (sic).[40]

It is not clear here, however, whether the term *"Cum forward"* is meant to
be taken literally or not. The problem of when to take the phrase "come
forward" literally or otherwise will be looked at later in this chapter.

Streett says that in 1785 John Taylor of Kentucky, one of the first
Baptist preachers to arrive in that state, called inquirers to the front of his
church, and "two men and their wives ... came forward".[41] Here Streett is
misinterpreting H.R. McLendon's "Mourner's Bench". McLendon
certainly says that, "two men and their wives ... came forward", but does
not say that it was as a result of an appeal by Taylor.[42] Indeed, in later
references to seemingly the same incident McLendon says that they went
forward of their own accord, and were not actually converted until later,[43]
though it could be argued that the fact that they did go forward suggests
familiarity with the practice.

Methodism in America

The precise date of the arrival of Methodism in America is debated,
but the establishment of the first regular Methodist societies in America
appears to have taken place in the mid 1760s.[44] American Methodism was
to have a key part to play in the development of the altar call.

Amongst the first preachers Wesley sent from England to assist his
struggling church in America were Thomas Rankin and George Shadford,
who arrived on 3 June 1773.[45] In the early to mid-1770s a revival sprang
up in Virginia under the ministry of Deveraux Jarratt, an evangelical
Anglican.[46] Rankin and Shadford and other Methodists joined forces with
Jarratt and the revival gained a new impetus. On 30 June 1776, Rankin
and Shadford were at a meeting at Boisseau's Chapel, and while Rankin
was preaching,

> such power descended, that hundreds fell to the ground, and the house
> seemed to shake with the presence of God. The chapel was full of white and
> black... Look wherever we would, we saw nothing but streaming eyes, and
> faces bathed in tears; and heard nothing but groans and strong cries after
> God and the Lord Jesus Christ... Husbands were inviting their wives to go
> to heaven, wives their husbands; parents their children, and children their
> parents; brothers their sisters, and sisters their brothers. In short, those who
> were ... happy in God themselves, were for bringing all their friends to him

in their arms. We [Rankin and Shadford] attempted to speak or sing again
and again; but no sooner we began than our voices were drowned.[47]

It is true that there is no clear mention of a public invitation, as it has been
defined, in that account. However, the record of a service on the following
day goes a step closer. It is from the pen of Jesse Lee (an American-born
preacher and historian), who was present as a youth. He says that
Shadford was invited to speak after another speaker (presumably Rankin)
had concluded. Lee continues that Shadford spoke

> with pleasure, and in a little time cried out in his *usual manner:* "Who wants
> a Saviour? the first that believes shall be justified." In a few minutes the
> house was ringing with the cries of broken hearted sinners and the shouts of
> happy believers.[48]

The definition of the altar call in use in this book included "calling out a
response" to a sermonic appeal, and this incident seems to fit that clause
of the definition. It could be argued that Shadford might not have expected
an audible response, or that the "cries" and "shouts" were not in direct
response to the appeal, but the account does sound like an authentic public
invitation. Now, Lee states that this was done in Shadford's "usual
manner". Precisely what he meant by this phrase is not clear. It could just
refer to Shadford's style of preaching, or it could mean that he regularly
made a form of direct invitation, even, possibly, for a public response. It
needs, however, to be stated that no other clear evidence of Shadford's
using the public invitation has been uncovered.

Neither does there seem any evidence that a regular invitation for
seekers to respond publicly was used in this revival, though regular after-
sermon prayer and counseling were given. Jarratt speaks of some people
in distress after one service refusing to leave the chapel, and of their being
counseled by "Some lively Christians". It was common for some of his
helpers to be "praying all at once, in several parts of the room, for
distressed persons."[49]

It should be noted that Rankin appears to have had some contact with
the Baptists in America,[50] and Shadford may have, so the possibility of
American Baptist influence in the above cannot be excluded. Certainly,
the Baptists were very strong in Virginia, where these events took place.[51]
As Shadford (and Rankin) returned to England in 1778,[52] his story will be
picked up again, when the origins of the altar call in Britain are examined.

Jesse Lee (1758-1816) does not seem to have been a great user of the
public invitation himself. The paucity of references to it in his *Journal*

either suggests he only used it rarely, or that he did not see it as a sufficiently significant thing to record. A reasonably frequent incidental mentioning of it, however, would seem inevitable, if he was using the practice often. Indeed, his own record of his preaching from 1785-89 seems to preclude the possibility that he was using it at that time, at least on a regular basis.[53] He does, though, write that in one revival in which he participated, in Virginia in 1787, several Methodist preachers preached outdoors, and many of their hearers fell to the ground. He says that, "the mourners were collected together," though he does not indicate the method used for doing so.[54] In June 1789, he speaks of some of his congregation staying to talk to him "about religion," and again in July,[55] but there is no indication that an appeal was used to assemble them. In September 1789, he preached at a meeting of Separate Baptists in Rhode Island. This sermon was followed by singing, then personal testimony and exhortation by members of the congregation (which included such invitations as "come to the Lord Jesus Christ", directed to a person by name), but there is no indication that he joined in or considered adopting this practice.[56] He once more mentions that several persons spoke to him to request his prayers, after a service had been dismissed in March 1790, but no mention is made of a public invitation.[57]

There is, though, one very clear mention of its use in his company, though it was not necessarily given by him. On 31 October 1798, in Paup's Meeting House, Virginia, Lee says that he was exhorting after Francis Asbury had preached, when they became very aware of the power of God. He goes on,

> many wept, and some cried aloud with deep distress. Then Miles Harper exhorted, and dismissed the assembly. The class was desired to remain. Brother Mead ... began to sing, and in a little while many were affected, and a general weeping began. John Easter proclaimed aloud, "I have not a doubt in my soul but what my God will convert a soul today!" The preachers then requested all that were under conviction to come together. Several men and women came, and fell upon their knees; and the preachers, for some time, kept singing, and exhorting the mourners... Then prayer was made in behalf for the mourners, and two or three found peace.[58]

"The preachers" who did the calling "together", presumably, would include Lee, though it may have just been one of the group who actually made the invitation, and if so, it was not necessarily him. It is also of particular interest here that only "The class" was still present, which presumably refers to the class or classes of that congregation into which

Methodist societies were divided. A class usually contained those already converted, plus those seeking Christ, and would normally have less than twenty members, but the phrase "many were afflicted" suggests more remained than just one class.[59]

In Baltimore, on 18 May 1800, after Lee had preached "several prayed with those that were under conviction", but he does not mention how those souls were identified.[60] Lee's ministry was mainly in the eastern, particularly the north-eastern states, rather than in the developing western regions, and this may be one reason why he may have used the public invitation rarely.

Early in 1789 James Haw, an early Methodist arrival in Kentucky, wrote to Francis Asbury telling him that at a quarterly meeting they

> had another gracious season around the Lord's table, but no remarkable stir until after preaching; when, under several exhortations, some burst out into tears, others trembled, and some fell. I sprang in among the people, and the Lord converted one more very powerfully.[61]

Though this is not clearly a public invitation as has been defined (this cannot be certainly determined without knowing the content of the "exhortations"), it is very overt, both on the part of preacher and convert, and there is a strong suggestion there of the preacher's expectation of a public response.

McLendon relates that around 1790 in Tennessee, the revivalist J.A. Granade conducted a protracted meeting for ten days, during which "Scores of mourners crowded the mourner's bench", though McLendon does not state how the seekers were assembled.[62]

William Burke, later a Methodist minister, says that in February 1791, he was in a congregation when the preacher after his sermon "opened the door to receive members. I went forward alone and gave my name."[63] In context, his comments make it likely that this was a conversion experience, rather than a formal reception into membership, and it seems probable that "opened the door" refers to some form of invitation for public response. On another occasion, speaking of a love-feast during a revival centered around the camp-meetings at the beginning of the next century, Burke could say, "the doors were thrown open, and the work became general," and from this "numbers experienced justification by faith".[64] However, two other uses of this phrase, "opened the door", one Methodist, one Baptist,[65] both seem to refer to reception into membership. This phrase may also refer to opening the door in the communion rail, so that those coming forward could sit or kneel around the communion table.

One very clear and early use of a public invitation in Methodism was in 1795 or 1796 in a house in Pennsylvania. Valentine Cook invited "the mourners to come to the vacated seats in front of the communion table" to be prayed for.[66] Though there seems to be some uncertainty about the date, it could not be later than 1798 for Cook was posted from Pennsylvania to Kentucky that year.[67]

One of the reasons for getting inquirers to come together or to come forward was because of the difficulty of dealing with them when scattered throughout a church. The German Methodist preacher Henry Boehm praised the practice when he saw it in action in Maryland in 1800, because "By bringing them together they were accessible to those who desired to instruct and encourage them."[68] The tone of his comments strongly suggests that this was the first time he had seen such an occurrence, which indicates that though in some parts of America it was becoming quite popular, in others it was rare or unknown.

Like Boehm, Stith Mead, another Methodist, found the method of getting the mourners to come to the front useful during a revival in northern Georgia in 1801-3. It had been Mead's method to counsel each inquirer privately, but owing to the large number in spiritual distress in one service he called them all to the front, that he might speak to them together.[69] On one occasion during this period, Mead decided to pray for the penitents and invited them to come and kneel around the communion table. The response, if not large, was most dramatic. Two young women went forward, "pressing over the benches and people with loud lamentations."[70]

Boehm was one of the preachers at an open-air service on 18 April 1802, about which William Colbert records that in the pouring rain "a great number of mourners came to join us in prayer when the invitation was given."[71] This is an early use of the term "invitation" in the context of the public invitation.

Another reason for using the altar call can be found in a letter written by Richard Sneath, about his practice in Philadelphia early in 1801. He wrote,

> I invited all the mourners to come to the communion table, that we might pray particularly for them. This I found to be useful, as it removed the shame which often hinders souls coming to Christ, excited them to the exercise of faith.[72]

From the above it can be seen that the Methodists in America were certainly using the public invitation by the beginning of the nineteenth century, but it is not clear how widespread the practice was amongst them. It will be seen in chapter four on the camp-meetings how it became their common practice.

A Change of Century

The possibility of American Baptist influence in the very early use of the altar call has already been noted. But if there is uncertainty about its use by Baptists in the 1770s and 1780s, there is none about its use right at the end of that century. In 1799 Jeremiah Vardeman,[73] a Separate Baptist lay preacher, later ordained, was confronted by a number of his Kentucky congregation coming forward in great distress after a sermon, asking for prayer, without an invitation having been given. In meetings immediately after the experience, Vardeman, "gave an invitation to all who felt conscious of their sinfulness and need of the power and grace of Christ, and who desired the prayers of God's people, come forward and give him their hands". According to James E. Welch, this was done without undue pressure.[74]

The Baptist preacher, Lemuel Burkitt recorded that in 1801 in North Carolina

> The ministers *usually,* at the close of preaching, would tell the congregation, that if there were any persons who felt themselves lost and condemned ... that if they would come up near the stage, and kneel down, they would pray for them.[75]

Yet, as Olive points out, it may not have been as common in Baptist circles as Burkitt there suggests, for writing of the following January, Burkitt says of one service at Cashie Church, North Carolina:

> Towards the close of the worship [the preacher said] "if there was any person in the congregation who saw himself in a lost condemned state by reason of sin, if he would come up to the table, at the pulpit, he would pray to the Lord for him." [About three came forward.] The people had never seen an instance of the like before.[76]

The probability is that at this time it was common in some areas but unknown in others, even in the same state, which may have been because only some ministers were using it and the practice generally only moved with them.

Another occurrence is recorded by Henry Smith, a Methodist itinerant. He wrote in his diary for 19 May 1803:

> I preached at Frontayel. I met the class, having invited all who wished to serve the Lord to stay with us. Eight or ten did so. After I had spoken to the class I opened a door to receive members into the society. None seemed disposed to join. I then proposed to pray for those who were mournin to know the love of God if they would come forward and kneelg down. Eight or ten came (sic).[77]

The examples given of the public invitation thus far appear mainly in the Separate Baptist and Methodist churches, and probably only represent the tip of the iceberg of what was actually taking place in this period in those denominations. But the practice also began to spread to other denominations.

New England Congregational Churches

The following account is reported from the childhood experience of Ebenezer Porter, who was ordained into the Congregational ministry around 1796/7,[78] though it is not clear under what denominational auspices this particular incident happened. It presumably took place, however, not later than 1790. Porter recalled that

> a zealous preacher, at the close of a public lecture, called on all impenitent sinners, "who could then make up their minds to be on the Lord's side", to rise and declare that purpose by speaking aloud ... After a dead silence of a few moments, five or six men rose made the declaration which was desired.

Porter indicates that this was one of two such incidents he could recall having seen before his own ordination.[79]

That the public invitation was used in American Congregational churches in the final decade of the eighteenth century and the first of the next could be supported by some accounts of revivals in New England in that period. One problem encountered in this research is when to take the phrase "came (come) forward" literally or otherwise. In most cases it is undoubtedly meant in a literal sense, whilst occasionally it appears to be used metaphorically. But at times the usage is unclear. A significant group of such usages is found in the book, *New England Revivals* by Bennet Tyler, which details a sequence of revivals in New England

Congregational churches at the turn of the century. This book repeatedly emphasizes the conservative and orderly nature of these revivals,[80] and they hardly seem the setting for new, controversial practices. In addition, Bennet Tyler, himself, strongly opposed the New Haven Theology and the "new measures" in revival it supported and most specifically the public invitation.[81] Yet, the phrase "come forward" keeps appearing, and it is hard not to take it literally on some occasions, as shall be seen.

Jeremiah Hallock, writing of revival in Canton, Connecticut, in 1798-9, could say: "The number who have made a public profession is fifty-nine, and it is expected that others will come forward, and subscribe with their hands unto the Lord." In similar circumstances in 1805-6, Hallock recorded that "Fifteen have joined the church, and others are expected to come forward, and subscribe with their hands unto the Lord."[82]

Again in 1798-9, Alexander Gillet of Torrington wrote:

> The number that came forward and made a profession of religion is forty-five ... There are besides upwards of thirty who have expressed a hope that they are the subjects of this wonderful work; but they have not as yet dared to come forward because they fear that they have been deceived. [83]

Elijah Lyman of Brookfield, Vermont, in 1801 hoped that he would see some of those concerned about their souls "coming forward publicly to profess Christ."[84] One converted at Killingworth, Connecticut, in that same year could later recall that he "went forward and made a public profession of religion" in April or soon after. But all was still not well, and in November he came under strong conviction of sin, and only after that was he "born again".[85] Of 1803, David Smith of Durham, Connecticut, could write that "forty persons came forward and publicly professed the religion of Jesus."[86]

One thing noticeable about most of these accounts is that coming forward is linked with some statement about public profession of faith, and though it is difficult to prove that a literal coming forward is meant, it is strongly suggested. One can only guess what Hallock's "subscribe with their hands unto the Lord" might mean (he uses this exact phrase on both occasions). It could refer to a handshake, signing a document (perhaps to do with membership), or just a reference to working for God after conversion.

However, a letter written in the 1830s might give the answer. In it a pastor by the name of Francis Robbins of the Congregational church in Enfield, Connecticut could speak of nearly twenty young people converted under the ministry of Asahel Nettleton, who "Not long after he left... came forward, and made a public profession of religion".[87] This is unlikely to refer to the Altar Call as such, because of Nettleton's known opposition to it, and may refer to acceptance into membership of that church. It is possible that this is also what the earlier occurrences mean, but that is far from certain.

The Lord's Supper and the Altar Call

In the mid-eighteenth century, in at least some of the churches in America, and, indeed, many in Britain, people taking communion would go forward to do so.[88] It is possible that this also played a part in creating the environment for the public invitation. T.J. Frelinghuysen, the Dutch pietist whose ministry was considered earlier, insisted that only the "penitent, believing, upright and converted persons" could come forward to take communion. In a series of sermons on that ordinance, he frequently urged his listeners to "approach" the table worthily, and "approach" is used literally here, as well as possibly figuratively. On one occasion when members of his congregation had accepted his invitation to move forward to receive the elements, he announced, "See! See! Even the people of the world and the impenitent are coming, that they may eat and drink judgment on themselves", at which some would-be communicants hastily returned to their seats.[89] In one of these sermons he forbade "the unconverted" to go forward to take communion, but for those truly showing evidence of conversion he stated that they "not only may, but must approach."[90] Earlier we considered Frelinghuysen to be a probable foundation stone upon which the public invitation system was built, rather than as its first user. Here his seeming emphasis on going forward for communion (or not doing so) suggests a link between the communion service and the public invitation, even though here those encouraged to go forward were those believing themselves to be already converted.

Thomas Olivers, an early English Methodist (writing in 1779) on the Sunday after his conversion in 1748 could speak of "the *invitation* to the Lord's supper, which was to be administered the next Sunday".[91] It is far from certain that the term "invitation" can conveniently be seen as an example of this suggested link, but neither can it be ruled out. Calvin Colton, a Presbyterian evangelist of the 1820s and 1830s, said that the practice of assembling candidates for full admission into the church that they might make confession of their faith, in front of the established congregation, prior to their receiving communion for the first time, was a custom used "extensively" in American churches. Colton immediately goes on from speaking about this practice to discussing the "anxious seat" (which he favored in moderation), suggesting that he too may have seen a link.[92] The evangelistic "altar" and its usage will be looked at in the chapter on camp-meetings, but this term also implies a link with the Lord's Supper, and in addition suggests Church of England/Methodist origins. John Wesley, of course, remained a staunch Anglican till the day he died, though the American Methodist church severed ties with the Church of England in 1784.[93] The Canadian, Robert More Jr. appears convinced of such a link with the term "altar call" at least, seeing the progression as: Church of England eucharistic practice and terminology - John Wesley - Methodism - American camp-meetings (Methodist dominated) - American evangelism.[94] He is probably correct with regard to the term "altar call", though definite proof is lacking so far.

Public Confession and the Altar Call

Another factor that may have influenced the emergence of the public invitation is the practice of public confession of sin. This was particularly evident in early Methodism, both in Britain and America. The medium for this was normally the class meeting. Class meetings were originally formed by John Wesley in 1742, and were expected to contain about twelve members. One aspect of them was for each member to confess his or her sins publicly, often at the prompting of the class leader.[95] Though this confession was not usually done before the whole Methodist Society, it was still public, and as the process towards conversion would also normally include confession of sin, it might be that some felt it necessary that that confession should also be made public.

In addition were the testimonies given by Separate Baptist baptismal candidates. It was the normal policy for each candidate to give an account of their conversion or some brief statement of their faith to the assembled congregation.[96] This would often, no doubt, include confession of sin. This also could have encouraged the development of the public invitation.

Summary

At this stage, then, the altar call appears to have been used only in America, though part of its base had been developed in Britain. (It shall be seen, though, in chapter seven that there are hints of its usage in Britain and one American using a form of it in the British Isles before the close of the eighteenth century). Its practice was not only to be found across a wide range of states, but also in several major denominations. Its usage thus far seems to be, for the most part, spasmodic rather than systematized, though Baptists, especially the Separates, and Methodists seem to have been using it quite frequently, and there appears to have been, at least, the germ of systematization in their practice.

Notes

[1] Francis Asbury, *The Journal and Letters of Francis Asbury* (3 vols. ed. Elmer T. Clark *et al.* London: Epworth, 1958), 1: 436.

[2] Iain Murray, *Revival and Revivalism* (Edinburgh: Banner of Truth, 1994), 226.

[3] Wesley M. Gewehr, The Great Awakening in Virginia, 1740-1790 (Gloucester: Smith, 1965), 4-5; William Warren Sweet, Revivalism in America: Its Origin, Growth and Decline (NY: Scribner's, 1945), 26.

[4] Sweet, *Revivalism*, 16.

[5] Sweet, *Revivalism*, 26, 46-51; W.O. Thompson Jr., "The Public Invitation as a Method of Evangelism: Its Origin and Development". Ph.D., Southwestern Baptist Theological Seminary, 1979), 26-30; Bernard A. Weisberger, *They Gathered at the River* (Boston: Little Brown, 1958), 54.

[6] Thompson, "Public Invitation", 28, quoting from Frelinghuysen's sermons in *Een Trouwhertig vertoog* (NY: 1729), translated by William Demarest.

[7] Thompson, "Public Invitation", 30.

[8] Details of others using this counseling can be found in Fawcett, *Cambuslang*, 100-101, 108-9, 133-34; John Gillies, *Historical Collection of Accounts of Revival* (Edinburgh: Banner of Truth [1845], 1981), 359-360, 368-372, 381-392, 396, 399, 402-4, 409; Joseph Tracy, *The Great Awakening* (Edinburgh: Banner of Truth [1842], 1976), 117, 138-141, 151, 157-58, 210-11.

[9] R.E. Davies, *I Will Pour Out My Spirit* (Tunbridge Wells, Monarch, 1992), 87-8; Fawcett, *Cambuslang* 101-125; MacFarlan, *Cambuslang*, 45-60, 224-28.

[10] Dallimore, *Whitefield*, 2:123; Fawcett, *Cambuslang*, 128-29; Gillies, *Revival*, 44; Tracy, *Great Awakening*, 270. See also MacFarlan, *Cambuslang*, 238-39.

[11] MacFarlan, *Cambuslang*, 48.

[12] MacFarlan, *Cambuslang*, 121.

[13] Richard Green, *Thomas Walsh: Wesley's Typical Helper* (London: Kelly, 1906), 48, 71. Walsh had a brief and vigorous ministry, dying at the age of 29.

[14] Though for some periods of his life he was quite rational, he was twice declared "judicially insane", C.C. Goen, *Revivalism and Separatism in New England, 1740-1800* (New Haven: Yale, 1962), 27. See also Tracy, *Great Awakening*, 230-255.

[15] Goen, *Revivalism*, 21.

[16] Bennett Tyler & Andrew Bonar, *Asahel Nettleton: Life and Labours* (Edinburgh: Banner of Truth, [1854] 1975), 442-43; Weisberger, *Gathered*, 57-58, both quoting from a sermon preached by Joseph Fish in 1763. Fish's overall comments do not sound like those of a bigoted man trying to get square, indeed, he twice calls Davenport a "good man" (Tyler & Bonar, 442, 446), so there is no reason to doubt his words.

[17] Goen says they were brothers-in-law, Goen, *Revivalism*, 25n51. Stout says they were cousins, Stout, *New England Soul*, 202.

[18] Gillies, *Revival*, 375-76; Tracy, *Great Awakening*, 166-68, 202. H.R. McLendon, "The Mourner's Bench" (D.Th., Southern Baptist Theological Seminary, 1902), 15, dates this as October (Streett follows him, 94 [101]), which is not an unfair deduction from Tracy's record on pages 166-68. But Tracy, 202, also has some extracts from Wheelock's Journal, and the entry for November 1 places him in Taunton and bears considerable similarity to Crocker's account recorded above (e.g. Wheelock had to stop preaching because of the uproar), though it lacks the crucial details about gathering "the distressed ... together". None of the recorded entries for October have Wheelock in Taunton. R.T. Kendall, *Stand Up and be Counted* (Grand Rapids: Zondervan, 1984), 46-47, and Streett states that the incident took place in Lebanon, Connecticut, but though Wheelock was the minister of the Lebanon church, he did itinerate and was preaching in Taunton on this occasion, see Gillies, 375-76; Tracy, 166-68.

[19] Tracy, *Great Awakening*, 167-68.

[20] Gillies, *Revival*, 404.

[21] Gewehr, *Great Awakening*, 9-18.

[22] Gewehr, *Great Awakening*, 59-61, quoting from a letter from Henry in the Dawson Manuscript in the US Library of Congress.

[23] Goen, *Revivalism*, 31-35. See also William L. Lumpkin, *Baptist Foundations in the South* (Nashville: Broadman, 1961), 13-14; William G. McLoughlin, *Isaac Backus and the American Pietistic Tradition* (Boston: Little, Brown, 1967), 15-32; Robert G.Torbet, *A History of the Baptists* (Valley Forge: Judson, 1963), 216; Tracy, *Great Awakening*, 287-88, 304-325.

[24] Tracy, *Great Awakening*, 253-54, 409.

[25] Goen, *Revivalism*, 4-5, 36-38; Tracy, *Great Awakening*, 318-19.

[26] McLoughlin, *Backus*, 16-18; Stout, *New England Soul*, 208-210.

[27] Goen, *Revivalism*, 143; 159-167; Tracy, *Great Awakening*, 316-18.

[28] Goen, *Revivalism*, 206-215; Lumpkin, *Baptist Foundations*, 15-20; McLoughlin, *Backus*, 57-88; Torbet, *Baptists*, 223-24; Tracy, *Great Awakening*, 324, 390.

[29] R.I. Devin, *History of Grassy Creek Baptist Church* (Raleigh: Edwards, Broughton & Co, 1880), 69.

[30] Lumpkin, *Baptist Foundations*, 56; Steve O'Kelly, "The Influence of the

Separate Baptists on Revivalistic Evangelism and Worship". (D.Th, Southwestern Baptist Theological Seminary, 1978), 129-130; Olive, "Evangelistic Invitation", 29; Streett, "Public Invitation", 102; Thompson, "Public Invitation", 69-71, all quoting from Devin, *Grassy Creek,* 69.

[31] Devin, *Grassy Creek,* 69-70, emphasis in the original. Thompson states that the Grassy Creek records were destroyed by fire in 1832, Thompson, "Public Invitation", 70-71n2. If this is correct, the records Devin researched were, presumably, from other churches in the same association.

[32] The Grassy Creek church was part of the Sandy Creek Baptist Association, see Lumpkin, *Baptist Foundations,* 46.

[33] Lumpkin, *Baptist Foundations,* 38-39; Joe M.King, *A History of South Carolina Baptists* (Columbia: SC Baptist, 1964), 70; H. Shelton Smith, Robert T. Hardy, & Lefferts A. Loetshcer, *American Christianity: An Historical Interpretation with Documents* (2 vols. NY: Scribner's), 1:363, the latter is quoting from Morgan Edwards, *Materials towards a History of the Baptists in the Province of North Carolina.* "The right hand of fellowship" was also given to newly ordained ministers in the Kehukee Baptist Association, C.B. Hassell, *History of the Church of God, from the Creation to AD 1885: Including especially the History of the Kehukee Primitive Baptist Association* (Middletown, NY: Beebe, 1886), 704-6; while John Leland says that in Virginia it was offered at baptism, O'Kelly, "Separate Baptists", 131, quoting John Leland, *The Virginia Chronicle* (Norfolk: Prentis & Baxter, 1790), 35.

[34] John B. Boles, *The Great Revival, 1787-1805* (Lexington: UP of Kentucky, 1972), 76, quoting Burkitt and Read, *History of the Kehukee Baptist Association* (Halifax: 1803), 144-45.

[35] O'Kelly, "Separate Baptists", 106, 128.

[36] The Separate Baptists were usually calvinists, but were reluctant to draw up confessions of faith, Goen, *Revivalism,* 284-7. See also Tom Nettles, *By His Grace & for His Glory* (Grand Rapids: Baker, 1986), 43-4. Sandy Creek did have a brief statement of faith as far back as 1757, which was also calvinistic, Lumpkin, *Baptist Foundations,* 62, quoting Devin, *Grassy Creek,* 43.

[37] H. Leon McBeth, *The Baptist Heritage* (Nashville: Broadman, 1987), 229, 234. The same might be said of another Separate Baptist, John Leland, Goen, *Revivalism,* 285-86.

[38] Goen, *Revivalism,* 296-97; Lumpkin, *Baptist Foundations,* 37-38, 40-59, 156.

[39] Richard B. Cook, *The Story of the Baptists in all Ages and Countries* (Greenwood: Attic, [1884] 1976), 259.

[40] Goen, *Revivalism,* 174, quoting from the records of the Congregational Church in Canterbury, 25 (spelling as in the original, emphasis added).

[41] Streett, "Public Invitation", 103.

[42] McLendon, "Mourner's Bench", 13, quoting from Taylor's book, *The History*

of Ten Churches, 47f. Streett also says that this was in Tennessee, but gives no reason for claiming this. He could be stumbling over McLendon's practice of abbreviating titles, and regarded Taylor's book as *Tennessee Churches* not *Ten Churches*. According to Robert B. Semple & G.W. Beale, *History of the Baptists in Virginia* (Lafayette: Church History, [1894] 1972), 415, Taylor originally ministered in Virginia, but in 1785 was experiencing revival in Kentucky.

[43]   McLendon, "Mourner's Bench", 22, 51.

[44]   W.E. Arnold, *A History of Methodism in Kentucky* (Winchester: Herald, 1935), 19-20; Nathan Bangs, *A History of the Methodist Episcopal Church* (2 vols. NY: Mason & Lane, 1839), 1:46-52; John O. Gross, *The Beginnings of American Methodism* (Nashville: Abingdon, 1961), 35-36, 40-43.

[45]   Bangs, *Methodist*, 1:77; Thomas Jackson (ed.) *The Lives of Early Methodist Preachers, Chiefly Written by Themselves* (6 vols. London: Wesleyan, 1878), 5:184-190; John Telford, *Wesley's Veterans: Lives of Early Methodist Preachers Told by Themselves* (2 vols. London: Culley, c.1909), 2:196-98.

[46]   Deveraux Jarratt, "A Brief Narrative of the Revival of Religion in Virginia. In a Letter to a Friend", Asbury, *Journal*, 1:208-211.

[47]   Thomas Rankin, extract from his Journal, Asbury, *Journal*, 1:221; Bangs, *Methodist*, 1:111-14. This is an abridgment of one of three different, but similarly worded, accounts of this incident. A very similar, but not quite as full, account appears in Rankin's brief autobiography, Jackson, *Methodist Preachers*, 5:207-8. The third account is in the third person and appears to be an adaption of the one quoted, and according to Thompson comes from Jesse Lee, though he quotes no actual reference to Lee's works, Thompson, "Public Invitation", 80-81. Thompson also says that Shadford was the preacher and not Rankin, and is presumably quoting Lee for that. But even though Lee seems to have been present on this occasion, he did not begin to keep a written record of events until eighteen months after this, see Minton Thrift, *Memoir of the Rev. Jesse Lee* (NY: Arno, [1823] 1969), 19, so Rankin's record, in diary form, is probably correct.

[48]   Thompson, "Public Invitation", 81-82, quoting Jesse Lee, *A Short History of the Methodists* (Baltimore: Magill & Clime, 1810), 58, emphasis added.

[49]   Two letters by Jarratt to Archibald McRoberts, dated 2 May 1776 and 7 May 1776, Asbury, *Journal*, 1:212-13.

[50]   Jackson, *Methodist Preachers*, 5:200.

[51]   Gewehr, *Great Awakening*, 106-137.

[52]   They returned to England because of the American Revolution, out of loyalties to their home country, Bangs, *Methodist*, 1:123-24; Jackson, *Methodist Preachers*, 5:185; Sweet, *Revivalism*, 101; Telford, *Wesley's Veterans*, 2:207-211; Thompson, "Public Invitation", 81n1.

[53]   Thrift, *Jesse Lee*, 82-83, 86, 93-5, 101-2. (A substantial part of Thrift's book is extracts from Lee's *Journal*, including the relevant material on these pages).

[54] Bangs, *Methodist,* 1:264-65, quoting Lee.

[55] Thrift, *Jesse Lee,* 110, 117, quoting Lee's *Journal.*

[56] Thrift, *Jesse Lee,* 124-25, quoting Lee's *Journal.*

[57] Thrift, *Jesse Lee,* 141, quoting Lee's *Journal.*

[58] Thrift, *Jesse Lee,* 243, quoting Lee's *Journal.* See also Asbury, *Journal,* 2:176; Robert More Jr., "The Historical Origins of 'The Altar Call'" *Banner of Truth* 75 (Dec. 1969): 30; Thompson, "Public Invitation", 83.

[59] According to Rankin, in Virginia at this time it was common practice for the Methodist preachers to meet and speak individually with each member of the local Society after a service, Thomas Rankin, Letter to John Wesley, 24 June 1777, Asbury, *Journal,* 1:219. For details of early class meetings see Wesley, *A Plain Account of the People Called Methodists,* in *Works,* 8:252-55.

[60] Thrift, *Jesse Lee,* 269-270, quoting Lee's *Journal.*

[61] Arnold, *Methodism in Kentucky,* 63-64.

[62] McLendon, "Mourner's Bench", 11, quoting from McFerrin, *Methodism in Tennessee,* 105.

[63] Olive, "Evangelistic Invitation", 25, quoting from James B. Finley, *Sketches of Western Methodism* (ed. W.P. Strickland, Cincinnati: Methodist Book Concern, 1857), 72.

[64] Arnold, *Methodism in Kentucky,* 201-2.

[65] Thompson, "Public Invitation", 85, quoting from John Atkinson, *Centennial History of American Methodism* (NY: Philips & Hunt, 1884). 469; King, *S. Carolina,* 154, quoting from the Black Creek Baptist Church records of 1802, in the Furman University Library.

[66] Thompson, "Public Invitation", 86, quoting Samuel W. Williams, *Pictures of Early Methodism in Ohio* (NY: Eaton & Mains, 1909), 71-73.

[67] Arnold, *Methodism in Kentucky,* 84, 154-57.

[68] Thompson, "Public Invitation", 86, quoting Atkinson, *Centennial History,* 469.

[69] Thompson, "Public Invitation", 87-88, quoting Samuel Williams, *Pictures,* 74.

[70] Letter from Stith Mead to Dr. Coke, 11 May 1802, *Methodist Magazine* 25 (Nov. 1802): 522.

[71] More, "Origins of 'The Altar Call'": 30-31, quoting from Atkinson, *Centennial History,* 468-69.

[72] Thompson, "Public Invitation", 91, quoting from a letter of Sneath's published in the (American) *Methodist Magazine* 16 (1803): 373.

[73] In some accounts Vardeman appears as Vardaman and Vardiman, but for consistency we will use only Vardeman.

[74] Nettles, *Grace & Glory,* 416-17, quoting William B. Sprague, *Religion in America, Annals of the American Pulpit* (NY: Arno Press, 1865), 6:422-23, 427. Ronald F. Deering, "A Restored Baptist Treasure: Portrait of Jeremiah Vardeman,

1775-1842" *Baptist History and Heritage* 21: 4 (Oct. 1986): 27-28.
    [75]   Nettles, *Grace & Glory*, 417-18; Olive, "Evangelistic Invitation", 30;
Thompson, "Public Invitation", 71, quoting Lemuel Burkitt, *A Concise History of
the Kehukee Baptist Association* (Halifax: Hodge, 1803), 145 (emphasis added).
    [76]   McLendon, "Mourner's Bench", 8, 51; Olive, "Evangelistic Invitation", 30-31,
quoting Burkitt, 203.
    [77]   Thompson, "Public Invitation", 85, quoting from Atkinson, *Centennial
History*, 469 (spelling as in the original).
    [78]   Bennet Tyler, *New England Revivals* (Wheaton: Richard Owen Roberts,
[1846] 1980), 309.
    [79]   Murray, *Revival*, 213-14, quoting E. Porter, *Letters on Revival*, 89-90.
    [80]   Tyler, *New England*, 18, 29, 56, 65, 133, 155, 158, 161, 228, 301. This book
is made up of abridgments of reports from the *Connecticut Evangelical Magazine*,
which were published soon after the revivals. Weisberger says, with some truth,
that "to be converted in Kentucky was likely enough to be an exercise of the body;
in Connecticut it was an exercise mostly of the mind", Weisberger, *Gathered*, 52.
    [81]   Keith J. Hardman, "Bennet Tyler" in *The New International Dictionary of the
Church* (ed. J.D. Douglas, Grand Rapids: Zondervan, 1978), 989-990.
    [82]   Tyler, *New England*, 49, 323.
    [83]   Tyler, *New England*, 85.
    [84]   Tyler, *New England*, 278.
    [85]   Tyler, *New England*, 294-97.
    [86]   Tyler, *New England*, 301.
    [87]   Bennet Tyler, & Andrew Bonar. *Asahel Nettleton: Life and Labours*
(Edinburgh: Banner of Truth [1854], 1975), 336.
    [88]   Fawcett, *Cambuslang*, 118; MacFarlan, *Cambuslang*, 114, 138-39, 160-61;
Sweet, *Revivalism*, 46-48; Tracy, *Great Awakening*, 183, 281n; Wesley, *Journal*,
in *Works*, 3:183.
    [89]   Sweet, *Revivalism*, 46-48; Thompson, "Public Invitation", 28-29, both quoting
from Abraham Messler, *Memorial Sermons and Historical Notes* (NY: 1873),
170.
    [90]   Smith & Handy, *American Christianity*, 1:319-321. See also Hardman,
Seasons, 53-54.
    [91]   Telford, *Wesley's Veterans*, 1:206-7 (emphasis added).
    [92]   Calvin Colton, *History and Character of American Revivals of Religion*
London: Westley & Davis, 1832), 91-98.
    [93]   Bangs, *Methodist*, 1:153-166.
    [94]   More, "Origins of 'The Altar Call'", 25-28.
    [95] Wesley, *Journal*, in *Works*, 1:357; 2:48; Wesley, *People Called Methodists*, in
Works, 8:252-55. See also Rupert E. Davies, *Methodism* (Harmondsworth:
Penguin, 1963), 73-74.

[96] O'Kelly, "Separate Baptists", 130-33.

Chapter 3

"It was the best of times, it was the worst of times" (Charles Dickens)

The Social Scene

Theological shifts and changes in church practice do not happen in a vacuum. In varying degrees they are influenced by, and frequently reflect, trends in society at large. It will be noted in chapter five that the end of the eighteenth century and the first half of the nineteenth heralded in a new theology which paved the way for the introduction and systematic use of the altar call. But behind even that theology were influences outside the church orthodox.

In 1789 a violent revolution began in France in the name of *liberte*, and continued for several years, with each new wave seemingly more bloody than that which preceded it. Since the seventeenth century, the Enlightenment had been preparing the world for a new age, with an emphasis on reason and education. In France philosophers such as Voltaire, Diderot, and Rousseau had loudly criticized the unjust social structures existing in their country. Upon this platform the French Revolution was launched, and it changed the face of France and sent shock waves throughout Europe.[1]

Even before this the American Revolution gained that nation an independence, the effects of which have since echoed around the world. It was an age when democracy, equality, individualism and freedom were on the agenda, and would not be ignored.

In America, Deists such as Thomas Paine (an Englishman) and Thomas Jefferson were constructing a similar platform to that seen in France. A.J. Ayer says that Paine's booklet *Common Sense* did more than anything else to persuade the American colonies to insist on independence (eventually declared on 4 July 1776), rather than some form of allegiance to the British Crown, advocating, as it did, representative forms of government in preference to monarchial ones. This pamphlet is said to have sold 150 000 copies by the end of its first year of publication, 1776.[2]

Jefferson (dubbed "Liberty's Philosopher")[3] urged equality of opportunity, and initiated a movement to bring about religious toleration, which led to the disestablishment of the authorized church in the various states, and the freedom for all to follow their consciences on religious issues.[4] It was mainly through his instrumentality that a *Bill of Rights* was brought into being at this juncture, which led to a freer and more democratic society. Without a doubt, this independence and democracy had a great influence upon Americans over time, both collectively and as individuals, and American society would appear to have been more individualistic after the Revolutionary War.[5]

This changing mood had a quicker and more pervasive influence upon America than it did upon Britain. Paine published his *Rights of Man* in Britain in two parts in 1791 and 1792, and by the end of 1793 it had sold over 200 000 copies.[6] The impact of this book on Britain, however, was nothing like as dramatic as the earlier one had been on America.

The three primary rights outlined by Paine were:

1/ Men are born, and always continue free, and equal in respect of their rights....
2/ The end of all political associations, is, the preservation of the natural and imprescriptible rights of man; and these rights are liberty, property, security, and resistance of oppression.
3/ The nation is essentially the source of all sovereignty....[7]

Once more freedom and democratic rights and even nationalism were being trumpeted forth.

Historians J.E. Johnson and Richard Carwardine both see a link between the developing democratic process in America in the first third of the nineteenth century and the new theology and evangelism. As Carwardine puts it, the egalitarian emphasis of the age and "the increased sense of individual participation in politics were paralleled by theological developments that asserted the 'democratic' and 'egalitarian' nature of Christ's atonement and the participation of the individual in determining his spiritual fate."[8] Thus Christ's death became, in the popular mind, democratically for all, not just the elect, and each person could have the opportunity and did have the ability to respond to the offered salvation.

Certainly, the force of outside events upon the church is well indicated by Samuel Porter, a Presbyterian minister, in an address in Pittsburgh in 1811. He complained that "a spirit of innovation, hostile to all existing systems, has gone forth into the world, and is to be found in operation within the precincts of the Christian Church.... Clergymen of ambition are under a strong temptation to sail with the wind and tide."[9] Simeon Harkey of Frederick, Maryland, could argue, however, that as America was "full of new inventions, improvements and innovations of every kind", it was only natural and proper that "this spirit" should "manifest itself" in the nation's religion,[10] though he seems to have found that "spirit" less hostile than Porter.

Amongst the American churches the democratic and nationalistic cause was supported very strongly by the Methodists,[11] and especially by the Baptists.[12] Indeed, it seems certain that not only did the political and social environment affect religion, but the increasingly democratic and individualistic thinking in the churches influenced the move towards political democracy, particularly in the area of granting religious liberty. Wesley Gewehr called the Great Awakening "one of the secret springs" out of which the democratic movement grew in America.[13] Thus the two movements fed off each other.

In America, at least, a new mood existed: the nation was free from colonial ties, and individuals, theoretically, had the right to make decisions for themselves. Not that the theory was always manifested in practice, as, for example, in the case of slaves. America's original inhabitants too became less free as the European settlers, exercising their freedom, moved more and more into Native American territory.

John Leland, a Baptist preacher from the 1770s, was greatly influenced by, and a supporter of, Jefferson, indeed, he was nicknamed the "Jeffersonian Itinerant".[14] He insisted that "religion is a matter between God and individuals".[15] The importance of the rising status of the individual for our study is supported by Weisberger, who regards the significance of the individual as one of the two main "props" upon which subsequent revivalism was to stand,[16] and it was, to use W.W. Sweet's term, "individualistic religion" which was stressed by the revivalists.[17] It was in this revivalist movement that the public invitation system became established.

Significantly, in 1791, Leland also wrote a book advocating freedom of religion, entitled, *The Rights of Conscience Inalienable.*[18] The concept of freedom was another key ingredient in the developing religious ferment. Nathan Hatch describes freedom as "a powerful engine", that was driven by Baptists, Methodists and other evangelicals "in ever wider circles of evangelization and cultural influence."[19] Robert Torbet also sees this changing social climate in America as having a great influence upon that nation's religious life, in that it fostered a democratic spirit in churches.[20] If the orthodox American churches rejected much of the "religion of reason" which stemmed from the Deists, there can be no doubt they were influenced by it. It is not hard to see shades of the Deists' understanding of a gentler, democratic God in theology and preaching since that time, than that previously perceived as the biblical one. Included in that Deistic influence too was the idea that people had the ability to obey God.[21]

Another field that was to have its part to play in the development of evangelistic method was the world of business. Modern business practice with its marketing techniques was beginning to develop at this time, and Frank Lambert and Harry Stout regard George Whitefield as the one who first saw the importance of taking religious issues outside church buildings and presenting them in the market place, competing, in a sense, with the goods and services on sale there.[22]

As was seen in chapter one, Whitefield began to take the Gospel into the great outdoors in 1739. This was because by this time he had been banned from preaching in many of the pulpits of his own denomination, though Stout suggests that he was planning this departure into the fields before he was forced into it, because he saw the opportunities it presented.[23] The enormous audiences who attended his meetings, at times attracted the strange phenomenon of traders erecting their stalls on the fringes of the crowds and doing a roaring trade.

Outdoor preaching, of course, in one sense was not new; Jesus had done it, as had the Apostles and others at different times in church history. In Whitefield's own time Howell Harris, the Welsh preacher, had been proclaiming the Gospel in the fields since 1735. But Lambert and Stout claim that Whitefield introduced a new factor into the practice: the religious equivalent of marketing a product.[24]

Certainly, Whitefield saw from early on the usefulness of publicizing his activities in the newspapers, which were just beginning to become popular in the second quarter of the eighteenth century. With encouragement from Whitefield and his associate William Seward, the newspapers on both sides of the Atlantic reported extensively on Whitefield's activities. Whitefield's tour of New England in 1740, for example, was widely covered by the newspapers, in a positive manner by most, but negatively by some. He received favorable treatment in the *Boston Gazette* and the *New England Weekly Journal*, but he was strongly criticized in the *Boston Evening Post*. Further south, in one period the *South Carolina Gazette*'s main front-page focus in 17 out of 52 issues was upon Whitefield and the controversies that surrounded him. But whether the publicity was positive or negative it always resulted in more attention on his ministry.[25]

More than a century later D.L. Moody, an experienced and successful businessman, probably unconsciously, incorporated business method into revivalism to form modern mass evangelism. One associate called Moody's work "a vast business enterprise, organized and conducted by business men, who put their money into it on business principles, for the purpose of saving souls".[26] It has been common for the crusades since Moody's time to have a strong business-like emphasis on publicity, organization and method. The evident need to "see converts" could also be regarded as the evangelist's equivalent of the accountant's "bottom line". The method of counting the converts has mainly been through the use of the altar call. It should be noted, however, that Moody himself did not like the idea of counting converts.

The Movement West

As these changes were occurring, European settlement in America began to move further and further west. After the Revolutionary War a massive new parcel of land was opened west of the Appalachian Mountains. New states were established, such as Kentucky (1792), Tennessee (1796), and Ohio (1803). These states play a key role in the next stages of the history of the altar call. In 1803 the American government made the Louisiana Purchase from France, which added another enormous piece of territory to the USA, stretching from the Mississippi River to the Rocky Mountains. Thousands upon thousands of settlers loaded their wagons and went to occupy these newly available regions. Historian, Steven Keillor says that this westward expansion happened in a little more than 70 years.[27]

The "frontier" became the name for the outer reaches of this settlement. Dickson Bruce, an authority on American culture, has a point, however, when he says that the "frontier" should be considered "a condition rather than a particular geographical area".[28] The literal frontier never remained in one place for long, but the mentality of each new group of settlers and the problems they encountered were less open to change. Indeed, when the physical frontier did move further west, frontier-type problems (lack of facilities, for example) still remained for the settlers in recently developed areas.

This westward movement of people did not usually stem from any religious motivation, unless one counts the desire that some had to escape from what was seen as the interference of the church in family life. Certainly, persecution played barely a part in it. The only significant religious group that was forced to move westward to observe their religion in peace was the Mormons. This vast movement of people was motivated by the desire for land and the hope of a better, more independent life style.[29]

Summary

The concepts of democracy, equality, individualism, freedom and human ability were all to play their part in the theological and evangelistic changes which were to emerge in the first part of the nineteenth century. The world of business was also to have its influence with a strong emphasis on marketing one's wares, organization, correct method and the need to see results. The great westward spread of people in America was to be the major stage upon which these changes would be acted out.

Some of these changes in evangelistic method, relevant to this study, will become evident in the next chapter on the camp-meetings. The story of the theological changes will be left until chapter five.

Notes

[1] Gerald R. Cragg, *The Church in the Age of Reason 1648-1789* (Harmondsworth: Penguin, 1970), 245, 279; J Edwin Orr, *The Light of the Nations* (Exeter: Paternoster, 1965), 18-19.

[2] A.J. Ayer, *Thomas Paine* (London: Secker, 1988), 31, 35-36; see also Richard B. Morris, *The Making of a Nation* (NY: Time-Life, 1974), 35.

[3] Morris, *Making a Nation,* 45.

[4] Lumpkin, *Baptist Foundations,* 116-120; Morris, *Making a Nation,* 40; Torbet, *Baptists,* 241; Henry C. Vedder, *A Short History of the Baptists* (Valley Forge: Judson, 1907), 319-320; see also Cragg, *Age of Reason* 183.

[5] R.D. Birdsall, "The Second Great Awakening & the New England Social Order" *Church History* 39: 3 (Sept. 1970): 350-51, 356.

[6] Ayer, *Paine,* 72.

[7] Ayer, *Paine,* 83.

[8] Carwardine, *Transatlantic,* 91; J.E. Johnson, "Father of American Revivalism", *Christian History* 7: 4 (Issue 20) 9.

[9] Murray, *Revival,* 279-280, quoting Porter in Joseph Smith, *Old Redstone,* 371-72.

[10] Simeon W. Harkey, *The Church's Best State* (Baltimore: Publications Rooms, 1842), 109-110.

[11] Gross, *American Methodism,* 64-65. It was noted in chapter two, however, that some English Methodists in America, such as George Shadford and Thomas Rankin, did remain loyal to Britain, but they usually returned to their homeland.

[12] Cook, *Baptists,* 229-251; Gewehr, *Great Awakening,* 134-6; Blanche S. White, *First Baptist Church Richmond: 1780-1955* (Richmond: Baptist Church, 1955), 9-11, 16.

[13] Gewehr's chapter "Contributions to the Rise of Democracy" deals with this in some depth, *Great Awakening,* 187-218. See also McLoughlin, *Backus,* 136-166, 169-170, 195-200; Sweet, *Revivalism,* 40-43.

[14] Goen, *Revivalism,* 289.

[15] Smith & Handy, *American Christianity,* 1: 469-470.

[16] Weisberger, *Gathered,* 19. "Emotion in religion" was the other.

[17] Sweet, *Revivalism,* 40.

[18] Gewehr, *Great Awakening,* 190; McBeth, *Baptist Heritage,* 274.

[19] Mark A. Noll, David W. Bebbington and George A. Rawlyk. *Evangelicalism* (NY: Oxford, 1994), 117, quoting Nathan O. Hatch, *The Democratization of American Christianity,* 6.

[20] Torbet, *Baptists,* 244.

[21] Weisberger, *Gathered,* 6.

[22] Lambert, *Pedlar,* 6-7, 38-39; Stout, *Divine Dramatist,* xvii-xviii, 66-67.

[23] Stout, *Divine Dramatist,* 66-71.

[24] Lambert, *Pedlar,* 37-39; Stout, *Divine Dramatist,* 85-86.

[25] Lambert, *Pedlar,* 52-55, 65-68, 103-9, 149; Stout, *Divine Dramatist,* 114-16, 119, 130-31.

[26] Hardman, *Seasons,* 192; William G. McLoughlin, *Modern Revivalism: Charles Grandison Finney to Billy Graham* (NY: Ronald Press, 1959), 166, 173-74, 185, 195; J.C. Pollock, *Moody Without Sankey* (London: Hodder, 1963), 28-29, 42-43.

[27] Steven J. Keillor, *This Rebellious House: American History & the Truth of Christianity* (Downers Grove: IVP, 1996), 105.

[28] Dickson D. Bruce, Jr. *And They All Sang Hallelujah* (Knoxville: Uni. of Tennessee Press, 1974), 14.

[29] Keillor, *Rebellious,* 104-108, 124-25.

Chapter 4

Camp-Meetings and Itinerant Preachers

The churches found it difficult to keep up with the rapid, widespread movement of people in America, and many new communities came into being with no clergy and little organized Christian witness. To meet this need several denominations employed itinerant preachers, most notably the Methodist Episcopal Church. Men like Francis Asbury and Peter Cartwright exercised a wide ministry, riding the ever-extending Methodist circuits. (It has already been seen in chapter two how Jesse Lee did this, mainly in the north-eastern states). Within this environment one of the most useful tools for reaching people with the gospel was the camp-meeting. It was in these gatherings that the public invitation became, in certain circles at least, common, accepted and even systematized.

Lorenzo Dow

One of these itinerants was Lorenzo Dow. For part of his early career Dow was licensed as a Methodist preacher, but most of the time he functioned independently, whilst remaining Methodist-like in doctrine and manner.[1] His first recorded use of a form of the public invitation was at the end of 1797 in Wilson's Hollow, New York. He made "a covenant" (this seems to be Dow's synonym for a public invitation)[2] with the small band gathered to hear him that "if they would attempt to pray three times a day, [for] four weeks ... [he] would remember them thrice" each day, and to indicate their acceptance of that challenge the people were urged to stand up. Twenty rose to their feet. This would appear to have been just Dow's way of challenging them to seek Christ. There is nothing in his account to confirm that any of that number then, or even later, became Christians, though he does record that soon after he had left the district eight young people in that town were converted. These eight may or may not have been from the twenty that earlier had stood.[3] If Dow's invitation here was not a direct appeal to accept Christ as such, it certainly seems to be related to it. Dow often asked people to stand to indicate some form of interest in the Christian faith.[4] There is not a hint in his autobiography of whether he was being innovative or copying someone else's practice in this.

Towards the end of 1804, on a visit to the Mississippi Territory, he appealed for "backsliders" to "come forward". One "old backslider" did so, and "several followed his example".[5] Clearly, even as early as this, the public invitation was used for purposes other than a conversion experience.

Sometimes Dow would use a combination of methods on the one occasion. In Virginia in 1805 he spoke of three thousand rising up "in covenant, sundry of whom came up to be prayed for".[6] Thus some of those who stood at Dow's request also went forward. Charles Sellars says that Dow was not averse to tricking his hearers into responding, though he does not elaborate.[7] On one occasion Dow made a most bizarre public appeal, and it had nothing to do with the gospel. Shortly after the death of his first wife, at the end of a sermon he declared himself "a candidate for matrimony", and asked any interested, eligible women to stand. Two did, and he selected, and eventually married, the first who rose. This story might be apocryphal, but it so fits the man it is quite probably true.[8]

As shall be seen, Dow and itinerant preachers like him were to have a significant impact upon the development of the altar call, though in Dow's case his major influence may have been in Britain rather than in America. Dow thus played an important part in the spread of this revivalist methodology.

Camp-Meetings

As the eighteenth century ended, a new type of religious gathering came into being in America, which saw the public invitation develop into a system, and become more accepted. The camp-meetings, originally, do not seem to have been planned as the explosive gatherings they did become, but explosive they were from their birth. They were an important part of the Second Great Awakening, which swept America at the beginning of the nineteenth century.

If one accepts the outdoor New Light Presbyterian communion service at Gasper River, Kentucky in July 1800 as their origin,[9] then the original aim was quite subdued compared with the reputation camp-meetings quickly earned. Presbyterians, traditionally, have conducted communion less frequently than most denominations, so a Presbyterian communion service can be of special significance, at least in part because of its comparative rarity. In this instance a series of services was organized in the open air, to which several congregations were invited. As it was impossible to house all the visitors, people were advised to bring tents or prepare to sleep in their wagons. The communion season lasted for several days.[10]

The tradition of protracted communion services in Presbyterianism went back a long way. They had been common in Scotland and Ulster from the seventeenth century, and, at times, had been the means of revival. The revival at Cambuslang in Scotland in the eighteenth century, mentioned in chapter two, was centered in one such communion season. Much of American Presbyterianism had its origins in Scotland and, particularly, Ulster, and had inherited those traditions.[11]

It wasn't long before the meeting at Gasper River took a dramatic turn, and one eyewitness reported that "sinners" were "lying powerless praying and crying for mercy", and such was the enthusiasm that the services went on well into the night. Only 45 professed conversion,[12] but in camp-meetings like it during the next two decades thousands would be brought into the kingdom, and new practices popularized in the face of fierce criticism.

A month earlier a similar meeting had been held on the banks of the nearby Red River. This too has been claimed as the commencement of the camp-meetings, though the foremost authority on these gatherings, Charles Johnson, rejects this as a genuine camp-meeting because only one man actually camped out.[13] We will not worry about the technicalities here, and for convenience regard this Red River gathering as an authentic camp-meeting, and the commencement of the concept as normally understood.

These meetings often crossed denominational boundaries, especially in the early years,[14] though not always happily.[15] The Red River meetings had as guest preachers the McGee brothers, William, a Presbyterian, and John, a Methodist.[16] These gatherings frequently included congregations from a mixture of denominations, and usually included more than a sprinkling of the "just curious" and those just out for a good time, and attracted many with no, or little genuine interest in religion.[17] They became especially popular with the Methodists, who perceived the strange phenomena often associated with them in a more positive light than, say, the Presbyterians. They also proved fairly popular with some Baptists, but not with others.[18]

To understand this phenomenon it is essential to realize that the majority of the early camp-meetings were held in the western frontier territories, such as Kentucky and Tennessee, where most of the people were, to quote the term used by Bruce, "plain-folk", i.e., small farmers and townspeople, generally of little education and influence.[19] Life for these people was a struggle, and the camp-meetings (held in many districts annually,[20] in other places more frequently), were to some extent an escape from the drudgery of life. It was a time to relax after, say, a tiring harvest, as well as an opportunity to spend time with one's neighbors.

On the frontier individualism was paramount, though cooperation and community spirit were certainly not absent.[21] The community spirit was built by the months spent in wagon trains on the trail west, and later evidenced by such events as barn raising when a whole community would join together to build a barn or house for, perhaps, a newly married couple. But in frontier situations one's neighbors usually lived hours away, so dependence upon others was often not possible. Thus self-reliance became essential, further developing the spirit of individualism. That individualism, as was suggested in chapter three, was a key factor in the development of the public invitation system.

Bruce argues that though their churches bore the same denominational labels as their European ancestors, the "plain-folk", brought to the camp-meetings both in "belief and practice ... something quite different" from that owned by their predecessors.[22] For example, American Methodism was now separated from its Anglican origins and also, in any governing sense, English Methodism. Though its body of tradition was largely from its English predecessors it did not regard these practices as being set in granite, and was prepared to experiment. The American Methodists, for example, appointed Bishops, which the English Methodists never did. Charles Johnson sees this flexibility as part of the reason for the success of Methodism in this medium. Certainly the organizers of these meetings were not much concerned about theology or ecclesiastical decorum; their prime concern was "saving sinners". Indeed, the clergy of the increasingly predominant Methodists were, for the most part, limited in education and training.[23] They were simple men preaching to simple folk, though they were not ignoramuses. John Wigger says, "In many cases, the only distinction between a Methodist preacher and his audience", as far as background and education was concerned, "was which side of the pulpit each was on".[24] In this largely non-intellectual, non-traditional environment the camp-meeting, seemingly inevitably, became the flower bed for new methods to sprout and develop, not least the public invitation. This would have been aided by the belief common to many of the preachers that it was important to be able to date precisely one's conversion experience.[25]

The most famous of these camp-meetings was held at Cane Ridge, Kentucky in August 1801. This was scheduled originally as a Presbyterian communion service, but, as it was widely publicized for a month previously, it became interdenominational and attracted between 10 000 and 25 000 people from a wide area, with about 140 wagons densely packed on site. It lasted for six days.[26] With ministers from different denominations preaching regularly at different sites, members of the "congregation" could drift as the mood led, hearing the gospel from a variety of mouths.[27] Estimates of the number of converts made at Cane Ridge vary from 500-3000. Though the number converted was clearly large, it is apparent from the wide divergence of the estimates that no one had any real idea how many there were. Conkin has a valid point when he suggests that in the confusion the "ministers lost all clear guidelines as to what marked conversion".[28] From John Wesley and Whitefield to Bill Bright it is very difficult to always know how seriously to take evangelists' estimates of crowd sizes and conversion numbers. It is not unfair to say that exaggerations are common, and the upper limit at Cane Ridge is probably another example of that. But Francis Asbury was still right in regarding camp-meetings as "fishing with a large net".[29]

It is not insignificant that historian Paul Conkin subtitles his book on Cane Ridge, *"America's Pentecost"*, for the influence of this series of meetings was felt well beyond Kentucky, and was out of all proportion to even the highest estimate of conversions. It attracted an enormous amount of interest throughout the country and appeared to act as a catalyst for many similar gatherings. To quote Conkin, the local event of Cane Ridge "took on almost cosmic significance."[30]

Certainly, from then on the popularity of camp-meetings increased rapidly, and just over half way through 1808 Asbury estimated that between 400 and 500 would be held in that year alone.[31] Yet less than thirty years later their use and influence had faded considerably, and their primary purpose in the second half of the century was often the promotion of holiness, rather than the conversion of sinners.[32]

The camp-meeting preachers varied from old men to mere boys, the trained and the untrained. Most preached extemporaneously, at length, and with considerable vigor and emotion.[33] Often there would be several preaching points from which the gospel would be preached simultaneously, and there was not usually any shortage of preachers to occupy them. Asbury wrote of there being 70 preachers at one camp-meeting in 1805. Sometimes the meetings went on into the night, and even lasted all night.[34]

It would be a mistake to tar all these meetings with the same brush, and it is probably best to understand their wilder aspects as occurring mainly in the first few years of the nineteenth century, but the following accounts of those early services give something of their flavor.

At the final service of the Red River camp-meeting mentioned above, John McGee, a visiting Methodist, was scheduled to preach after his Presbyterian brother, William, and a Rev. William Hodge. As they spoke, the "temperature" of the congregation began to rise, with shouts of praise coming from the assembly. As the excitement increased, John McGee descended from the pulpit to exhort the people at eye level. Some of the Presbyterians advised him against encouraging emotionalism. Let John McGee himself give the account of what followed. He wrote:

> I turned to go back, and was near falling. The power of God was strong upon me; I turned again, and, losing sight of the fear of man, I went through the house, shouting and exhorting with all possible ecstacy (sic) and energy, and the floor was soon covered with the slain.[35]

The term "the slain" referred to those who had literally fallen to the floor under conviction of sin or some religious ecstasy. At one camp-meeting in 1801, it is said that 800 experienced this falling.[36]

Richard M'Nemar, a Presbyterian, described the early meetings this way:

> At first appearance those meetings exhibited nothing to the spectator but a scene of confusion that would scarce be put into human language. They were generally opened with a sermon, near the close of which there would be an unusual outcry; some bursting forth into loud ejaculations of prayer ... others breaking out in ... exhortation ... others flying to careless friends with tears of compassion, beseeching them to turn to the Lord; some struck with terror ... others trembling, weeping ... and swooning away ... others collecting into circles around the variegated scene, contending with argument for or against.[37]

Another minister recalled seeing

> Sinners dropping down on every hand, shrieking, groaning, crying for
> mercy, convoluted; professors praying, agonizing, fainting, falling
> down in distress, for sinners, or in raptures of joy! [Some were] talking
> to the distressed, to one another, or to opposers of the work, and all this
> at once.[38]

James B. Finley went along to Cane Ridge out of curiosity, but was
converted on his way home. He describes the noise made by the
densely packed throng as being "like the roar of Niagara". He went on,
"Some of the people were singing, others praying, some crying for
mercy in the most piteous accents, while others were shouting most
vociferously." He retreated for a while, overcome by the scene, but
returned and climbed upon a log to gain a better view. What he then
saw astonished, even frightened him.

> At one time I saw at least five hundred swept down in a moment, as if a
> battery of a thousand guns had been opened upon them, and then
> immediately followed shrieks and shouts that rent the very heavens.[39]

A secondhand, but contemporary, account relates that at such
gatherings:

> In time of preaching, if care is taken, there is but little confusion; when
> that is over, and the singing, and praying and exhorting begins, the
> audience is thrown into what I call real disorder. The careless fall
> down, cry out, tremble, and not infrequently are affected with
> convulsive twitchings. Among these the pious are very busy, singing,
> praying, conversing, falling down in extacies (sic), fainting with joy ...
> a number, too, are wrought upon in the usual way, and hopefully get
> religion without any of these extraordinary appearances.[40]

But this extravagant behavior was, for the most part, only at the
beginning of the century. According to Charles Johnson, such bodily
manifestations as mentioned above were much rarer after 1805, though
not particularly at the expense of conversions.[41]

Frances Trollope, an English visitor, wrote disapprovingly of an
1829 camp-meeting experience in this fashion,

> The preachers came down from their stand and placed themselves in
> the midst of [the altar], beginning to sing a hymn, calling the penitents
> to come forth ... above a hundred persons, nearly all females, came

forward, uttering howls and groans, so terrible that I shall never cease to shudder when I recall them. They appeared to drag each other forward ...[42]

But what were the distinctive features of the camp-meeting relevant to our subject? First, is the fact that the displays of religious experience common in them, such as outlined above, and to which can be added such phenomena as the "jerks", "laughing", and "barking",[43] though not directly related to "public invitations" as such, were very public displays of religious feeling.

One intriguing camp-meeting phenomenon that has some bearing upon our subject is that sometimes when the preacher warmed to his theme, very nearly the whole congregation would rise, and, without invitation, move closer to the preacher. W.E. Arnold mentions such incidents in the ministries of James Axley and Miles Harper.[44] But the main, relevant camp-meeting features were the "altar" and the work of the exhorters.

It is probable that in the first three or four years of camp-meetings the public invitation played little part in the proceedings. With many under presumed religious conviction falling down where they had stood or sat, often comatose,[45] calling people forward was not only unnecessary, but frequently impossible.

The Altar

It is significant that when the outward manifestations, particularly falling down, began to decline at these meetings, the public invitation seems to have become common. Whether this increase in usage of the public invitation was deliberately intended to replace the falling down, or something which just emerged to fill the gap is not clear. The device most commonly used in these camp-meeting invitations was the "altar".

The camp-meetings, depending on size and the methods of individual organizers, generally had one central preaching point, with others as required. The preacher usually spoke from an elevated pulpit, in front or to the side of which was the altar. These altars were quite different from traditional altars. They were fenced enclosures, frequently from six to ten yards square, with seats.[46] Their purpose was to provide the opportunity for "the mourners" or "the anxious" to be gathered together for counsel, away from the noise and activity of camp life. There does not appear to be any evidence that they were used in the earliest camp-meetings, but from the middle of the first decade of the nineteenth century they became a regular feature.[47]

On 24 July 1804, William Heath wrote a letter to Ezekiel Cooper, the Methodist Book Steward, stating that during the previous five days there had been a camp-meeting at Bedford, Virginia, in which 110 "came forward and gave testimony of their faith that God had converted their souls", but Heath makes no mention of the altar as such.[48] Dow writes of "several mourners" coming forward to be prayed for at a camp site in Albany on 31 August 1804, but there is still no mention of an altar.[49]

True, Peter Cartwright could say of an 1806 camp-meeting that "The altar was crowded to overflowing with mourners".[50] But this was written years after the event, so it only proves that the device or something similar to it was in use by that year, not necessarily the name, which may have been transplanted from later usage. Henry Smith, another itinerant, makes mention of its use in Maryland in October that same year, though he calls it a "pen".[51] In addition, Aaron Hunt, a Methodist minister in New York City, spoke of calling people forward to the front of his church in 1806, following the example of the "altar" being used in camp-meetings, in which it appeared to have been only recently adopted. The term "altar" seems to have been used by one of Hunt's colleagues to Hunt actually in that year.[52]

In one of Asbury's letters in 1806, he speaks of "houses or huts" being built for camp-meetings, and it seems that at about this time, as these meetings became regular, permanent structures, often including altars, appeared on many sites. Certainly, Asbury was advocating the creation of "mourner's benches" in the meeting houses on camp-meeting sites in August 1810.[53] In the printed "Order of Meeting" at one camp-meeting in Tennessee in 1820, it was announced that an "invitation to the altar" would follow both the 2 p.m. sermon and the 7 p.m. service on the Friday,[54] indicating that the practice had already been systematized in these circles at least, as prior planning and regular usage were clearly involved.

An alternative to the altar was the "praying circle" or "prayer ring", which appears to have been used mostly in the eastern states. The idea was for a group of preachers and leading laymen to stand in a circle holding hands, and the mourners were invited to enter that circle.[55] Praying circles also operated in the west, but in a slightly different form. According to Cartwright, at some camp-meetings between the services many Christians "would retire to the woods and hold prayer meetings", and if any seekers could be identified they would be taken along too, and "many of them obtained religion in these praying circles".[56] Another, later, alternative was the "mourner's tent". These canvas shelters, some as large as 16 yards by 10, began to appear around 1820.[57]

In the Fishing River Methodist Circuit, Illinois, in 1823, two preachers had taken it in turn to preach and exhort. When the congregation began to sing a hymn, "the Almighty came down in such a wonderful manner as is seldom witnessed." As one of the preachers collapsed in the pulpit, the other gave an invitation to the congregation, and "the mourners came pouring forward in a body for prayers till the altar was filled with weeping penitents."[58] A "filled" altar was not unique to Fishing River. Four years earlier in Indiana an English visitor recorded that the altar "was so much crowded that its inmates had not the liberty of lateral motion".[59]

Peter Cartwright, though a staunch advocate of the altar call, experienced some problems with it in Russellville, Kentucky, in 1822. He too found the altar "filled", but largely with "idle professors" and "idle spectators", and had to police those entering the enclosure, admitting only those showing genuine concern about their souls. On another occasion, Cartwright invited sinners to come forward and over 500 came,[60] far too many for the altar's capacity, and presenting a tiring task for the usually energetic exhorters.

At another time Cartwright was conducting a camp-meeting with Valentine Cook, in which they took turns to preach. Though the altar was available for the expected seekers, it was eventually not used, for, in the chaos resulting from one of Cartwright's sermons, "several hundred fell in five minutes; sinners turned pale; some ran into the woods, some tried to get away, and fell in the attempt, some shouted for joy", and the seekers were counseled where they were found.[61] This incident offers some confirmation to the earlier suggestion that calling people forward was not normally done when many were falling down.

One unnamed circuit rider recognized that the altar could be more of a hindrance than a help on some occasions. In Ohio in 1818, this man encouraged those who found the tumult in the altar to be a distraction to go instead to the nearby grove to seek God privately. "Many" took his advice.[62]

It is apparent that considerable psychological pressure was often brought to bear on people to "convert". Gregory Schneider relates an eyewitness account of an incident when the pressure became decidedly physical as well. One new female convert was being dragged away from the camp ground by her unbelieving husband, when a powerfully built preacher forced the man to the ground, sat on him and ordered him to pray. He then told the man that he would not get off until the husband prayed to God. It wasn't long before the man "began to weep and cry out to God for mercy to his soul" and was soon "converted".[63]

How genuine a conversion this was one can only guess. Whilst it should not be thought that this was normal camp-meeting practice, there are hints of other similar incidents. Certainly, Cartwright was not loath to use physical persuasion when the going turned rough,[64] but it was a "language" the frontier dwellers understood and respected.

Keillor says that many men who took their families west did so, at least in part, to escape the church's influence.[65] Perhaps this man "converted" above was one of many who were frustrated and angry that the church had followed them.

The possibility of a link between the communion service and the public invitation has already been discussed in chapter two, but a few more comments are appropriate here. Does the title "altar" suggest such a link between the two, and also Methodist/Anglican origins of the term? In the early years of Methodism, almost until the death of Wesley, Methodism contained very few ordained ministers, and though Wesley permitted lay preachers, he did not allow them to administer the sacraments. If his people wished to take communion and no ordained Methodist minister was available, they had to go to the local Church of England church.[66] In this setting the communicants usually went forward to kneel around the altar to take the elements, a practice later followed in Methodist churches, though the altar was usually renamed the "communion table".[67] Indeed, in 1801, in Philadelphia, Richard Sneath, a Methodist preacher, "invited all mourners to come to the communion table."[68] As we saw earlier, Robert More Jr. has a valid point when he posits a link through Wesley between Church of England eucharistic practice and terminology and the camp-meeting altar.[69] The giving of the name "altar" to the collecting place for camp inquirers does, indeed, suggest Methodist/Anglican influence. While no record of a definite link between the practice of moving forward to take communion and doing so for personal counseling and prayer has so far been forthcoming, the above, particularly the example of Sneath, suggests there is one.

Exhorters

Exhorters and exhorting have been mentioned a number of times in this chapter. What is precisely meant by these terms, and how does the practice fit into this subject? Exhorters originally appear to have been lay preachers or teachers, who filled in when a member of the clergy was not available. As far back as 1558 John Knox, the Scottish Reformer, could write of five exhorters being used to teach the Word, because of a lack of clergy. In the early 1740s, Thomas Prince Snr. criticized James Davenport for encouraging laymen "to pray and exhort" (i.e. like ministers). Davenport was a most enthusiastic supporter of exhorters. In 1741 John Porter of Bridgewater, Massachusetts referred to two young visitors to his church as "the only two exhorters we have had". The ministry of these two men seems to have been a more informal kind of preaching.[70]

The nature of the exhorters' role seemed to undergo gradual changes over the centuries, and in America by the early nineteenth century it seems to have been less formal and less cerebral than in earlier years. These exhorters became key figures in the evangelism of this period, particularly at camp-meetings. They were often clergymen, but lay men or women could also fill the position. Though some were appointed to the role, others just assumed it as the need arose and the "Spirit moved". At Cane Ridge hundreds exhorted, including young children and slaves. Even some of those who had been comatose or weeping on the floor suddenly sprang up with joy and began to exhort others. According to M'Nemar, exhortations from those who had recently fallen to the ground and been in a trance-like state showed special evidence "of a Divine power", [71] Olive suggests (with justification) that exhortation might be "one more link in the chain" leading to the use of the altar call.[72]

One task of the exhorters was to move through the congregation, during the sermon or after, on the lookout for "mourners" to counsel, and to urge sinners to respond to the gospel message.[73] Exhorters usually spoke after a preacher had concluded his sermon, and applied the subject, so as to "move the congregation to action."[74] Thus the exhortation appears to be similar to the modern "appeal". At some of these gatherings singing was a continual background to the work of the exhorters, and the message presented in those songs was often an interesting contrast to the exhorter's words. Whereas the exhortations were full of dire warnings, the songs (often specifically coined for frontier Christianity) were often full of hope, and in some instances encouraged a public response.[75]

Exhortations could be very direct and to the point, or little more than just shouts of praise.[76] In later camp-meetings they were often a quite formal, lengthy appeal.[77] In the early days one exhorter cried, "Go, sinner; go to hell and be ruined forever, and I will say, amen! Go on, if you want to, after all that has been done for you by a dying Saviour and a living ministry." Another urged, "Cry aloud and spare not." It was also not unknown for some to encourage visible manifestations, such as "the jerks".[78]

Charles Johnson says that Asbury "placed more faith in exhortation than in formal preaching", though how true this is may be debated. Certainly, he often exhorted rather than preached, but this seems to have been because of sickness or time restraints rather than preference.[79]

Though at these meetings many people walked unaided to the altar or mourner's bench in direct response to the preacher's message, in a way not dissimilar to that seen in modern "crusades", many others only did so after persuasion from an exhorter. At the altar they were then further counseled by a minister or lay person. Thus, often, considerable pressure was brought to bear on the unconverted to respond to Christ.[80] It is not always easy, though, to determine the extent or even the precise nature of the exhorter's role, for the terms "exhort" and "exhortation" do not always seem to be used in the same way. Sometimes, as above, the nature of the exhortation was to urge people to believe in Christ, but Asbury could speak of giving "a short exhortation before the sacrament" at a Methodist Conference in Maryland in 1799,[81] and this suggests that it was used in other ways too. On other occasions the terms are used with no clue to their meaning, though usually exhortation is seen as distinct from preaching.[82]

Conkin distinguishes between preaching and exhortation by describing the former as being "prepared" and having "a theme or text taken from the Bible and carefully developed points or arguments" and the latter as "extemporaneous or even impromptu practical advice, or tearful appeals and warnings".[83] From a British perspective, H.B. Kendall said that exhortations lacked "the formality of a previously announced text", were "essentially hortatory in character", and consisted "of appeals based on the elemental evangelical facts and declarations of Scripture, as confirmed by personal experience".[84] Dow also gives the impression that preaching was normally from a text, but exhorting was not.[85] As far back as 1769, John Wesley, a little uneasy about the propriety of women preaching, told one of his female followers:

> intermix short exhortations with prayer; but keep as far from what is called preaching as you can: therefore never take a text; never speak in a continued discourse without some break, about four or five minutes.[86]

But Asbury states that one of his men "exhorted long ... proposing causes of conscience, and answering them, and speaking about Christ, heaven and hell,"[87] though the term "exhorted long" is probably relative to the usual length of exhortations.

There is in these comments a degree of uniformity about the differences between preaching and exhorting, but often, especially in the mayhem of a camp-meeting, sermons could as easily be described by Conkin's definition of exhortation, and exhortations could also bear some of the marks of a sermon, e.g. based upon a text of Scripture.[88] It is probably best, though, to understand exhortations as varied in nature, but usually short,[89] informal and direct, and intended to make people take action upon what they had heard.

Peter Cartwright could speak of his childhood Methodist society in the late eighteenth century as containing "thirteen members, one local preacher, one exhorter, and a class leader".[90] Indeed, in 1802, as a sixteen-year-old, Cartwright was officially appointed as an exhorter himself. Exhorters, then, in some cases seem to have held an official position in the church, but were distinct from preachers.

In early nineteenth century English Primitive Methodism, which was greatly influenced by the American camp-meeting scene, one preaching plan for a circuit lists over 40 "Preachers", and, separately, seven "Exhorters". The preachers are listed first (numbered 1-40), then the preachers "On Trial" follow (numbered 41-45), following them are the exhorters (numbered 46-52).[91] These exhorters seem to have been preacher-like, but not genuine preachers, though according to the plan they would appear to have preached on occasions. Their most common function was probably to apply the preacher's words to the congregation, and, increasingly as time went by, to invite their hearers to make a public response.

There is, then, justification to regard the camp-meeting exhortation as a forerunner of the modern appeal, and as such is, indeed, "a link" with the public invitation system This is especially so in cases where exhorters led people to the altar or urged "mourners" to believe where they were sitting or had fallen.

More Itinerant Adventures.

A public invitation in unusual circumstances took place in Indiana in 1808. In that territory (it did not become a state until 1816) many Christians were leaving different denominations to join the Shakers, an offshoot of the Quakers,[92] and Peter Cartwright was invited to visit in an attempt to redress the situation. A public debate was held, in which Cartwright spoke last. At the conclusion of his three hour address he "invited all that would renounce Shakerism to come" and shake hands with him. Forty-seven went "forward, and then openly renounced the dreadful delusion". The following day he visited from cabin to cabin interviewing both those who came forward and any others who would receive him. By the end of the day he had 87 adults to form into a Methodist society.[93]

Another method of public invitation he used on at least one occasion was the raising of the hand. Around 1822 he was preaching out doors to a vast congregation on the person of Christ in a district in which, in his words, "Arianism was rife". At the conclusion of his sermon, he announced:

> If there is a single man, minister, woman, or child, in this assembly, that will dare to ascribe Divine honours to Jesus Christ and not believe in his supreme Divinity, let them show it by raising the hand.

Not a hand was raised, Then he

> desired that everyone ... that believed that Jesus Christ was justly entitled to alone supreme honour and glory, and expected to get to heaven through his merits

to raise their hands. This time "the hands went up by the thousand, and with hands, triumphant shouts of glory". Two hundred were said to have "professed religion" at that gathering, and 170 were added to the Methodist Episcopal Church.[94]

Camp-meeting method spread well beyond the circles of wagons and tents. Wilson Thompson, a Baptist pastor, left a critical, eyewitness account of the methods of another Baptist, Jeremiah Vardeman. At a service in Cincinnati, Ohio, in the late 1820s, after another speaker had concluded his address, Vardeman stood up, and began instructing people in the front seats to vacate them, so that those pews might be free for "the mourners". The account continues,

> He started a song and ... many voices joined in the singing ... Every few minutes he would raise his voice and tell the mourners to "come on" ... "come and receive offered mercy" ... he would order runners to go up every aisle and lead the mourners to these benches. Yet with all this they came but slowly. He stepped upon one of the long seats, and turning his eyes upward and raising his ... arm stretched out above his head, he roared at the top of his voice ... "Stop Gabriel, stop; don't speed your golden pinions again, nor attempt to take the news to the throne of God, until you can report at least fifty humble mourners on these anxious benches seeking the salvation of their souls".

After some further attempts by Vardeman to whip up some enthusiasm, the runners

> began to lead in the mourners very fast. They were handed up to him; he would slap them on the shoulders and halloo, "Glory to God," and motion them to their seats. The seats were soon filled. [He then] passed between the benches where the mourners had been placed, and stooping down to each one he would ... converse a short time with them, and in many cases he would rise up erect, clap his hands together, and shout "Glory to God, here is another soul born for heaven".

Wilson Thompson reflected, "I had not seen one among the whole number that I thought looked like a contrite mourner ... at least as far as I could judge..."[95] Even allowing for a possible coloring of events by the disapproving witness, there would seem to be considerable pressure being applied by Vardeman upon his hearers. Undue pressure does tend to result in false conversions, as shall be seen.

Camp-Meeting Results

If one seeks to examine the results (i.e., the number of genuine conversions) of these meetings, and thus to some degree the success of the methods employed, including the altar call, the task is not easy. Many hundreds of camp-meetings were held in a variety of states, over several decades, under the auspices of a number of different denominations. Perhaps the major indicator is the church membership figures of the period of the denominations most heavily involved. For example, in Kentucky between 1800 and 1803 the membership of the Baptist and the Methodist churches increased by about 10 000 each. From the wider perspective, the Methodist Episcopal Church in America had annual increases of 12.3%, 19.02%, and 19.99% in the years 1801-3, and even though some of this was because of immigration, Carwardine shows that in the first thirteen or fourteen years of that century American Methodism nearly doubled its membership as a percentage of the American population.[96] This indicates that large numbers were being added to the church from among those, presumably, previously right outside it. As the camp-meetings were the major scenes of evangelism in this period for Methodism, at least, much of that growth must be attributed to them. So, though there were certainly problems with the camp-meetings, much good did result.

Yet, even Asbury, one of the most ardent advocates of camp-meetings, recognized in 1809 that many of the "conversions" made at them were not genuine. In "many" cases professed converts displayed "neither the form nor power of goodness", and he feared there would be much "backsliding". Charles Johnson concedes that "for a great number" the regenerating effect of the camp-meetings was "short-lived". How much of that decline was to do with the altar call is difficult to determine; a great deal would seem to be due to the excessive emotionalism of the services, and not particularly to any device used in them.

Though a few regarded the extreme bodily manifestations of the hearers as no certain sign of conversion, the common view seemed to accept them as such, or, if not, at least some form of divine working. A.P. Mead, who recorded details of many of the early camp-meetings, said that, "Physical demonstrations are no infallible marks of a divine work", for though some of them were genuine others were not.[97] Yet, as one reads the many eyewitness accounts of these paroxysms, one cannot help but conclude that most viewed them as proof of divine working.[98]

The camp-meeting was mainly an American phenomenon. The British Methodist Conference banned them in 1807. A breaking of that ban led to the formation of the Primitive Methodist Connexion, and the new church then embraced camp-meetings eagerly, though in a modified form.[99] Camp-meetings in Britain and Australia will be looked at in chapters seven and nine.

Summary

The public invitation does not seem to have been used very often in the early days of the camp-meetings, but when the physical manifestations declined it became popular. The "altar" was developed in these meetings about half way through the first decade of the nineteenth century. The work of the exhorters bore some resemblance to the later appeal, in that its primary aim was to urge "mourners" to immediately respond to Christ. The very existence of the altar indicated that the use of the public invitation in this setting was usually planned, and it was certainly used both frequently and regularly. It would seem, then, that it was in the American camp-meetings, in the first decade or two of the nineteenth century, that the public invitation became systematized.

Notes

[1] Lorenzo & Peggy Dow, *History of Cosmopolite, Polemic Writings & The Journey of Life* (Cincinnati: Martin & Robertson, 1849), 56, 148-152; Charles Coleman Sellars, *Lorenzo Dow: The Bearer of the Word* (NY: Minton, 1928), 44-50, 63-64.

[2] Dow, *Cosmopolite*, 45, 51, 66, 76, 135. Dow's writing style is often not clear. He seems to have his own jargon, and often tells his stories in a way which leaves one guessing about important detail. Dow's lack of clarity is also noted by Sellars, *Dow*, 78.

[3] Dow, *Cosmopolite*, 45.

[4] Dow, *Cosmopolite*, 51.

[5] Dow, *Cosmopolite*, 218.

[6] Dow, *Cosmopolite*, 244.

[7] Sellars, *Dow*, 46.

[8] Sellars, *Dow*, 197-99.

[9] Bruce, *Hallelujah*, 51-52; Murray, *Revival*, 152. See also Boles, *Great Revival*, 53-54.

[10] Murray, *Revival*, 151-52. .

[11] Paul K. Conkin, *Cane Ridge: America's Pentecost* (Madison: Uni. of Wisconsin Press, 1990), 13-29.

[12] Weisberger, *Gathered*, 29-30, quoting from William Speer, *The Great Revival of 1800* (Philadelphia: 1872), 13-14.

[13] Charles A. Johnson, *The Frontier Camp Meeting* (Dallas: Southern Methodist UP, 1985), 34. McLendon, "Mourner's Bench", 9-10, gives the year for Red River as 1799. According to Johnson, John McGee, one of the organizers of these meetings, in different writings gave both 1799 and 1800 as the year in which they were held. The latter date accords with the accounts of others and is probably correct, see Johnson, *Camp Meeting*, 273n26; Conkin, *Cane Ridge*, 59-60; J. M. Gready of Kentucky, letter to Dr. Coke, c. 1802, *Methodist Magazine* 26 (Apl. 1803): 182. Outdoor services as such were no new thing, and Christians in new townships often had no choice but to worship in the open, because they lacked church buildings. The Baptists in Virginia, however, were also holding outdoor gatherings from 1769, which they appear to have named "camp meetings" by the mid-1770s, Johnson, *Camp Meeting*, 27, 265, 272; O'Kelly, "Separate Baptists", 157-59 (quoting various people, most notably John Waller, who held "camp meetings" in the 1780s and died on 4 July 1802, see Benedict, *History of the Baptists*, 2:394-96); Semple, *Baptists in Virginia*, 23-24. Yet William Burke, a camp-meeting preacher, says that that term was still unknown in 1801, Arnold, *Methodism in Kentucky*, 205, quoting Burke. Galli says that the phrase "was not coined until 1802", Mark Galli, "Revival at Cane Ridge", *Christian History* 14: 1 (Issue 45): 11, while Boles says that Asbury was the first to use it in October 1802, Boles, *Great Revival*, 55, 72-73. Certainly, from 1803 it became a common term, see letters from Stith

Mead of South Carolina, 4 Jan. 1803, *Methodist Magazine* 26 (Sept. 1803): 419; Zachary Myles of Baltimore, 11 Jan. 1803, *Methodist Magazine* 26 (June 1803): 285; Rev. N. Snethen, 4 Oct. 1803, *Methodist Magazine* 27 (May 1804): 233-34; Mr. J Hagerty to Dr. Coke, 11 Oct. 1803, *Methodist Magazine* 27 (Mar.1804): 137-38.

[14] Asbury, *Journal*, 2:649; Boles, *Great Revival*, 55; J. Chappell, letters to Mr John Edwards, 7 Aug. and 23 Oct. 1801, *Methodist Magazine* 25 (June 1802): 262-63; Conkin, *Cane Ridge*, 90-91; Johnson, *Camp Meeting*, 38; King, *S. Carolina*, 151-52; unnamed Presbyterian minister in Kentucky, letter Aug. 1801, *Methodist Magazine* 25 (June 1802): 264.

[15] Conkin, *Cane Ridge*, 96; Johnson, *Camp Meeting*, 126.

[16] Boles, *Great Revival*, 53.

[17] Bangs, *Methodist*, 2:107-8, 268-69; Johnson, *Camp Meeting*, 53-54.

[18] Arnold, *Methodism in Kentucky*, 105-6; Johnson, *Camp Meeting*, 82-90. Possible reasons for the lesser use of camp-meetings by Baptists when compared with the Methodists include: the Baptist's more restricted use of the circuit rider system. (The Methodist circuit riders traveled further and fitted into the camp-meetings more effectively), Lumpkin, *Baptist Foundations*, 132; the general Baptist unease at this time about excessive emotionalism, Lumpkin, *Baptist Foundations*, 145; and their reluctance to participate in communion with other denominations, King, *S. Carolina*, 151-52. See also O'Kelly, "Separate Baptists", 160-63.

[19] Bruce, *Hallelujah*, 4-5.

[20] Bruce, *Hallelujah*, 51.

[21] Bruce, *Hallelujah*, 25-29, 30-31, 33-4; Johnson, *Camp Meetings*, 14, 17; Weisberger, *Gathered*, 21.

[22] Bruce, *Hallelujah*, 6-7.

[23] Bruce, *Hallelujah*, 36-39. Bruce says that Methodists did not establish permanent seminaries in the West and the South until the 1830s, *Hallelujah*, 57; though they did commence one further east in Maryland as far back as 1785, but after two fires it was closed, Johnson, *Camp Meeting*, xv. See also Carwardine, *Transatlantic*, 40; W.R. Cross, *Burned-over District* (Ithaca: Cornell UP, 1982), 8. Johnson gives details of the Methodist system of appointing and training preachers at this time, 20-21. He also makes it clear that Methodist itinerant preachers, though often lacking in formal education, were keen readers and encouraged their listeners to be too, 161-67.

[24] John H. Wigger, "Holy 'Knock-'em Down' Preachers", *Christian History* 14: 1 (Issue 45): 23.

[25] Boles, *Great Revival*, 39, 47.

[26] Rev. G. Baxter, letter to Rev. Dr. Archibald Alexander, 1 Jan.1802, *Methodist Magazine* 26 (Feb. 1803) 86-93; Boles, *Great Revival*, 64-65; Bruce, *Hallelujah*, 52; Conkin, *Cane Ridge*, 83-86; Galli, "Revival at Cane Ridge", *Christian History* 14: 1 (Issue 45): 9-10; Johnson, *Camp Meeting*, 62-63; Colonel Robert Paterson, letter to Rev. Dr. John King, 25 Sept. 1801, *Methodist Magazine* 26 (Feb.1803) 82-86; Weisberger, *Gathered*, 31.

[27] Boles says that eighteen Presbyterian ministers were seen on site, and

there were probably even more Baptist and Methodist preachers, Boles, *Great Revival,* 65; see also Conkin, *Cane Ridge,* 95-96; Weisberger, *Gathered,* 31.

[28] According to Galli estimates of conversions varied from 1000-3000, Galli, "Revival at Cane Ridge", *Christian History* 14: 1 (Issue 45): 14, though he seems to have ignored Barton Stone, one of the organizers, whose more moderate estimate was 500-1000, Conkin, *Cane Ridge* 95.

[29] Asbury, *Journal,* 3:251.

[30] Conkin, *Cane Ridge,* ix. For further consideration of the significance of Cane Ridge Conkin's concluding chapter (164-178) gives valuable insights. See also Anthony L. Dunnavant, "From Precursor of the Movement to Icon of Christian Unity: Barton W. Stone. In Memory of the Christian Church (Disciples of Christ)" in Anthony L. Dunnavant, *Cane Ridge in Context: Perspectives on Barton W. Stone and Revival* (Nashville: Disciples of Christ, 1992), 1-2.

[31] Asbury, *Journal,* 2:576.

[32] Bruce, *Hallelujah,* 56; Johnson, *Camp Meeting,* 78, 80, 242-251; Samuel Miller, letter (8 Mar. 1832) in Sprague, *Revivals,* 35. Yet a massive national camp-meeting was conducted by the Methodists in Philadelphia in 1867, A McLean & J.W. Eaton (eds.) *Penuel; Or Face to Face with God* (NY: W.C. Palmer, 1869), 3-15.

[33] Bruce, *Hallelujah,* 73-74; Johnson, *Camp Meeting,* 184-86; Richard M'Nemar, *The Kentucky Revival* (NY: Jenkins, 1846), 25-26.

[34] Asbury, *Journal,* 3:270, 321; J. Chappell, letter to Mr. John Edwards, 7 Aug. 1801, *Methodist Magazine* 25: (June 1802): 263; Conkin, *Cane Ridge,* 93; Colonel Robert Paterson, letter to Rev. Dr. John King, 25 Sept. 1801, *Methodist Magazine* 26 (Feb. 1803) 83.

[35] Arnold, *Methodism in Kentucky,* 195-96, quoting a letter from John McGee to Rev. Thomas Douglass; Johnson, *Camp Meeting,* 34-35; Murray, *Revival,* 164.

[36] Johnson, *Camp Meeting,* 58.

[37] M'Nemar, *Kentucky Revival,* 23. See also Olive, "Evangelistic Invitation", 32-33. M'Nemar was a Presbyterian at this time, but later became a Shaker, Conkin, *Cane Ridge,* 102.

[38] Conkin, *Cane Ridge,* 93-94.

[39] Arnold, *Methodism in Kentucky,* 207-9; Johnson, *Camp Meeting,* 64-65, quoting from J.B. Finley, *Autobiography,* 166-67. James Crawford, a minister at Cane Ridge, is said to have tried to keep an "accurate ... account" of those who "fell" during the meetings, and ended up with the figure of 3000, M'Nemar, *Kentucky Revival,* 26.

[40] Murray, *Revival,* 166, quoting the words of Moses Hoge.

[41] Johnson, *Camp Meeting,* 94-98.

⁴² Johnson, *Camp Meeting*, 255, quoting Francis Trollope, *Domestic Manners of the American* (London: 1832), 1:240-45. But Carwardine describes Trollope's reporting of the camp-meetings as "impish", *Transatlantic*, 67.

⁴³ Conkin, *Cane Ridge*, 130-1; Galli, "Piercing Screams and Heavenly Smiles", *Christian History* 14: 1 (Issue 45): 15; Johnson, *Camp Meeting*, 58-62; Weisberger, *Gathered*, 34-35. The "jerks" were wild and apparently uncontrollable jerkings of the head or body, or both, while the other two manifestations are adequately described by their nicknames. M'Nemar describes various occurrences of such manifestations M'Nemar, *Kentucky Revival*, 64-67. Peter Cartwright believed that sometimes those experiencing the jerks became Christians, at other times not. He regarded this manifestation "as a judgment sent by God, first to bring sinners to repentance; and, secondly, to show professors that God could work with or without means", Peter Cartwright, *The Backwoods Preacher: An Autobiography of Peter Cartwright* (London: Hall, Virtue, 1859), 15-16. Dow's view was similar. He saw them as "partly a judgment for the people's unbelief, and yet as a mercy to convict people of divine realities", Dow, *Cosmopolite*, 182-84. Bangs viewed such manifestations unfavorably, calling them "unseemly", Bangs, *Methodist*, 2:161-62. These phenomena were not by any means new, and such were also found in the revivals amongst the Separate Baptists and the Methodists in the 1780s and before, Gewehr, *Great Awakening*, 110-111, 152-53, 170-72, and of course since.

⁴⁴ Arnold, *Methodism in Kentucky*, 282-86.

⁴⁵ S. Coate of Baltimore, letter c. 1803, *Methodist Magazine* 27 (May 1804): 235; John Couser of South Carolina, letter, 21 Apl. 1802, *Methodist Magazine* 26 (Mar. 1803): 131; Rev. J.E. Findley of Kentucky, letter, c. 1801, *Methodist Magazine* 26 (Mar.1803): 126; Rev. James Hall of North Carolina, letter, 4 May 1802, *Methodist Magazine* 26 (June 1803): 273-76; William Hodge of Tennessee, letter, c. 1801, *Methodist Magazine* 26 (June 1803): 269-270; Colonel Robert Paterson of Kentucky, letter, 25 Sept. 1801, *Methodist Magazine* 26 (Feb. 1803): 84-85.

⁴⁶ Johnson, *Camp Meeting*, 132-33; J.B. McFerrin, *Methodism in Tennessee* (c. 1890), 337.

⁴⁷ Bruce, *Hallelujah*, 71-73; McLendon, "Mourner's Bench", 10, 23-24; Murray, *Revival*, 185-86.

⁴⁸ Dow, *Cosmopolite*, 189-191.

⁴⁹ Dow, *Cosmopolite*, 207.

⁵⁰ Cartwright, *Autobiography*, 28.

⁵¹ Johnson, *Camp Meeting*, 258, quoting a letter from Smith dated 11 Nov. 1806. The editors of *Christian History* also state that the name "the pen" was used in New York camp-meetings, "Camp Meetings & Circuit Riders", *Christian History* 14: 1 (Issue 45): 16-17. Some opposers of the camp-meetings called it the "glory pen", Sellars, *Dow*, 20.

⁵² Carwardine, *Transatlantic*, 13, quoting Samuel Seaman, *Annals of New York Methodism*, 170-171.

⁵³ Asbury, *Journal*, 3:357,436.

[54] Johnson, *Camp Meeting*, 90.

[55] Johnson, *Camp Meeting*, 133-34.

[56] Cartwright, *Autobiography*, 18-19.

[57] Thompson, "Public Invitation", 92, quoting Elizabeth K. Nottingham, *Methodism on the Frontier* (NY: Columbia, 1941), 61.

[58] Johnson, *Camp Meeting*, 135, quoting Methodist circuit rider, Stephen R. Beggs.

[59] Johnson, *Camp Meeting*, 135-36, quoting James Flint, *Flint's Letters from America 1818-1820*, 258-261.

[60] Cartwright, *Autobiography*, 100; Johnson, *Camp Meeting*, 138, quoting J.B. Finley, *Autobiography*, 322-25.

[61] Cartwright, *Autobiography*, 48.

[62] Johnson, *Camp Meeting*, 136-37, quoting from the (NY) *Methodist Magazine* 2 (1819): 234-35.

[63] Gregory Schneider, "Focus on the Frontier Family", *Christian History* 14: 1 (Issue 45): 40.

[64] Peter Cartwright, "Wrestling with God and Man", *Christian History* 14: 1 (Issue 45): 21.

[65] Keillor, *Rebellious*, 105-8.

[66] Leslie F. Church, *More About the Early Methodist People*, (London: Epworth, 1949), 258-263.

[67] At the English Methodist Conference of 1795 it was agreed to permit the communion service in any Methodist church wishing to conduct it, but it was to be administered "according to the form of the Established Church", Church, *More Early Methodist*, 267. American Methodism had been granted independence by Wesley in 1784, when he sent "superintendents", later termed "Bishops", to administer the sacraments and to ordain others, Bangs, *Methodist*, 1:151-55.

[68] Carwardine, *Transatlantic*, 13.

[69] More, "Origins of 'The Altar Call'": 25-28.

[70] Fawcett, *Cambuslang*, 63, quoting from John Knox, *Works*, 1:299-300n2; Gillies, *Revival*, 356, 365; Tyler & Bonar, *Nettleton*, 443-44, quoting Joseph Fish.

[71] Conkin, *Cane Ridge*, 93-94; Galli, "Revival at Cane Ridge", *Christian History* 14:1 (Issue 45): 14. See also Bangs, *Methodist*, 2:104-5; M'Nemar, *Kentucky Revival*, 21-22, 34-35.

[72] Olive, "Evangelistic Invitation", 23.

[73] Bruce, *Hallelujah*, 74-76; Johnson, *Camp Meeting*, 54-55.

[74] McFerrin, *Methodism in Tennessee*, 338-39.

[75] Bruce, *Hallelujah*, 80-81, 127; see also his chapter on the musical side of camp-meeting religion, 96-122.

[76] Johnson, *Camp Meeting*, 127, 131-32.

[77] In McLean & Eaton, *Penuel*, the text of a number of sermons at an 1867 camp-meeting are given along with the exhortations which followed some of them. These exhortations were in each case delivered by different clergyman from the one preaching, and are probably best described as prolonged appeals.

Though of varied length, they are on average about half the size of the sermon they followed. None of them make any mention of a public invitation as such. See 38-56, 283-296, 334-351.

[78] Bruce, *Hallelujah* 77, quoting from A.P. Mead *Manna in the Wilderness* (Philadelphia: Perkinpine & Higgins, 1859), 56; Johnson, *Camp Meetings*, 140, quoting James Flint, *Letters from America*, 262; Conkin, *Cane Ridge*, 154.

[79] Johnson, *Camp Meetings*, 286n27; Asbury, *Journal*, 2:213, 330, 334, 369, 535-36.

[80] Bruce, *Hallelujah*, 75, 85-87.

[81] Asbury, *Journal*, 2:192.

[82] Asbury, *Journal*, 1:75, 118, 387; Olive, "Evangelistic Invitation", 23; Thrift, *Jesse Lee*, 277-78, 294, 304, quoting Lee's *Journal*.

[83] Conkin, *Cane Ridge*, 91.

[84] H.B. Kendall, *History of the Primitive Methodist Church* (2 vols; London: Dalton, c 1906), 1:89-90.

[85] Dow, *Cosmopolite*, 29.

[86] Church, *More Early Methodist*, 39.

[87] Asbury, *Journal*, 1:308-9.

[88] Asbury, *Journal*, 2:213.

[89] Asbury speaks of exhorting for "about fifteen minutes". Sermons in those days usually lasted considerably longer. Asbury, *Journal*, 2:338.

[90] Cartwright, *Autobiography*, 4.

[91] Kendall, *Primitive Methodism*, 1:278. (A further six names follow after the exhorters, under the heading "Women"). See also the preachers' plan of 1819, which also lists exhorters separately, again with consecutive numbering, Kendall, 1:508.

[92] The Shakers held that God was both male and female; Jesus Christ was the male incarnation of God, whilst their leader, Mother Ann Lee, was the corresponding female manifestation of the Deity. Their worship included dancing, laughing, barking and shaking. Robert Linder, *The New International Dictionary of the Christian Church*, 900-901.

[93] Cartwright, *Autobiography*, 17-18.

[94] Cartwright, *Autobiography*, 23-24.

[95] Murray, *Revival*, 310-312, quoting Wilson Thompson, *Autobiography*, 312-321.

[96] Johnson, *Camp Meeting*, 67; Carwardine, *Transatlantic*, 46-49.

[97] Johnson, *Camp Meeting*, 173-74, quoting Mead, *Manna in the Wilderness*, 17-19.

[98] Peter Cartwright, for example, frequently gives this impression, see Cartwright, *Autobiography*, 7, 15-16, 32. ,

[99] Frank Baker in Asbury, *Journal*, 3:343n141; Hugh Bourne, *History of the Primitive Methodists* (Bemersley: Primitive Methodist, 1835), 24-31; Carwardine, *Transatlantic*, 106-7; John Petty, *History of the Primitive Methodist Connexion* (London: Davies, 1864), 30-39.

Chapter 5

Theological Changes

In chapter three it was noted that significant changes were happening to society in the late eighteenth and early nineteenth century, especially in America, bringing about a new emphasis on such issues as democracy, individualism and freedom. It is now time to examine the theology which predominated in Protestantism at that time, and to note the relevant doctrinal changes that came about, influenced, to some degree at least, by what was happening in society. A thorough study of this is not possible here, so just a brief outline will be given. Those wishing to examine this more thoroughly should consult those books that specifically examine the relevant areas.[1]

A great deal of Protestant theology in Europe and America up until the mid-eighteenth century had been varying shades of calvinism, though arminianism had not been absent. Yet, it needs to be noted that the arminianism of, say, Arminius and the Remonstrants and the Wesleys was considerably closer to calvinism than much of what is called arminianism today. Some of the proponents of these teachings evangelized little, but others, though their methods were conservative, preached the gospel energetically and, in some cases widely. Amongst the Puritans, for example, preaching was paramount, though personal counseling and catechizing were perceived as useful adjuncts to this. Richard Baxter in seventeenth century England and David Hall in America in the 1730s were excellent examples of the latter.[2] Important components of this theology, as it impinged upon evangelistic practice, were: first, limited atonement; secondly, that both justification and the faith that led to that justification were gifts of God; and thirdly, that human beings were unable to respond to God until empowered to do so by the Spirit of God. Whilst the first of these beliefs was rejected by arminians, the second and third were commonly held by both calvinists and arminians.

To demonstrate this it is necessary to return to John Wesley, George Whitefield and Jonathan Edwards to examine their teachings as representative of the arminian (Wesley) and calvinist (Whitefield and Edwards) traditions in the area of Christian salvation. The remarkable similarity of the teaching of the three men should be noted.

The Beliefs of Wesley, Whitefield and Edwards

It needs to be first recognized that though Edwards and Wesley are justly regarded as theologians, Whitefield, to use Stout's term, "was a visionary not a thinker",[3] a man of action rather than a scholar. Whereas Edwards could spend thirteen hours a day in his study, Whitefield sometimes spent as much as forty hours a week preaching. This does not mean, though, that Whitefield lacked firm doctrinal convictions, but that these were not as well formulated as his two contemporaries.

All three men had a negative view of humanity's natural condition. Whilst believing that Adam and Eve were created perfect,[4] the Fall saw mankind descend, so that all "became ... naturally God's enemies" (Edwards), "earthly, sensual, devilish ... a mere lump of ungodliness" (Wesley), and "like the beasts that perish, nay like the devil himself" (Whitefield).[5] Consequently, everybody stands under the eternal judgment of God, for, as Edwards puts it, "Sin is a violation of infinite obligation [to love honor and obey God], and so is an infinite evil [deserving] an infinite punishment".[6] All three of these evangelists believed that because of this sin and judgment, men and women needed saving, but that they were incapable of saving themselves. The only means of salvation was the grace of God, through the Lord Jesus Christ.[7]

Differences do emerge, however, when one considers the three evangelists understanding of grace. To Wesley, prevenient or preventing grace is available, to some degree to everybody, and frequently manifests itself in what we call "conscience", and, by human definition at least, good behavior.[8] But though no one "has a natural power to choose anything that is truly good", human will naturally being "free only to evil", "every man has a measure of free will restored to him by grace".[9] But that limited endowment of grace does not itself save, for additional gifts of grace are necessary before one can be justified,[10] and the source of that grace is solely through Jesus Christ, the Son of God.

Edwards also spoke of a generally available "restraining grace", but his concept is not to be equated with Wesley's prevenient grace, for this is not a universal endowment which can lead to justification, but God's "setting bounds to [mankind's] wickedness". Like Wesley, Edwards sees it as manifest in conscience, and also in providence. To Edwards, though, "natural men have no ... free willingness" to come to Christ, and they "obstinately refuse to" do so.[11] For Edwards, grace to move the human will Christ-ward is not given universally.

Wesley and Whitefield, of course, clashed over their different understandings of God's grace. Shortly after Whitefield had launched forth into field preaching, he invited his Methodist colleague to substitute for him in Bristol while he went into other districts. It was at about this time that Wesley preached his famous sermon on free grace, which was the original cause of the division between them. In this sermon Wesley proclaimed that grace was "Free in all" and "Free for all".[12] Wesley's understanding of the term "free grace" was, as Allan Sell has it, "grace freely available to all", while to Whitefield it was that which was "given or withheld freely by God".[13]

Yet, Wesley agreed with Whitefield that God had "unconditionally elected some persons to eternal glory", though Wesley did not hold that *all* those not so elected would of necessity perish. Wesley also rejected preterition.[14] In the free grace sermon he logically concluded that if God had predestined the elect to salvation, by implication one must believe He has decreed "to damn" others.[15]

Later Wesley's views seemed to change a little, and he appears to have moved a bit towards calvinism. In 1745 he said that his brand of arminianism "touches the very edge of Calvinism", indeed it was just a "hair's breadth" from calvinism.[16] In addition when he published a selection of 12 sermons in 1746 as a standard of Methodist belief, the free grace sermon, probably his most arminian statement, was not included. It was still omitted when he added sermons to that selection in later editions in 1748, 1750, 1760 (*Forty Four Sermons*), and 1771 (*Fifty Three Sermons*).[17] Why he omitted this sermon is unknown, but he certainly always regarded himself as an arminian.[18] When he published a magazine for the Methodist people in January 1778, he nailed his colors firmly to that mast, by naming it the *Arminian Magazine*.

In the free grace sermon Wesley stated that he considered the teaching that "one part of mankind [being] infallibly saved, and the rest

infallibly damned made preaching useless".[19] That Whitefield and
Edwards strongly disagreed with Wesley here is clearly proved by their
practice. They believed that the "infallibly saved" became effectually
saved through preaching.[20]

Yet, to Wesley, if grace was "the source" of salvation, faith was "its
condition".[21] But what was the nature of that faith? In a conversation
with Wesley in 1739 the Bishop of Bristol suggested that "faith itself is
a good work". But Wesley would have none of that. After all, even
faith "is the gift of God, and a gift that presupposes nothing in us but
sin and misery", a view he confirms in his sermon on justification by
faith.[22] Edwards and Whitefield echoed this. They stated that faith is
the condition upon which justification rests, though Edwards added,
Christ Himself is the "ultimate condition", and not surprisingly they
also agreed with Wesley that faith itself is given by God.[23]

None of the three men regarded good works as in any way
meritorious, whilst they all recognized that good works were naturally
manifested in those who had been saved and an evidence of that
salvation.[24] But even though good works could not save, all three urged
upon their unconverted hearers the necessity of seeking salvation. At
that time some of the Moravians and others had slipped into a doctrine
of passivity that taught that the only way to true salvation was through
"silent prayer and quiet waiting upon God", even advising prospective
converts against church attendance and the reading of Scripture.
Wesley opposed that strongly, and urged his listeners not to "rest short
of this prize of thy high calling" and to "cry unto Him day and night ...
until thou knowest in whom thou hast believed".[25]

To Edwards, too, seeking was vital, for "God does all, and we do all.
God produces all, and we act all". Therefore "If we would be saved, we
must seek salvation". Indeed, in his sermon "Pressing into the
Kingdom" he informs his hearers that seeking salvation needs to
include "strength of desire", "firmness of resolution", and "greatness of
endeavour". Yet this seeking, of itself, is doomed to failure. It is only
intended to make sinners despair of their own efforts, and to propel
them into the arms of a gracious God.[26]

Whitefield also urged his hearers to seek Christ. In one sermon he
pleaded with sinners to "awake", to "fly, fly, fly to Jesus Christ ... and
beg of God to give you faith, and to enable you to close with Jesus
Christ". In another sermon he said, "let me persuade you to close with
Christ, and never rest until you can say, 'The Lord our
righteousness'".[27]

None of these three men believed that the sinners should just wait
passively for God to save them.

Wesley generally rejected the concept of the perseverance of the saints.[28] Yet for Edwards "all that have true grace shall persevere", for that perseverance is grounded in God's grace not human effort. Whitefield, in a letter to Wesley in 1740, indicated his firm conviction in "the final perseverance of those who are truly in Christ", though he conceded that though a Christian cannot fall "finally", as to lose salvation, he or she "may fall foully" into sin.[29]

In the doctrinal areas relevant to the altar call that have been considered here, for the most part there is harmony between the three evangelists. The primary areas of difference are with regard to the universality or otherwise of the offer of God's saving grace to sinners and the subsequent extent of its influence on the human will, and the possibility of a Christian falling totally from grace. In those areas Wesley takes the traditional arminian viewpoint, and Edwards and Whitefield the calvinistic.

The Theological Ferment

From the end of the eighteenth century there was a gradual, uneven theological shift, led by Methodist arminianism (which at times had a stronger belief in an individual's natural ability to believe the gospel than did Wesley), and more moderate forms of calvinism. Indeed, some of those claiming to be calvinists were probably not really such at all, at least not in the traditional sense. Historian Douglas Frank quotes an unnamed source as saying that the theologians of the nineteenth century twisted calvinism "almost beyond recognition."[30] By the end of the nineteenth century even those claiming to be calvinists were in a distinct minority.

It is a moot point whether the theology of salvation changed to allow for new evangelistic practices, or those practices grew out of the new theology. It is probably correct to say that there is some truth in both contentions. For example, the American Baptist, John Leland noted the emergence of an apparently successful hybrid. In 1791 he said that

> the preaching that has been most blessed of God, and most profitable to men, is the doctrine of sovereign grace in the salvation of souls, mixed with a little of what is called Arminianism.[31]

David Rice, a Presbyterian minister, made a similar observation in 1803 about the theology of revival sermons. He said,

> Sometimes there is in our discourses a strange heterogeneous mixture
> of antinomianism, arminianism, and I may add, calvinism; calvinism,
> perhaps in the beginning, antinomianism in the middle, and
> arminianism at the end.[32]

These comments suggest that the theological shift was at least in part
pragmatic, though this may also reflect the fact that whilst it may be
easy to be a consistent calvinist in the study, it is probably harder in the
pulpit.

Deism and Unitarianism had a considerable influence upon changes
in Christian theology, especially in America. Traditionally, says
William McLoughlin, calvinists "stressed man's depravity and
untrustworthiness" and his lack of free will. By contrast Deists
"stressed his innate goodness, free will and reasonableness".[33] Christian
teachers, in an effort to defeat these spreading new teachings, felt the
need to respond to them, and did so by adjusting their own beliefs to
meet the rationalists, if not half way, at least somewhere on middle
ground. McLoughlin also states that in the process of unseating deism,
American calvinism had to make these major concessions to it:

> that God was benevolent and not wrathful, merciful not stern,
> reasonable not mysterious; that he worked by means and not miracles,
> that man was active and not passive in his salvation, that grace was not
> arbitrarily or capriciously dispensed ... but offered freely to all men as a
> gift of a loving Father to his children ...[34]

If McLoughlin, perhaps, sees it too much as a progression from one
extreme to the other, his point is largely valid. Most significantly for
the subject of this book was the new understanding of man's role in his
own salvation.

S.E. Mead, in his biography of Nathaniel Taylor, has commented
that total depravity was a major target in the attack by the Unitarians on
orthodox Christianity. He says that the adjustments that Taylor (see
below) and his successors made to that doctrine were part of an attempt
to "restate calvinism in more acceptable terms".[35]

In addition was the considerable influence of the "Common Sense"
school of philosophy in eighteenth century Scotland,[36] which advocated
the idea that humanity had developed to the stage where people learned
to be happy, moral beings through innate common sense and the
benefits of experience. This philosophy was not anti-Christian. Indeed,
it was intended to support Christianity, but its underlying basis was

reason rather than Scripture,[37] and as such its influence moved some of evangelical Christianity a step away from its earlier position. Not only was this philosophy prominent in Britain, but also in America, particularly at Princeton, where John Witherspoon, a Scottish advocate of this system, became president in 1768.[38]

Nathaniel Taylor (1786-1858) of Yale was, perhaps, the first major theologian to put forward a theological system (New Haven Theology) to suit the changes already occurring in evangelism. Indeed, Ahlstrom claims that he "consciously formulat[ed] a reasonable revival theology" to suit the democratic ethos of that time.[39] Starting with the premise that "The clear, unperverted deductions of reason" were as reliable as the "Word of God",[40] Taylor accepted to some degree the calvinistic idea of human depravity, in that to him the nature of each individual would lead him or her inevitably to commit sin, but could not accept the traditional calvinistic concept of a sinful human nature (stemming from Adam) that made it impossible for one to believe.[41] For "the sinner" is able to choose and act on the issue of salvation "just as voluntarily, as when he yields in any case to the solicitations of a friend". True the Holy Spirit was an "influence" upon the unbeliever in the process of salvation, but He did not compel him or her.[42] These principles were also later adopted by C.G. Finney,[43] and opened the way for "decision" evangelism. Indeed, J.W. Nevin claimed that, "Finneyism is only Taylorism reduced to practice".[44]

Frank says that Taylor's theology also presented "a relatively tame and friendly God", in whom love was far more prominent than judgment.[45] This was a definite shift from the position of a host of calvinists, or even Wesley and many of his followers. Finney, a few years after Taylor, still had a strong emphasis upon God's judgment, though Taylor's teaching did have its influence upon Moody, directly or indirectly, and many other evangelists, theologians and teachers since. Once one has a friendlier, more easy-going God, it follows that the road to Him is simpler, quicker and less painful. These facts are particularly evident when one compares modern evangelistic expectations and "results" with those of two hundred years ago and more.

A half generation after Taylor, Edwards Amasa Park (1808-1900), a Congregationalist theologian at Andover Seminary (originally established to preserve calvinistic teaching), was teaching that human beings did not have a sinful nature, and leading from that they were not automatically guilty at birth, nor would they of a certainty sin, for they naturally had the power to obey God.[46]

On both sides of the Atlantic, many in traditionally calvinistic churches were reworking their theology. In America, the debate had raged from the time of Jonathan Edwards, and "new theology" was ushered in. This new theology (theologies, more accurately) rode in some measure on Edwards' back, though to what degree it was true to him is still hotly argued.[47] Even Finney used Edwards' name (selectively) to justify his use of the "New Measures", much to the annoyance of Albert Dod and others, who, with justification, challenged his claims.[48]

Mark Noll says that in the nineteenth century Edwards' *Freedom of the Will* encountered no less than "twenty-nine serious refutations".[49] Edwards opponents, in varying degrees, opened up the way for, and supported the belief that human beings are free to decide for Christ.

The Denominations

Amongst the denominations, arminian Methodism grew rapidly in England,[50] and, after a later start, even more so in America, where in the nineteenth century, it exercised considerable influence, particularly where it mattered most at the local church level. It is not insignificant that when Wesley in England and Asbury in America each introduced a Methodist magazine for their people, they both chose the name *The Arminian Magazine*.[51] As has already been suggested, nineteenth century Methodism generally had a more optimistic view of the human will than did Wesley himself. Methodism became, if you like, more arminian than its founder. Carwardine says that this arminian theology, with its "individualistic, democratic and optimistic emphasis" played a significant part in Methodism's rapid expansion in America, where it became the largest denomination by the mid-nineteenth century.[52]

There had been calvinist and arminian wings amongst the American Baptists probably from the end of the seventeenth century, and some congregations included members of both persuasions.[53] The leaning appears to have moved in favor of the calvinists with the advent of the Separates (mainly calvinistic, though of varying shades) in the mid-eighteenth century,[54] but towards the end of that century the tide began to drift slowly towards arminianism, a trend which continued into the next century. Though Nettles speaks of leading Baptist teachers still propagating calvinism well into the nineteenth century,[55] the same cannot necessarily be said of Baptists at grass roots level. David Benedict, writing of his 50 years experience of American Baptist life, lamented in 1860 that "the old-fashioned doctrines of Predestination, Total Depravity, Divine Sovereignty, etc., if referred to at all, must be by the way of circumlocution and implication", a marked difference from his earlier experience, when they were clearly preached.[56] If such doctrines were still widely held in American Baptist circles, it would seem that they were not much proclaimed by that time.

In 1833, the Separate Baptists adopted a new confession of faith, which spoke of "the free agency of man", and stated that, "nothing prevents the salvation of the greatest sinner on earth except his own voluntary refusal to submit to the Lord Jesus Christ."[57] This represented a clear shift from the earlier position of the majority of the Separates.

A new group of Presbyterians emerged in America at the beginning of the nineteenth century, under the influence of the early camp-meetings. One leader of this movement was Richard M'Nemar, who was charged with heresy by his elders at the Cabin Creek Church on the Ohio River in 1801 for preaching arminianism. The following year he crossed the river to pastor another church in Turtle Creek. Once more the accusations surfaced. John Thompson, another Presbyterian minister in the same area, found himself similarly accused. Charged by the Presbytery, both of them decided to withdraw from that church, and with three other ministers, Barton Stone, Robert Marshall and John Dunlavy, formed a new church, which retained few characteristics of traditional Presbyterianism.[58] This church avoided having a confession of faith as such, and Stone, its most theologically articulate leader, held a number of ideas that troubled the orthodox. Some of these do not need to be investigated here,[59] but others are relevant to this study, for his views were decidedly "arminian", believing that Christ died for all, and that people had the free will to accept Christ.[60]

This new denomination grew quite rapidly, but suffered fairly substantial defections to the Shakers, including M'Nemar. But in the early 1830s Stone's group joined with another new arminian church under the leadership of the father and son team of Thomas and Alexander Campbell, and formed the Disciples of Christ. This group underwent rapid growth, and eventually became the Churches of Christ.[61] For the most part Alexander Campbell rejected the idea of the activity of the Holy Spirit in conversion, and reduced faith to an intellectual assent to truth.[62] Walter Scott, one of the key Disciples' evangelists in America at this time, believed that people had the inherent power of mind, heart and will to respond to the gospel, and this seems to have been the common view of the Disciples.[63] Thus in this period emerged another important denomination preaching an "arminian" theology, with a strong emphasis on human ability.

Another splinter group (influenced by the camp-meetings) was the Cumberland Presbyterian Church, a splinter but not a small one, for it had over 60 churches by 1813. This group retained the Presbyterian label and much of the Westminster Confession, but dissented on such doctrines as the atonement (they believed Christ died for all), and original sin, which they rejected. Early in the twentieth century most of the Cumberland churches united with the Presbyterian Church in the United States of America, which Conkin says modified its confession along more arminian lines to accommodate the Cumberlands.[64]

In Britain

In this period in England there was also a theological upheaval. The Congregational Church, for example, generally preached a more moderate form of calvinism. One of this theology's major advocates, Edward Williams of Rotherham Academy, taught: a) that Christ's death was sufficient for all, and b) that though mankind's depravity extends to its nature, the individual's will is entirely free. Whether this could be accurately described as calvinism must be questioned, but it certainly represented a significant shift. Sell states that Williams' influence "was considerable".[65] In 1876, citing R.W. Dale (a leading Congregational preacher and writer), the *General Baptist Magazine* could observe that "Calvinism is almost an obsolete theory" in Congregationalism.[66]

In Particular Baptist circles Andrew Fuller led most away from the stifling hyper-calvinism of Gill and Brine to a distinctly evangelical calvinism,[67] which some dubbed "moderate Arminianism".[68] C.H. Spurgeon, a generation or two later, proclaimed largely the same message as Fuller to thousands of hearers and millions of readers. He, too, was dubbed by some an arminian, though his doctrine was genuinely calvinistic.[69] But other Baptists went further. John Howard Hinton took a very strong stand against the concept of human inability to repent without divine aid, going as far as to state at one point that "a sinner has power to repent without the Spirit",[70] a view that would have horrified Wesley, let alone traditional calvinists. Hinton described himself as "at the same time, both a Calvinist and an Arminian", though, in whatever sense that can be true, Sellars is probably correct when he says that the latter was preeminent.[71] By 1870, John Clifford could say that, "For all practical ends what might be called the Calvinism of" the Particular Baptists "is exactly the same as the Arminianism of" the General Baptists.[72]

This era also saw a liberalizing of theology in the Calvinistic Methodist, Congregational and Baptist Churches in Wales, so that what became known as "the New System" (a more "arminian" theology) was, according to Carwardine, dominant by 1840. Though the

Calvinistic Methodists adopted a new confession of faith based on the Westminster Confession in 1823, this was moderated after disputes in the 1820s and 1830s.[73]

In Scotland, which was for the most part, a stronghold of calvinism (Methodism, for example, had made little headway there), the changes were slower, but James Morison's Evangelical Union could state that it held "tenaciously to the doctrine of free will", and criticized the concept of unconditional election. A leading Presbyterian layman, Thomas Erskine, caused a stir when in 1828 he wrote a book entitled *The Unconditional Freeness of the Gospel* and John McLeod Campbell was dismissed from the Presbyterian ministry in 1831 for teaching universal atonement.[74]

American Presbyterian, Calvin Colton wrote a book on American revivals for the British market in 1832. In it he said that conversion "should not be regarded as a mystery ... It is a plain, common sense, practical business, intelligible to all. It is a decision in mind and heart of the simplest question: 'Shall I love and serve God, or shall I love and serve the world?'"[75] He thus presented a picture quite different from the majority of his Presbyterian predecessors.

Summary

Peter Toon states "that in this period three important characteristics were incorporated into evangelical Christianity ... pietism, individualism and reductionism": pietism in the sense of a stress upon "a subjective experience of religion", and reductionism in that "creeds, rituals and ceremonies were pared down to a minimum".[76] It would be a mistake of course to suggest that this form of pietism or even individualism were completely new to the period under consideration. It was rather that they became much more significant, and they were crucial factors in the development of the altar call, where individual experience is paramount. The decline in creeds too has had its part to play in this process, in that as the church became less clear about its theology, it became less aware of what constituted conversion, and more prepared to experiment with evangelistic method.

For the most part the changes in the Protestant church's understanding of the theology of salvation have been considerable, and this has occurred in a wide range of denominations on both sides of the Atlantic. As W.O. Thompson puts it, "What was heresy to [Albert Dod and others in the 1830s and before] was by the next generation orthodoxy".[77] The field was by then, and even earlier, wide open to a whole army of new evangelists using methods which would have puzzled or horrified their predecessors. For example, in the 1840s in England, American Methodist evangelist, James Caughey could urge his hearers to "Decide now ..." and come forward,[78] based on this new theology.

Notes

[1] These include: R.C. Sproul, *Willing to Believe: The Controversy over Free Will* (Grand Rapids: Baker, 1997), which is an examination of how certain major theologians have understood the subject of free will, from Augustine to Lewis Sperry Chafer; Alan Sell, *The Great Debate* (Worthing: Walter, 1982), which gives a useful summary of the history of the calvinist/arminian debate; Peter Toon, *Born Again* (Grand Rapids: Baker, 1987) which examines how the doctrine of regeneration has been perceived in various eras of church history and by different groups; and Alistair E. McGrath, *Justitia Dei: A History of the Christian Doctrine of Justification* (2nd ed. Cambridge: Cambridge UP, 1998).

[2] Richard Baxter, *The Reformed Pastor* (ed. William Brown; Edinburgh: Banner of Truth, 1974); Packer, *God's Giants,* 393, 401-5; Tracy, *Awakening,* 162-63.

[3] Stout, *Divine Dramatist,* 211.

[4] Edwards, "Original Sin" in *Works,* 1:178; Wesley, *44 Sermons,* 50; Whitefield, *Sermons,* 140.

[5] Edwards, "Men Naturally God's Enemies" in *Works,* 2:130, 137; Wesley, *44 Sermons,* 69; Whitefield, *Sermons,* 140.

[6] John Carrick, "Jonathan Edwards and the Deists", *Banner of Truth,* 299-300 (Aug.-Sept., 1988), 29, quoting from Edwards, *Eternity of Hell Torments,* in *Works,* 2:83.

[7] Edwards, *Freedom of the Will,* in *Works,* 1:51; Edwards, *Remarks on Important Theological Controversies,* in *Works,* 2:547, 551-53; Wesley, *44 Sermons,* 70-71; Whitefield, *Sermons,* 129, 155.

[8] Wesley's sermon on conscience, in *Works,* 7:187-88. See also *Works,* 6:512; 7:373-74; and Williams, *Wesley's Theology,* 41-42.

[9] Wesley, "Some Remarks on 'A Defence of the Preface to the Edinburgh Edition of Aspasio Vindicated'", in *Works,* 10:350; Wesley, "Some Remarks on Mr. Hill's 'Review of all the Doctrines taught by Mr. John Wesley'", in *Works,* 10:392; Burtner & Chiles, *Wesley's Theology,* 132-33.

[10] Williams, *Wesley's Theology,* 42.

[11] Edwards, "Men Naturally God's Enemies", in *Works,* 2:137-38. See also his sermon on divine light, *Works,* 2:13.

[12] Wesley, *Works,* 7:373-74.

[13] Sell, *Great Debate,* 70; Williams, *Wesley's Theology,* 53-54, quoting a letter from Whitefield.

[14] Wesley, *Works,* 1:426-27.

[15] Wesley, *Works,* 7:375.

[16] Wesley, "Minutes of Some Late Conversations", in *Works*, 8:284-85. See also Sell, *Great Debate*, 67.

[17] Wesley, *44 Sermons*, ii, v; John Wesley, *Sermons on Several Occasions: Fifty Three Sermons* (London: Methodist [1771]).

[18] See David Bennett, "How Arminian was John Wesley?" *Evangelical Quarterly* 72:3 (July, 2000) 237-48, for a more detailed exploration of his views in this area.

[19] Wesley, *Works*, 7:375-76.

[20] Edwards, *Affections*, 115; Whitefield, *Journals*, 575.

[21] Wesley, *44 Sermons*, 2.

[22] Wesley, *Journal*, 2:256-57; Wesley, *44 Sermons*, 58-59.

[23] Edwards, "Discourse on Justification by Faith", in *Works*, 1:622-23; Edwards, "Remarks on Important Theological Controversies", in *Works*, 2:545, 547; Edwards, "Wisdom Displayed in Salvation", in *Works*, 2:146-47; John H. Gerstner, *Jonathan Edwards: A Mini-Theology* (Wheaton: Tyndale, 1987), 79, quoting Edwards; Whitefield, *Sermons*, 100, 135, 155.

[24] Dallimore, *Whitefield*, 1:223-24; Randall E. Otto, "Justification and Justice: an Edwardsean Proposal", *Evangelical Quarterly*, 65:2 (April 1993) 137; Wesley, *Journal*, 4:419; Wesley, *44 Sermons*, 164-174.

[25] Wesley, *Journal*, 2:419; 3:258; Wesley, *44 Sermons*, 19.

[26] Edwards, "Theological Controversies", *Works*, 2:557; Edwards, *Works*, 1:655; 2:52-53; "Narrative of Conversions", in *Works*, 1:352. See also Jenson, *America's Theologian*, 58-59.

[27] Whitefield, *Sermons*, 90, 135.

[28] Wesley, *Works*, 1:426-27; Williams, *Wesley's Theology*, 123.

[29] Edwards, "Theological Controversies", in *Works*, 2:596-98; Dallimore, *Whitefield*, 1:155; Whitefield, *Sermons*, 88.

[30] Douglas W. Frank, *Less Than Conquerors* (Grand Rapids: Eerdmans, 1986), 18. On the "coalface" D.L. Moody seems to have considered himself a calvinist, and was certainly believed to be such by some English Methodists, but an examination of his sermons makes that view untenable, see chapter eight of this book. Moody also argued with J.N. Darby against the latter's calvinistic views, see Max S. Weremchuk, *John Nelson Darby* (Neptune: Loizeaux, 1992), 143.

[31] Goen, *Revivalism*, 285, quoting from the *Writings of John Leland*, 172. Leland, himself, was dubbed by one of his hearers "a kind of Methodist", White, *First Baptist Church*, 9, quoting from the diary of Henry Toler.

[32] Boles, *Great Revival*, 66n51, quoting from *A Sermon on the Present Revival of Religion in this Country: Preached at the Opening of the Kentucky Synod* (Lexington: 1803), 32. See also Boles, 100.

[33] William G. McLoughlin, *Revivals, Awakenings and Reform* (Chicago: Uni. of Chicago, 1978), 99.

[34] Thompson, "Public Invitation", 98, quoting William G. McLoughlin, *The American Evangelicals, 1800-1900. An Anthology* (NY: Harper & Bros., 1968), 4.

[35] Murray, *Revival*, 260-61, quoting S.E. Mead, *Nathaniel William Taylor,*

213.
[36]   Ahlstrom says that this influence was mainly indirect, Sydney E. Ahlstrom, *A Religious History of the American People* (New Haven: Yale, 1972), 355-56.
[37]   Michael Gauvreau, *The Evangelical Century: College and Creed in English Canada from the Great Revival to the Great Depression"*. (Montreal: McGill-Queen's UP, 1991) 17. See also Ahlstrom, *Religious History*, 355; Thompson, "Public Invitation", 96-98
[38]   Ahlstrom, *Religious History*, 355; Thompson, "Public Invitation", 96-98.
[39]   Ahlstrom, *Religious History*, 420.
[40]   Frank, *Conquerors*, 16-17.
[41]   Nathaniel W. Taylor, "Concio ad Clerum", a sermon preached in 1828, in Keith J. Hardman, *Issues in American Christianity* (Grand Rapids: Baker, 1993), 138-140; Frank, *Conquerors* 17.
[42]   Frank, *Conquerors*, 17.
[43]   Charles G. Finney, *The Memoirs of Charles G. Finney* (ed. Garth M, Rosell & Richard A.G. Dupuis, Grand Rapids: Zondervan, 1989), 154-55.
[44]   Nevin, *Anxious Bench*, 104.
[45]   Frank, *Conquerors*, 17.
[46]   Mark A. Noll, in Hatch & Stout, *American Experience*, 265.
[47]   William Breitenbach, in Hatch & Stout, *American Experience*, 178. Breitenbach gives some of the recent literature and viewpoints on this issue, 195-97n1.
[48]   Charles G. Finney, *Lectures on Revivals of Religion* (NY: Revell, 1868), 241-42; Noll, in Hatch & Stout, *American Experience*, 261-62.
[49]   Noll, in Hatch & Stout, *American Experience*, 270. Noll is using data from M.X. Lesser, *Jonathan Edwards: A Reference Guide* (Boston: 1981).
[50]   There were an estimated 70 000 Methodists in Britain by the time of Wesley's death, and this number increased rapidly in the following century as Methodism both divided and multiplied, Telford, *Wesley*, 362; Carwardine, *Transatlantic*, 45-52.
[51]   Asbury, a letter "To the subscribers for *The Arminian Magazine*", *Journal*, 3:67; Murray, *Revival*, 177-79; Wesley, *The Journal* in the *Works of John Wesley*, 4:108, 113, 467.
[52]   Carwardine, *Transatlantic*, 10, 45-52; Orr, *Light of Nations*, 28. See also Sweet, *Revivalism*, 128.
[53]   Lumpkin, *Baptist Foundations*, 60-65; McLoughlin, *Backus*, 89-91; Semple, *Baptists in Virginia*, 99-101, 197-98, 201-2.
[54]   Goen, *Revivalism*, 284-87; Lumpkin, *Baptist Foundations*, 62-63; Nettles, *Grace & Glory*, 43-44; O'Kelly, "Separate Baptists", 118-120.
[55]   McLoughlin, *Backus*, 167-175; Nettles, *Grace & Glory*, 187-205.
[56]   Hassal, *Kehukee* 763, quoting David Benedict, *Fifty Years Among the Baptists* (NY: Sheldon, 1860).
[57]   Goen, *Revivalism*, 286, quoting W.J. McGlothlin, *Baptist Confessions of Faith* (Philadelphia: 1911), 302-5.
[58]   Ronald P. Byars, "Cane Ridge from a Presbyterian Point of View" in

Anthony L. Dunnavant, *Cane Ridge in Context*, 94-97; Conkin, *Cane Ridge,* 124-130, Leroy Garrett. *The Stone-Campbell Movement* Joplin: College Press, 1981, 106-111; M'Nemar, *Kentucky Revival,* 43-47.

[59] For example, accusations were made that Stone held Arian views, Conkin, *Cane Ridge,* 132-3. Further details of this group's beliefs can be found in M'Nemar, *Kentucky Revival,* 47-58.

[60] Conkin, *Cane Ridge* 134, 141; Max Ward Randall, *The Great Awakenings and the Restoration Movement* (Joplin: College, 1983), 53; James R. Rogers & B.W. Stone, *The Cane Ridge Meeting House and A Short History of the Life of Barton W. Stone* (Cincinnati: Standard, 1910), 149-153, 165-6. M'Nemar also believed that Christ died "for all", M'Nemar *Kentucky Revival,* 30, 51.

[61] Conkin, *Cane Ridge,* 102, 145-150; Toon, *Born Again,* 168.

[62] Alexander Campbell, *Christian Baptism: With its Antecedents and Consequents* (Bethany: Campbell, 1853), 63-76; Alexander Campbell, *The Christian System* (Cincinnati, Standard, n.d.), 37-38, 47-48; Alexander Campbell, "Confession unto Salvation", *Millennial Harbinger* 1-1 (4 Jan. 1830): 28; Tom Nettles, *An Introduction to the Southern Baptists* (Liverpool: Carey, 1986), 11, 25.

[63] H.R. Taylor, *The History of Churches of Christ in South Australia: 1846-1959* (Adelaide: Churches of Christ, c. 1960), 14.

[64] Conkin, *Cane Ridge,* 157-162.

[65] Carwardine, *Transatlantic,* 60-61; Sell, *Great Debate,* 89.

[66] J.H.Y. Briggs, *The English Baptists of the Nineteenth Century* (Didcot: Bapt. Historical Soc., 1994), 120, quoting from the *General Baptist Magazine* (1876), 66.

[67] Andrew Fuller, *Memoirs of the Rev. Andrew Fuller and his Works* (London: 1816 [publication details assumed, as the title page is missing]), *Memoirs,* xv-xvi, xxv-xxvi; *The Gospel Worthy of all Acceptation,* 150-190. See also Briggs *Nineteenth Century,* 98-99, 159; Carwardine, *Transatlantic,* 61; Sell, *Great Debate,* 82-87, 93-94.

[68] Briggs, *Nineteenth Century,* 109, quoting the *Baptist Magazine* (1888): 129-131.

[69] Iain H. Murray, *Spurgeon v. Hyper-Calvinism* (Edinburgh: Banner of Truth, 1995), 48-49, 54, 56-57.

[70] Carwardine, *Transatlantic,* 63, quoting from John H. Hinton, *The Work of the Holy Spirit in Conversion* (London: 1830), xviii, xxii-xxiv, 81. See also Briggs, *Nineteenth Century,* 163-64.

[71] I. Sellars, "John Howard Hinton, Theologian", *Baptist Quarterly* 33: 3 (July 1989): 122.

[72] Briggs, *Nineteenth Century,* 119, quoting from W. Underwood, *Centennial Survey* (1870), 14f. See also Murray, *Spurgeon v. Hyper-Calvinism,* 101-2

[73] Carwardine, *Transatlantic,* 91-92; Sell, *Great Debate,* 91.

[74] Sell, *Great Debate,* 92.

[75] Colton, *American Revivals,* 218-19.

[76] Toon, *Born Again,* 168.

[77] Thompson, "Public Invitation", 118.

[78] Carwardine, *Transatlantic,* 118-19.

Chapter 6

Charles Grandison Finney

Background

C.G. Finney's name will always be associated with what became known as the "new measures" of the Second Great Awakening. These "new measures" included the use of the altar call, particularly what was known as the "anxious seat". Finney defined this "seat" as "some particular seat in the place of meeting, where the anxious may come and be addressed particularly, and be made subjects of prayer, and sometimes be conversed with individually." Though an ardent advocate of these "new measures", and innovations generally, he was the originator of few, if any, of them.[1] With regard to the altar call, as has been seen, he was not the first to use it, nor the first to develop a theology that would allow for it, nor even the first to form it into a system. Yet there can be little doubt that by practice and the written word Finney above all people made it widely acceptable, and established it in the evangelical mind as the essential accompaniment of evangelistic preaching.

Finney was born in Warren, Connecticut in 1792. It is generally believed that he received little religious education during his childhood, though Charles Hambrick-Stowe argues that as the Bible was used frequently in almost all schools in America at that time he may have received more than is usually thought. But what he did receive appears to have been largely counter-productive. He became a schoolteacher and later studied law.[2] He was converted in October 1821, appropriately during a revival under the leadership of the Presbyterian minister G.W. Gale and an itinerant, Jedediah Burchard .

His own account of his conversion, in some respects, seems to argue with his teaching and his methods. He said that he then believed that all he had to do to be saved was to consent to "give up" his sins, and "give" himself to Christ. On the day he entered the woods, he said, "I will give my heart to God, or I never will come down from there." Yet, on his own word, this seemed to be the very thing he could not do. He tried to pray, but he found that his heart "would not pray." He tried to give his "heart to God," but found that he could not. Later that morning, however, he did "seize hold" with his "heart" some of God's promises, and trusted in "God's veracity." That night he had a vision of Christ, and almost immediately after that he experienced what he terms, "a mighty baptism of the Holy Ghost." It seems that God did the job for him, for the next morning he could say, "God has taken possession of my soul."[3] Though, in an 1852 comment on his state just before his conversion, he said, "At that time I had never received such instruction as I needed, for if I had, I should have been converted at once."[4]

Finney already attended his local Presbyterian church and had often had contact with its minister, G. W. Gale. It was now to Gale that he went with his questions about the Christian faith, and found himself in strong conflict with Gale's calvinistic views. Whether his theology was as well developed at this stage as he indicates is open to some doubt,[5] which would mean that the dispute may not have been as marked as Finney states. However, later he certainly did reject calvinistic teachings such as limited atonement, and the powerlessness of human beings to believe in and of themselves. That his legal background played its part in his rejection of calvinism is clear. Finney himself could relate that he found Gale's rules of biblical interpretation "much less definite and intelligible" than those used in his own legal studies, and Finney endeavored to read and interpret the relevant passages of Scripture as he would with "the same or like passages in a law book."[6]

Ministry

In 1823 he put himself forward as a candidate for the Presbyterian ministry. According to his account, he refused to go to Princeton, though encouraged to do so, because, he said, those ministers who had been educated at Princeton "had been wrongly educated; and they were not ministers that met my ideal at all of what a minister of Christ should be."[7] But Gale recalled it differently. He said that he approached Princeton, Andover and Auburn on Finney's behalf, "to see if they would admit him as a student and aid him from their funds." There was no positive response from any of the three, and Gale encouraged his protégé to embark on a course of study under the older man's supervision. It is difficult to know for sure which account is true, but one of Finney's biographers, Keith Hardman says that in his opinion Gale's memory "played fewer tricks" than did Finney's, so the truth may rest with Gale.[8] But whatever the truth here, he did go on to become a Presbyterian minister (later he joined the Congregationalists), and it was not long before he was involved in controversy.

His first charge (1824) was in the villages of Evans' Mill, Antwerp and Le Raysville in the state of New York. He launched forth, preaching vigorously and dramatically (eyewitnesses described his preaching as being accompanied by a wealth of descriptive arm waving and gesture),[9] and expecting results. After a handful of sermons in Evans' Mill, he felt frustrated at the lack of visible response, so he told his congregation that he "did not come there to please them but to bring them to repentance." His account of his sermon and application that night runs thus:

> quoting the word of Abraham's servant [I] said to them: "Now will you deal kindly and truly with my Master? If you will, tell me; and if not, tell me, that I may turn to the right hand or to the left." [He continued] I turned this question over, and pressed it upon them, and insisted upon it that I must know what course they proposed to pursue. If they did not purpose to become Christians, and enlist in the service of the Savior, I wanted to know it that I might not labor with them in vain. I said to them: "You admit that what I preach is the Gospel. You profess to believe it. Now will you *receive* it? Do you *mean* to receive it? Or do you intend to reject it?"

He pressed it home further, then concluded:

> "Now I must know your minds... You who now are willing to pledge to me and to Christ that you will immediately make your peace with God, please to rise up... you that mean that I should understand that you are committed to remain in your present attitude, not to accept Christ - please, those of you who are of this mind, to sit still." They looked at one another, and at me; - and all sat still, just as I expected. After looking around upon them for a few moments I said: "Then you are *committed*. You have taken your stand. You have rejected Christ and his Gospel."

According to Finney, the congregation appeared "angry, and arose en masse" and walked from the church. As the people left, Finney told them that he would preach again the following night, which he did. This time he closed the service without an appeal, yet a number of the congregation, under spiritual concern after the nightly bombardment, sought his aid later in the night.[10]

What does one make of this? This seems to have been Finney's first venture into an invitation for a public response to his preaching. The people were not called to come forward, yet their response, be it standing, or even remaining seated, was decidedly public, and viewed by the preacher as an acceptance or a rejection of Christ. It does not seem to have occurred to Finney that some in that congregation may already have been Christians, and therefore could neither rise to indicate their desire to "accept the Gospel", nor remain seated to "reject" it. In addition, we do seem to have here confusion in Finney's mind between the physical act of standing and the spiritual reality of conversion. We will return to this point later.

Finney makes no clear comment as to whether the above mentioned method was something he copied from others, whether he devised it himself and decided before the service to do it, or whether he had just thought of it "on his feet". Finney's full account has the feel of premeditation and he had preached in that church several times in the days immediately preceding the outlined event, and he recorded that he "was very much dissatisfied with the state of things", which suggests the possibility of a planned change of procedure.[11] Finney was not necessarily copying someone else, but he had heard the young Jedediah Burchard preach shortly before the former's conversion. Burchard was certainly using some forms of the public invitation, and that aggressively in the mid-1830s, but whether he was doing this when Finney heard him in 1821 is not clear.[12]

It should be noted here that Finney did vary his method of public invitation. This was deliberate policy, for he felt that getting "stuck in a rut", using the same method all the time, was harmful to the work, and innovations were necessary to keep it fresh.[13]

In the middle of 1825 he was preaching in a Baptist church in Rutland, when he made his first use of what was later to become known as the "anxious seat", (that is, he called inquirers to come forward to occupy vacant seats at the front of the church. This, however, seems to have been an isolated incident and he did not again call people forward that year.[14] His ministry from about this time was highly successful, and revival just seemed to follow him. In a two-month campaign in one church at the end of 1825, for example, about 140 conversions were recorded.[15]

Early the next year, during a remarkable revival in Rome in New York State, he did once more call people forward. He held regular inquiry meetings in Rome, usually during the day after a nighttime sermon. To help identify those being converted, Finney decided that at the end of his sermons he would invite to the front of his church those who had been converted during the previous twenty four hours, either during that service, the earlier inquiry meeting, or in some other circumstance. The inquirers would then be given (further) counsel.[16] Catherine Huntington, a witness of these events, recalled that the officiating ministers would shake the hands of those coming forward,[17] something which, as has been noted, was a common practice in some Baptist circles.

But at this stage in his career the "anxious seat" was rarely used, and he never became a slave to it. He did not use it frequently until 1830. During a revival in Rochester that year, Finney decided that something was necessary to bring people "out from among the mass of the ungodly to a public renunciation of their sinful ways, and a public committal of themselves to God." So Finney had the front seats of the churches in which he was preaching left vacant, and at the end of his sermons he invited inquirers to come forward to occupy them. He could recall that in that place he made appeals night after night, "calling forward those that were prepared to give their hearts to God; and large numbers were converted every evening."[18] From that time the invitation to come forward became a common part of Finney's armoury.

In his lecture on "one to one" work, and thus presumably an exposition of part of his own counseling technique, he urges his workers, if possible, to get the "careless sinner ... to repent and give themselves to Christ at the time." He also instructs them to "Carefully avoid making an impression that" they do not expect the inquirer "to repent NOW."[19]

Criticisms of Finney's methods with inquirers, if true, indicate that in his early days at least he did assert undue, even appalling, pressure on people at times. One account tells of his visit to a family, during which he asked one lady, "Do you love God?" She replied, "I think I do." Finney, then, is said to have shook his fist in her face and roared, "You lie!" and then he urged her to repent. She said that she could not, but Finney countered that with, "You lie! You can repent and be converted immediately."[20] This account was penned by strong opponents of Finney, so the accuracy, even basic truth, of it should be questioned, but it must be said that it is not entirely out of step with his words and attitudes at Evans' Mill (see above), which are from his own account of events.

The above accounts of his practices confirm, what is generally claimed of Finney, that he disagreed with the orthodox calvinism of the time. We have already noted the dilemma of what came first the "new measures", which included the public invitation, or the new theology/theologies. With Finney, as with his predecessors, it is not always easy to establish whether his evangelistic method grew out of his theology or vice-versa. An uncritical reading of his *Memoirs* would lead one to believe that, very soon after his conversion, he developed ideas contrary to the common theology of his day, and his methods grew out of that. But, as has been noted, leading Finney scholars doubt the accuracy of his observations about his early theological development, and tend to regard his firm anti-calvinistic sentiments as emerging some years after his early Christian experience. It seems apparent that his adoption of new evangelistic methods happened gradually, and it may well be that these methods developed hand-in-glove with his maturing theological views. In other words, each development influenced the other.[21]

Finney ran into conflict with two of the most noted evangelists of his early days, Asahel Nettleton and, initially, Lyman Beecher. Whilst not doubting the genuineness of the early revivals that accompanied Finney's work, they strongly criticized his methods and the theology behind them, though, at the time of their attack in the late 1820s, the public invitation does not appear to have been of particular concern.[22] Beecher later softened his opinion of Finney.[23]

What, then, was his theology, with regard to his understanding of conversion? First, what did he believe about humanity and sin? Finney did agree with the calvinists that mankind was "wholly *disinclined* to obey" God's word and was morally depraved, indeed, all had an "enmity against God."[24] But his understanding of that depravity was different from his antagonists. Moral depravity was not because of some nature with which all human beings were born, rather it was "a voluntary attitude of the mind; that it did and must consist in the committal of the will to the gratification of the desire ... of the lusts of the flesh, as opposed to that which the law of God requires."[25] Thus, to Finney, human beings were not morally depraved by nature but by choice.

Secondly, there is the atonement and its effect upon the salvation of individuals. Finney believed Christ's death "rendered the salvation of all men *possible*", but "did not of itself lay God under any obligation to save *anybody*." Thus, whereas in the calvinistic scheme it is believed that Christ died for the elect, and them alone, Finney held "that Christ died for all men," but this did not mean that all would be saved, for people had to respond.[26] Not that Finney denied the concept of the elect. His view, with Arminius and Wesley, was that "The elect were chosen to eternal life because God foresaw" those who in freedom would "embrace the Gospel,"[27] though, as shall be seen, his theology went far beyond that of Arminius and the founder of Methodism.

Thirdly, what were the respective roles of human beings and the Holy Spirit in conversion? In the final analysis, the determining factor as to who was to be saved and who was not was human decision, for each individual had free will, granting "the power and liberty of choice."[28] He attacked those who told their hearers just "to use the means of grace, to pray for a new heart, and wait for God to convert them." Instead, he urged his listeners "to make themselves a new heart and a new spirit", and he pressed upon them their "duty of instant surrender to God." Seekers had to give "their hearts to God", to "submit", and to "commit" themselves to God. They had the ability to obey God and repent, indeed, "repentance" and even "faith" were in the sinner's own power.[29] To achieve this end any suitable means may be employed by the evangelist.[30] Whereas the calvinist (and, indeed, John Wesley) would say the individual was unable to do these things of themselves because of sin, Finney proclaimed that he or she *was* able. Indeed, there was "nothing in religion beyond the ordinary powers of nature."[31]

If people are able to decide for Christ themselves, where does the Holy Spirit fit in? The Spirit certainly convicts of sin, awakens sinners to "the plan of salvation",[32] and teaches and persuades the sinner, exercising a "*moral* influence" upon them. But He has no "*physical*" influence,[33] though He does urge "the truth home upon (the sinner) with such tremendous power as to induce him to turn".[34] So "it is perfectly proper to say, that the Spirit turned" one who becomes converted, "just as you would say of a man, who had persuaded another to change his mind on the subject of politics, that he had converted him." But the Spirit does not actually change the nature of the convert.[35] It is presumably only in this context that he could say such things as: "The Holy Spirit is engaged in a great work within the soul. It is nothing less than to renovate the whole character of life", and God "caused" a repentant sinner "to act". In addition he said that "regeneration is always induced and effected by the personal agency of the Holy Spirit".[36]

But according to his own accounts, Finney did teach a limited work of the Holy Spirit in conversion. As Erroll Hulse puts it, Finney believed that "conversion was the direct result of moral persuasion by the appropriate use of means".[37] (It must be said, however, that Finney meant moral persuasion on the part of the Holy Spirit as well as the preacher.) But to him it was not a complete converting process conducted by the Holy Spirit. Later (1845 or 1846), Finney did admit that he had not placed enough "stress ... upon the necessity of divine influence upon the hearts ... of sinners", but did not substantially change his view.[38]

J.I. Packer states that "for Finney evangelistic preaching was a battle of wills between himself and his hearers, in which his task was to bring them to breaking-point"[39] (in fact, like a lawyer arguing a case). To be fair, one might expect Finney to add that a further factor was the Holy Spirit persuading the sinner to respond, but Packer has a valid point.

Finney, particularly in his later years, was strongly opposed to excessive emotionalism. Though emotion was not absent in his understanding of the conversion process, the key to it was the will. To him "the more calm the soul can be kept while it gazes on" the truths of the Gospel, "the more free is the will left to comply with obligation as it lies revealed in the intelligence."[40] Indeed, the preacher's appeals should be made "to the intelligence" rather than "the feelings",[41] for appeals to the emotions usually lead to false conversions.[42]

J.F. Thornbury says that Finney added a new concept to the public invitation, in that he perceived it to be "a *means of grace*, a test of piety". That is that Finney believed, on the one hand, that "The physical act of coming to the front" was an "outward sign of submission to God", and on the other, that "To fail to move to the ... anxious seat was rebellion against God."[43] Thus he appeared to confuse the outer act of moving forward with the inner spiritual reality of conversion. There are a number of places where Finney does give that impression. We gave, above, part of Finney's own account of his 1824 ministry at Evans' Mill[44] in which we noticed this tendency. Even later, in his *Lectures on Revivals*, he could say:

> If you say to (the sinner) "There is the anxious seat, come out and avow your determination to be on the Lord's side", and if he is not willing to do so small a thing as that, then he is not willing to do *anything* ... It uncovers the delusion of the human heart, and prevents a great many spurious conversions, by showing those who otherwise imagine themselves willing to do anything for Christ, that in fact they are willing to do *nothing*.[45]

Finney does here appear to confuse the act of going forward with genuine conversion to God.

There had been a hint of that idea before. In the chapter on camp-meetings it was noted that in 1804 William Heath, a Methodist, could say that 110 "came forward and gave testimony to their faith that God had converted their souls",[46] which suggests some confusion in his mind between the physical act and the inner reality. Jeremiah Vardeman, a Baptist, was also noted as one whose words and behavior at meetings in the late 1820s show a similar confusion.[47] But the fusion of the two factors in Finney is more evident, and more significant because of his prominence, thus Finney can here be considered to have started a dubious trend.

Finney believed it was his duty to preach his distinctives widely and vigorously.[48] He taught them in sermon, lecture and book, and in his long life exercised an enormous influence, especially in America, but also to a significant degree in Britain, and, through those nations, the world. Many American clergymen appear to have been dissatisfied with the evangelistic methods that were the norm up to the end of the eighteenth century, but hesitated to adopt new ones. But Finney's persuasive ways, the apparent success of his methods, and his development of an intelligent, theological rationale to justify them were the catalyst for many to use such innovations as the "anxious seat".[49] How this worked out will be especially apparent in chapter seven, when his influence on the British churches is noted.

How successful was Finney as an evangelist? The answer is that he was highly successful. In the early years of his ministry revival seemed to follow almost everywhere he went, though this declined to some degree later in his career.[50] If that is agreed, the reasons for the decline are not. Finney himself felt it was due to a deterioration in method of some other evangelists[51] and the opposition he, himself, experienced.[52] Yet he experienced considerable opposition even in his early days,[53] and cannot God overrule method? James Johnson suggests that it was because of confusion over his strong views on Christian perfection.[54] Murray regards it as evidence of the sovereignty of God, and that revival cannot be brought down simply by the efficient use of means.[55] R.E. Davies points out that Finney's early ministry occurred during extensive pre-existing revival, and he just "shared in the harvest",[56] while much of his later preaching did not have that advantage, and so was not as successful. As is so often the case, it is most likely a mixture of reasons, and there is, no doubt, some truth in all the above. Finney's methods did depend on a questionable understanding of revival. To Finney, revival could be brought about by the correct use of means, but a study of the history of revival suggests that it is not so mechanical, and is subject to the sovereignty of God.[57]

It is also true, of course, that many of the "converts" gained during his ministry did not endure. Indeed, he said on one occasion that "the great body of them are a disgrace to religion", and though his opposers saw this as because of faulty evangelistic method, Finney put it down to what would now be called poor follow up, a practice he advocated from the mid-1830s.[58] Whether the falling away rate after Finney's meetings was unusually high is difficult, probably impossible, to determine.

Specifically, how successful were his use of the "anxious seat" and other forms of the public invitation? He did not use such means regularly until 1830 in Rochester. Yet prior to that, revival had burned vigorously through his ministry. It is clear, then, that his work was not dependent upon such means, or necessarily helped by them, but later he did view them as very important to his work.

It is probably true, however, that his 1830 mission in Rochester, in which he used the public invitation, was the most successful in his career. Among the host of converts were many leading figures, which led not just to changes in the lives of individuals but changes in the life of the town. Also crime was said to have declined then and for some years afterwards.[59] Yet, even with further use of the invitation in the following years, this level of success was never quite repeated, suggesting that the method was not the cause, at least not on its own.

Finney was neither the originator of the public invitation, nor the first to use it systematically, but it is not without significance that in 1832, the same year that Finney began his ministry in New York City, the revival-inspired *New York Evangelist* ran a series of articles on how to conduct "revivals", which included instructions on how to use the "anxious seat", and how to deal with inquirers. The series began on April 14, and ran on and off until the end of the year. Finney arrived in New York City on May 1. Finney had some involvement in the original publication of the *Evangelist*, but it would appear that he was not directly involved in any of these articles, though no doubt an influence on their publication.[60]

His lectures on revival two years later encouraged the systematic use of the public invitation. He proclaimed his ideas to eager audiences, then the lectures were published in the *New York Evangelist*, and later appeared in America and Britain in book form. His influence through these printed lectures was immense, and it continues through those who adopted his practices.

It can be fairly said, with Lewis Drummond, that Finney was the "watershed" between the evangelism of the eighteenth century and the mass evangelism of the nineteenth and twentieth.[61] In addition, as McBeth has it, Finney tamed "the exuberant camp meeting and tailor[ed] it to fit the local church." [62] Thus the modern practice of evangelism, both nationally and locally, built, as so much of it is upon the altar call, owes probably more to him than anyone else.

Packer makes some astute observations with regard to Finney and his influence on modern evangelism. He says:

> If Finney's doctrine of the natural state of sinful man is right, then his evangelistic methods must be judged right also, for, as he often insisted, the "new measures" were means well adapted to the end in view ... But if Finney's view of man is wrong, then his methods must be called in question - which is an issue of importance at the present time: for it is Finney's methods, modified and adapted, that characterise a great deal of evangelism today ... I ... question, whether the use of them is really consistent with any other doctrine than Finney's ... if Finney's doctrine is rejected, such methods are inappropriate to a degree, and actually detrimental to the real work of evangelism.[63]

It is not hard to see in Finney's teachings and practice the idea that if one masters the right methodology, then conversions will inevitably follow. But as Ian Hawley reminds us, though methodology is "vitally important", it "must always be subordinate to a dependence on the activity of God's Spirit. Christian conversion is impossible apart from God's sovereign presence and action."[64]

Summary

Finney used the public invitation in a systematic way, in that he used it frequently, though not always regularly, and his use often appeared to be planned. His public invitation method varied, though it was most often calling people forward to occupy the "anxious seat". Success in his ministry, however, does not seem to have been dependent upon his use of the public invitation. His intelligent, theological rationale for the public invitation system appears to have been a major factor in the widespread acceptance of the practice.

Notes

[1] Finney, *Lectures on Revivals,* 238-262; Keith J. Hardman, *Charles Grandison Finney 1792-1875* (Darlington: Evangelical Press, 1990), 84. The "new measures" included: protracted meetings, women praying in meetings in which men were in attendance, praying for individuals by name in public meetings, and the hasty admission of new "converts" into membership. *Finney,* 84; James E. Johnson, "Father of American Revivalism", *Christian History* 7: 4 (Issue 20): 7; Thompson, "Public Invitation", 113.

[2] Charles G. Finney, *The Memoirs of Charles G. Finney* (ed. Garth M. Rosell

and Richard A.G. Dupuis, Grand Rapids: Zondervan, 1989), 4-10, 17; Charles E. Hambrick-Stowe, *Charles G. Finney and the Spirit of American Evangelicalism* (Grand Rapids: Eerdmans, 1996), 5-8; Hardman, *Finney*, 33, 36. (The Rosell & Dupuis edition of Finney's *Memoirs* contains a substantial amount of material which appeared in Finney's original manuscript [dictated and later edited by him], that did not appear in the published volume, edited by J.H. Fairchild, see xliv-xlvi). With quotations from Finney's *Memoirs* it must be remembered that they were written when he was 75 years old, and on his own admission he had to rely on his memory, not having kept a written record of the events recalled. So even though his claim to having a "very tenacious memory" no doubt was true, their accuracy is sometimes in doubt, Finney, *Memoirs*, xxiv, xxvii, 2-3. At times there are inaccuracies, or an apparent reading back of later ideas coloring his record of events, points noted by a number of scholars, including: Rosell and Dupuis, Finney, *Memoirs*, xxvii; Hambrick-Stowe, *Finney*, 10-11; Hardman, *Finney*, 444; Murray, *Revival*, 256-58; Thompson, "Public Invitation", 104n1. For example, his youthful criticism of G.W. Gale's theology (*Memoirs*, 11-12) seems somewhat advanced for one who claimed so little religious education, which suggests that either one or the other owes a little to tricks of the memory. This is not to discount what Finney says, just to advise an element of caution.

[3]   Finney, *Memoirs*, 14-26.

[4]   Hardman, *Finney*, 40, quoting from the *Oberlin Evangelist* (Oct 13, 1852).

[5]   Cross, *Burned-Over*, 158; Hardman, *Finney*, 44-46; Murray, *Revival*, 256-57.

[6]   Finney, *Memoirs*, 44-45. See also Hardman, *Finney*, 46-47. Hambrick-Stowe repeatedly refers to Finney as being in the calvinistic fold or generally in harmony with his evangelical forefathers, though holding to a new form of calvinism, *Finney*, 12, 27, 29-30, 65, 153, 156, 182-83, 189, 196, 217. It is very hard to agree with that view when one compares Finney's teachings with that of Calvin, the Puritans and Jonathan Edwards. The differences are significant, as will become evident.

[7]   Finney, *Memoirs*, 47-48; Hardman, *Finney*, 49-51.

[8]   Finney, *Memoirs*, 47n21; Hardman, *Finney*, 49-51, both quoting from G.W. Gale, *Autobiography of G.W. Gale* (NY: n.p.), 185.

[9]   Weisberger, *Gathered*, 101-2.

[10]   Finney, *Memoirs*, 65-68 (his emphasis). This method of Finney's is one that F.D. Whitesell (Professor of Evangelism at Northern Baptist Seminary for forty years) suggests for use today, though he does so cautiously, F.D. Whitesell, *65 Ways to Give Evangelistic Invitations* (Grand Rapids: Kregel, 1984), 58-59.

[11]   Finney, *Memoirs*, 65.

[12]   Murray, *Revival*, 287, quoting F.A. Cox & J. Hoby, *Baptists in America*, 180-81.

[13]   Finney, *Lectures on Revivals*, 172-74.

[14]   Finney, *Memoirs*, 114-15; Hardman, *Finney*, 75.

[15]   Hardman, *Finney*, 70.

[16] Finney, *Memoirs*, 161-62.

[17] Miss Huntington says that this was done "every other evening", Finney, *Memoirs*, 162n32, quoting from *Reminiscences of Gardiner Spring*, 222.

[18] Finney, *Memoirs*, 306-8, 315; Hardman, *Finney*, 199-200.

[19] Finney, *Lectures on Revivals*, 154. W.B. Sprague, speaking and writing from a calvinistic perspective, also urged counselors to encourage "awakened sinners" to repent "now", Sprague, *Revivals*, 160-61.

[20] Weisberger, *Gathered*, 115-16; Hardman, *Finney*, 109. Both quoting from *A Brief Account of the Origin and Progress of the Divisions in the First Presbyterian Church in Troy*, By a number of the late Church and Congregation (Troy: Tuttle & Richards, 1827), 19-20.

[21] Cross says that "His doctrine ... grew out of actions that met the pragmatic test" of numerical success, Cross, *Burned-over*, 160. Though there is, no doubt, some truth in that, it does not seem to be the whole picture.

[22] Lewis A Drummond, *Charles Grandison Finney and the Birth of Modern Evangelism* (London: Hodder, 1983), 115-123; Hardman, *Finney*, 112-132; J.F. Thornbury, *God Sent Revival* (Welwyn: Evangelical Press, 1977), 156-57, 164-179. The main concerns seem to have been such issues as addressing God in overly familiar terms, Tyler & Bonar, *Nettleton*, 343, 367, the indiscriminate praying for individuals by name, often in their presence, 351-52, 367, and that such methods were causing division 345-47.

[23] Hardman, *Finney*, 223-28.

[24] Finney, *Lectures on Revivals*, 16-17 (Finney's emphasis); C.G. Finney, *Revival Fire: Letters on Revivals* (Minneapolis: Dimension, n.d.), 9.

[25] Finney, *Memoirs*, 152, see also 154, 265.

[26] Finney, *Memoirs*, 51 (Finney's emphasis).

[27] Drummond, *Finney*, 227, quoting from a Finney sermon, in *Sermons on Important Subjects* (NY: Taylor, 1836), 229-53. See also Hambrick-Stowe, *Finney*, 154.

[28] Hardman, *Finney*, 230, quoting from one of Finney's sermons.

[29] Finney, *Lectures on Revivals*, 101, 156-59; Finney, *Memoirs*, 190-91, 264-270, 351.

[30] Finney, *Memoirs*, 152-53; Murray, *Revival*, 245.

[31] Finney, *Lectures on Revivals*, 12.

[32] Finney, *Lectures on Revivals*, 16-17, 134; Finney, *Memoirs*, 154-55, 200, 444.

[33] Finney, *Memoirs*, 155, 350, emphasis in the original; Hardman, *Finney*, 230-31, 335; Murray, *Revival*, 245-46.

[34] Finney, *Lectures on Revivals*, 187.

[35] Drummond, *Finney*, 255, quoting from a sermon of Finney's, in *Important Subjects*, 21-22; Finney, *Memoirs*, 350.

[36] Hambrick-Stowe, *Finney*, 21, 81, 220. Hambrick-Stowe has no footnotes in his book, so examining these quotations in their original context has not been possible.

[37] Hulse, *Great Invitation*, 94.

[38] Finney, *Revival Fire*, 10-11.

39 Packer, *God's Giants*, 386.
40 Finney, *Revival Fire*, 15.
41 Finney, *Revival Fire*, 17.
42 Finney, *Revival Fire*, 16, 36.
43 J.F. Thornbury, *God Sent*, 201 (these are Thornbury's words and emphasis).
44 Finney, *Memoirs*, 65-68.
45 Finney, *Lectures on Revivals*, 254 (Finney's emphasis).
46 Dow, *Cosmopolite*, 190.
47 Murray, *Revival*, 310-12. This was presumably after Finney's Evan's Mill experience, at the commencement of Finney's preaching career, but it is unlikely that the two had any contact.
48 Finney, *Memoirs*, 266-67.
49 Hardman, *Finney*, 153, 220.
50 Finney, *Memoirs*, 3; Hardman, *Finney*, 381-82; Murray, *Revival*, 285-86; Thompson, "Public Invitation", 122.
51 Finney, *Revival Fire*, 8-10. See also Hardman, *Finney*, 381-82.
52 Finney, *Memoirs*, xxi-xxii, xxiv-xxv; Murray, *Revival*, 286.
53 Lyman Beecher, Charles Hodge, Asahel Nettleton and Asa Rand were all influential men who had criticized Finney in the late 1820s or early 1830s, see Hardman, *Finney*, 111-117, 121-132, 229-238.
54 James Johnson, "Father of American Revivalism", *Christian History* 7/4 (Issue 20): 8.
55 Murray, *Revival*, 283-86.
56 Davies, *My Spirit*, 135.
57 Murray, *Revival*, 285-86. Murray's argues that "revival" is not something that can be brought down by means and thus is entirely brought about by the sovereignty of God, and he contrasts it with "revivalism" in the Finney mold. Davies takes a similar view, Davies, *My Spirit*.
58 Finney, *Revival Fire*, 81-87; Hardman, *Finney*, 380-81, see also 322-23.
59 Finney, *Memoirs*, 299-327; Hardman, *Finney*, 210.
60 Weisberger, *Gathered*, 146. See Drummond, *Finney*, 159-160 for the origins of the *New York Evangelist*. The year 1832 also saw the publication of W.B. Sprague's *Lectures on Revivals* (gently opposed to the public invitation) in America, and Calvin Colton's *History and Character of American Revivals* (moderately in favor of the public invitation) in England.
61 Drummond, *Finney*, 12.
62 Drummond, *Finney*, 17, quoting Leon McBeth, *Women in Baptist Life* (Nashville: Broadman).
63 Packer, *God's Giants*, 386-87.
64 Ian Hawley, *Christian Conversion* (Lilydale: Centre for World Mission, 1990), 26.

Chapter 7

The Public Invitation in the British Isles

Dow and the Primitive Methodists

Did the Invitation System first develop in America and then arrive in Britain through the writings of Charles Finney and the visits of various American evangelists, such as Calvin Colton and James Caughey? Or is it possible that the system developed independently in Britain, remained fairly low key until the 1830s, when it was stimulated by the American example? Is it even possible that the system began in Britain, but made no great inroads into church life until it had crossed the Atlantic with Christian migrants and become popular in the American camp-meetings? Certainly, the climate for its acceptance existed in the eighteenth century British religious scene, at least in Methodism.

In fact the first recorded definite usage of the public invitation in the British Isles, so far uncovered, was by an American visitor, but one who predates Colton and Caughey. At the age of 22 Lorenzo Dow fell ill, and decided that what he needed was a recuperative sea voyage to Ireland. His health grew worse on the trip, but after arriving in Ireland greatly improved, and he quickly seized every opportunity to preach that was offered him. He disembarked at Larne on 27 November 1799 and preached in a home that night. He hired a "ball-chamber" and preached in it the following evening and "caught near the whole [congregation] in a covenant, which the greater part, I suppose, broke that night."[1] If, as previously suggested, "a covenant" is a Dow synonym for a public invitation, then this would seem to be the first time such an invitation was given in the British Isles.

But if there may be a little doubt as to what happened on November

28, there is none about what occurred the following nights. Dow tells us,

> After preaching, said I to the people, as many of you as will pray for yourselves twice in twenty-four hours for two weeks, I will endeavour to remember you thrice, God being our helper: and you that will, come forward, that I may take your names in writing, lest that I forget. A few came forward that night, some more next day, and so on.

There are two main points of interest here, apart from the surprisingly early date. First, it is clear that this was not an isolated incident. Dow's invitation to come forward was repeated on several subsequent nights. It is possible, though he does not state it, that he regularly gave a public invitation throughout his first Irish ministry, which lasted until April 1801. Secondly, this is the earliest incident of the recording of the names of those who had come forward so far discovered. (People often gave slips of paper with their names on to George Whitefield during or after his sermons to elicit his prayers, but this appears to have been on the initiative of the inquirers not the preacher.) Dow's purpose here was also for prayer not some form of follow up. It needs to be noted, as with Dow's practice in America, that it is not completely certain that these invitations were related to conversion, or the need thereof. The context, however, suggests that they were, as Dow goes on to tell of people from these congregations "telling what God had done for their souls".[2]

Dow says that on his second trip to the British Isles, he "invited the mourners up to be prayed for" at a meeting at Mount Melick in Ireland in mid-1806. He also mentions another occasion in Athlone early in 1807 when he "called for mourners, but none came forward", though on the following day "about twenty" responded publicly.[3]

Dow spent time in England early in 1806, then went to Ireland, and returned to England for the second half of that year. The first time that he mentions the use of a public invitation in England was in Congleton, Cheshire on 18 November that year. His account runs:

> At the close of the meeting I invited the mourners to come forward: about fifty distinguished themselves. I prayed with them; several professed to find deliverance. I retired, leaving a number of mourners with those who were helping me.[4]

Yet Dow, according to Peggy his wife, seems to have used it even earlier that year in Warrington. She speaks of two women who came "up to be prayed for in the public congregation", both of whom "got religion".[5] Neither of the Dows date their time in Warrington precisely, though Peggy says that they "stayed in and about Warrington until May". They seem to have arrived there some time in March and left for Preston on May 10,[6] so this incident should be dated during that period.

As it seems to have been Dow's common practice to make some form of public invitation after preaching, it is possible that the first use of it in England was at his first preaching appointment. This seems to have been in the last week of December 1805, when he preached in a calvinistic church in Liverpool. Afterwards the minister of that church called Dow "crazy", but whether this was because of Dow's doctrine, practice or manner was not recorded.[7] It is possible, then, that the first use of a public invitation in England was in the final week of 1805, but if not, then it was most probably in January 1806, when Dow preached frequently in different places in Lancashire.

In 1801 a group of Methodists in the English county of Staffordshire, under the leadership of Hugh Bourne, considered holding an all-day prayer meeting. In May of the next year news began to appear in the *Methodist Magazine* (previously the *Arminian Magazine*) about the American camp-meetings. For the following two years a series of letters was published in that magazine, giving red hot, eye-witness accounts of the remarkable occurrences.[8]

Bourne's idea of holding an all-day prayer meeting began to change into thoughts of organizing a camp-meeting, but he and his associates could not reach agreement, and interest declined and the matter was abandoned. Dow's visit to that region created a new interest in camp-meetings. Bourne himself not only heard Dow, but purchased two pamphlets about these meetings from him, and Dow seems to have encouraged him to hold camp-meetings.[9] In one of those tracts Dow told about the American camp-meeting practice of "an invitation (being) given for mourners to come forward to be prayed for".[10]

The first camp-meetings in Britain were organized by Bourne and his associates in 1807, though most of these gatherings appear to have been lengthy open-air meetings rather than camp-meetings in the American style. Most lasted for just one day, a few for longer, and others just a matter of hours (the latter gaining the name "small camp-meetings), and though in some cases tents were erected, these seem to have been to hold services in during inclement weather, rather than to house people overnight.[11] According to Bourne, dealing with "mourners" was a common part of the meetings' activities. He makes no mention of how these people were identified or assembled in those early years,[12] though from an account of a meeting in 1819 by another early "Primitive" it is clear that sometimes "mourners" were identified simply because their condition was visible, for they "were down on the ground crying out for mercy",[13] similar to the situation in the early American camp-meetings.

The British Methodist Conference frowned upon this new venture and decided to discourage, and so effectively ban, camp-meetings.[14] Bourne and his followers disagreed with that decision, and that led to the expulsion of some of them and the resignation of others. This split resulted in the formation of the Primitive Methodist Connexion,[15] which began holding camp-meetings frequently.

In Primitive Methodist camp-meetings after 1819, brevity and variety were the catch cries. Bourne felt that too much time was being given to overlong sermons and urged changes. The recommended format allowed a total of forty-five minutes for the preliminary acts of worship and the sermon (or sermons!), which were then followed by a prayer meeting lasting about half an hour, during which prayer was made for "the mourners". Then other services in the same style followed later in the day. Yet, read the instruction, "When mourners are in distress ... the exercises may be lengthened".[16] Though Bourne does not acknowledge it, John Kent sees Dow's influence here. Kent says with justification that "Dow deeply influenced the first phase of Primitive Methodism" on his English visit in 1806-7. He goes on to state that during Dow's final trip to England in 1818 Bourne met him again, and Dow may well have suggested some of the changes Bourne introduced.[17]

It is probable, though no historian makes clear mention of it, that the Primitives were using some form of the public invitation between Dow's two visits to England. Certainly, they knew of such a method through Dow's writings and, presumably, his practice.

Though Bourne does not date it clearly, the first known use of the public invitation by the Primitives was about 1820. It was common for "praying companies" to position themselves around various locations within the camping ground after sermon, usually some distance from "the preaching stand", and it was the people in these groups who had the responsibility for counseling "mourners".[18] Sometimes, though, some in the congregation would cry out or show some other form of distress during the sermon, at which the preacher would have the "companies" remain, and they would form "a ring or opening" into which the "mourners" were called for prayer.[19] This method appears to have emulated the "praying circle" or "prayer ring" used in some camp-meetings in the eastern American states.[20] The Primitive Methodist use of this method instead of the "altar", may have, once more, owed much to Dow. Certainly Dow used the method. After the sermon at an open-air meeting in Bingham in September 1818, on his final trip to Britain, Dow instructed the faithful to stand in a circle, then issued an invitation for penitents to kneel within its confines. So many did so that those forming the circle had to enlarge its circumference repeatedly.[21] In addition, in 1816 Bourne had actually been given a copy of a journal by Joshua Marsden who had witnessed and written about New York camp-meetings,[22] where this method was in vogue. It would appear, then, that Lorenzo Dow, both by practice and writing, was the first major American model for British preachers adopting the use of the public invitation.

In the 1820s the Primitives not only held post-sermon prayer meetings at camp-meetings, but also at their ordinary services.[23] The primary reason for these was to speak to and pray for those concerned about their souls, and thus they were forerunners of later inquiry meetings, but there is little evidence as to how the inquirers were assembled.

In 1823 Thomas Batty was evangelizing in the north of England when he found his congregation reluctant to go home. Three times he dismissed it, but each time nobody moved. In seeming frustration he finally announced:

> I have attended two prayer-meetings to-day, have led two classes, have walked about nine miles, and have preached four times, and I am now weary. I am going into the house adjoining, and those who are determined to give their heart to God may follow me!

Petty records that "several" did follow him, and "four of them found freedom there from the bondage of sin".[24]

In spite of extensive research into British Primitive Methodism prior to 1835, no usage of the terms "altar" or "mourner's bench" appear in the early days of that church, though they were certainly using "penitents' forms" in the 1850s and 1860s.[25] Spurgeon's famous account of his own conversion in a Primitive Methodist chapel in 1850 showed that that church's preachers were not afraid to address their remarks to a specific member of a congregation, though it is not entirely clear whether that preacher expected some form of public response.[26] Joseph Ritson writes of an early Primitive preacher named Robert Key who was probably amongst the first to urge his listeners to "decide for Christ", but Ritson does not provide a date for this.[27]

Wesleyan Methodism

Wesleyan Methodism (the largest of the British Methodist groups formed after the death of Wesley) had its own, home grown equivalent of Dow, William Bramwell (1759-1818). He definitely used the public invitation but it is not clear when he started to do so. It may not have been until towards the end of his ministry, but certainly in May 1817 he was leading a meeting in a chapel at West Moor Colliery, and after some had given testimonies, he invited penitents to "stand up and show themselves". Fifteen or sixteen did. Bramwell then instructed everyone to kneel down to pray, and very soon one man "was set at liberty". Then Bramwell prayed again, and "several more were made happy" ("made happy" was a common Methodist synonym for conversion on both sides of the Atlantic at this time). He did the same at Cawe Hill six months later.[28]

Kent suggests that this is an example of an independent English tradition of the invitation,[29] but this independence is by no means certain, though use of some forms of the public invitation in Britain may go back thirty years prior to these incidents involving Bramwell. In 1785 Bramwell served in the Kent Methodist circuit alongside George Shadford.[30] Shadford, as was noted in chapter two, had been to America, and seems to have used a form of the public invitation there. Searching amongst the limited material available on Shadford[31] has not turned up any evidence that he used it back in Britain, but the possibility cannot be ruled out. If Shadford used it, then it not only means that Bramwell may have learned it from him, but it also could put the use of at least occasional public invitations in British Methodism as early as 1778, when Shadford returned to England,[32] though evidence to confirm this is lacking. James Sigston, one of Bramwell's biographers, says that Bramwell "never ceased to remember and imitate his venerable colleague" (Shadford).[33] Precisely what Sigston meant by that is not clear, but it does appear that Shadford had a considerable influence on the younger man.

There is a little more information on Bramwell's evangelistic methods than there is on Shadford's, but it is still rather limited and imprecise. In 1795 he wrote to a friend that after a weekday evening meeting, "We desired all in distress to come into the vestry, when eight souls were delivered from the bondage of sin." Then of another such meeting he says that

> the power of God came upon us. We concluded at the usual time, but
> begged all in distress to stay, and before eight o'clock it appeared to

many good men, that more than twenty souls were delivered.[34]

Though it is not certain that these two incidents precisely fit the altar call definition being used for this book, the phrases inviting people "into the vestry" and begging "all in distress to stay" could mean that they do.

In another letter six years later to a woman preacher named Barrett, Bramwell gives further clues as to his methods. He advises her

> *First* to dismiss the people, - all who choose to go after preaching. *Then*, to have what kind of meeting you choose, but to dismiss them again in an hour. *Then*, to go yourself, positively. If any remain in distress, leave the work in the hands of others.[35]

Presumably his advice reflects his own practice, and suggests that his preferred method for dealing with inquirers at this time was to have some form of meeting after the service had concluded, apparently during which some help was given to those "in distress". The exact method of identifying them or whether they were brought together is not mentioned.

A Nottingham lay preacher called Tatham, said of Bramwell that he had "frequently known him detect imposters who have stepped forth to exercise in various meetings".[36] This sounds as though it refers to people moving forward in response to an appeal, and there is clear indication there that it was something Bramwell did frequently. It is not quite clear what period of Bramwell's life this practice occurred, but as Bramwell ministered in Nottingham between 1798 and 1801 it presumably refers to those years.

So then we have the distinct possibility that the public invitation was being used in Wesleyan Methodism by at least one preacher by the end of the eighteenth century, and was definitely being used by him in the second decade of the next.

Transatlantic Exchange

American evangelicalism benefited from a continual stream of migrants from Britain in the late eighteenth and early nineteenth centuries, and this included many ministers and lay preachers.[37] Such favors were duly returned when a number of American evangelists began to visit Britain from the 1830s. Presbyterian minister Calvin Colton, an advocate of the public invitation, visited Britain in 1831, and in the following year published a book in London which defended the new measures used in American revivals, and encouraged their use in Britain.[38]

In this book, Colton says of the "anxious seat",

> It is not considered prudent to employ it except when there is manifestly a special degree of feeling in the congregation. On such occasions, and ordinarily towards the close of the meeting, a challenge is formally made on all who are willing publicly to signify their anxiety to secure an interest in the great salvation - to separate themselves from the congregation and come forward and be seated by themselves that public prayer may be offered on their behalf, and that they may receive advice and exhortation. [As one moves forward] immediately the sympathies of [most of the] congregation ... are roused to unwanted energy ... And when all who have come whose feelings have urged them, the minister rises and asks: "And are there no more? No more?" ... And another, and perhaps another press forward to claim a place with those whose example has decided them. And now the offer is suspended and fervent, importunate prayers are offered on behalf of those anxious souls, who kneel weeping before the Altar of God ... The same amazing power of the circumstances, instrumentally seems to bring out their feeling to enforce them to the crisis submission to God.[39]

There are a number of points here worth noting. First, Colton urged that the public invitation only be used when circumstances justified it. Secondly, he attached great store on the example of those moving forward being an encouragement to others to do likewise. Thirdly, the term "altar", which in this context never became popular in Britain, is used differently from the early camp-meeting use of the term. In the camp-meetings the inquirer entered the altar, here he or she comes "before" it, and it is described as "the Altar of God". Colton acknowledged, though, that no evangelistic method was sacrosanct. What was usable and successful in one culture, area or country was not necessarily usable everywhere,[40] which is a point that needs to be remembered.

Colton's visit to Britain was followed by New School Presbyterian Edward Kirk in 1839, who had been calling sinners to come to the front of his church in New York since the early 1830s. Another American Presbyterian, Benjamin Chidlaw, visited Wales in 1839, and at the conclusion of one service in December of that year asked those who were seeking or had found salvation to stand up. One hundred and fifty did.[41]

Another significant visitor with regard to the acceptance of the public invitation into the British evangelical scene, especially in

Methodist circles, was James Caughey. Born in Ireland, but resident in America since early childhood, Caughey visited Britain in 1841. He began a series of extensive campaigns in major cities, mainly in the north of England, frequently preaching six evenings a week, and using the public invitation regularly.[42] At the end of his sermons he urged his hearers to walk forward to the communion rail, sometimes shouting, "Come out, man! and save your soul now." At other times he would leave the pulpit and walk from pew to pew, urging concerned sinners to rise and go forward. Lay workers were also used to lead those convicted of sin to the front of the church, where they were counseled by Caughey and his helpers.[43]

Caughey seems to have been among the first to urge people to make "a decision" for Christ. One of his favorite texts was "How long halt ye between two opinions?" (1 Kg. 18:21). "Decide now", he would urge his listeners, "you are reaching the point on which your destiny turns; the fearful crisis approaches that decides your fate."[44] The developments in theology in the previous generation or so helped clear the way for that type of approach, which blended perfectly with the altar call.

But Caughey did not just invite sinners forward to decide for Christ, he also invited Christians to respond to experience "purification" or "perfect love", as Caughey called the Methodist form of holiness. In one three-week campaign by Caughey church leaders could report 486 conversions plus 262 persons "entirely sanctified". The latter could be seen as a forerunner of the modern call to rededication, which follows Caughey's regular practice of using the invitation for purposes other than an initial conversion experience. Indeed, many of those going forward for a supposed conversion experience may have already been Christians, or at least been considered so by their peers. Carwardine puts it neatly: "many who thought themselves converted took out a double indemnity at Caughey's communion rail."[45] The problem of people responding repeatedly will resurface when, in chapter fourteen, we examine the results achieved through the public invitation system.

Perhaps, though, the major influence on the British churches was not a visit but a book. In 1837 Finney's *Lectures on Revivals* was published in Britain, with a Welsh edition following soon after. The impact it made can be partly seen in that the English edition alone sold 80 000 copies in Britain by 1850.[46] But its impact, allied of course with the visits of Finney and others, is best judged by the influence it had upon British evangelistic thinking and practice. James Morison, a Scottish Presbyterian, adapted his theology after being deeply impressed upon reading Finney, and urged his own father to read Finney's book, and to "preach like him". John Kirk and Fergus Ferguson Jr., influential Congregationalists, also quickly adopted Finney's ideas.[47]

Joseph Belcher, an English Baptist, began editing a paper named *The Revivalist*, which promoted the work and thought of American evangelists in Britain, particularly Finney. Belcher was also a key figure in the Baptist Home Missionary Society (BHMS), which sent out evangelists to needy areas. The secretary of the BHMS in the late 1830s was Charles Roe. Roe was also a keen advocate of Finney's methods, and was amongst those who invited the American evangelist to Britain.[48] Thomas Pulsford, the "Evangelising Agent" of the BHMS in northern England for eight years from the end of the 1830s, read Finney's book and used some of his methods, but stopped short of inviting people forward. This was because it was regarded as likely to cause disharmony in the Baptist churches, because some disapproved of that practice. He preferred to dismiss the congregation and ask the "anxious" or "seriously impressed" to stay behind for counseling.[49]

It would also appear that these examples of changes in method were just the tip of the iceberg. The change in thinking and method became so common that, as in America, denominations were split because of these new measures.[50] John Angel James, a leading British Congregationalist, lamented the fact that "Finney's books have done a little harm in this country". He noted that eleven students had been expelled from the Scotch Congregational College for promoting the Finney-inspired "heresy" of "a virtual denial of the Spirit's work in conversion",[51] though he seems to have under-estimated the influence of Finney's *Lectures*.

The Salvation Army leaders William and Catherine Booth both read Finney's *Lectures on Revivals*, Catherine when she was in her early teens, and she later urged her eldest son to read it.[52] In addition, when the Salvation Army became established it was made standard reading for officers in training. With knowledge of Finney's writings and William Booth's first hand experience of James Caughey's methods, it is not surprising that the altar call has been an integral part of Salvation Army evangelism and worship from its earliest days.[53]

In Wales the impact was perhaps even greater than in other parts of Britain. Carwardine sees similarities in the Welsh situation to that on the American frontier. In some respects Wales was as isolated linguistically and culturally as the American pioneers were by distance. The population was also "unsettled", and the established church very weak, which left Christian work more in the hands of the evangelical denominations, which, like their American cousins, made extensive use of itinerant and lay preachers and camp-meetings. In addition, the

Welsh appeared culturally more open to revival than, say, the English. Indeed, Finney's book arrived there at a time of awakening which encouraged its use. How much influence the book itself had on this revival is debatable, but it was popularly dubbed "Finney's revival", which indicates that many saw it as being very influential. Indeed, one Congregational minister said that it had been "chiefly promoted" by Finney's book. It is probable that between 1839 and 1843, 20 000 were added to various Welsh churches, thus in many minds "Approved" was stamped upon Finney's methods, including the public invitation. As in Scotland, Finney's book caused strife in several denominations, encouraging, as it did, not just new evangelistic method, but a "new" theology of conversion.[54]

In this way Finney probably had more influence on Britain in his absence than by his presence.[55] His visits to Britain (1849-51 and 1858-1860) did not have the impact of Moody's visits twenty years later, nor in some respects those of Caughey before him, even though Finney worked from a wider, interdenominational base than Caughey, and did appear to have more converted through his ministry. Surprisingly, his use of the public invitation in Britain was fairly limited, often preferring to use inquiry rooms, or a semi-public invitation. For example, in 1850 he commenced a series of meetings in Whitefield's Tabernacle, London. It was several weeks before he even held an inquiry meeting. When he finally did so after one sermon, he invited those "anxious for the salvation of their souls" to move to a large schoolroom nearby. To "respond" the inquirers had to leave the Tabernacle and walk a few yards down an adjoining street, and then into the designated room. The room held about 1500, and on this occasion was said to be crowded. At that meeting he urged those gathered immediately to "submit themselves" to God. The previous year it appears that he had used the invitation and inquiry room more frequently in Birmingham, now, after this remarkable response in London, he began to use it more regularly. So great were the numbers responding on some occasions that the previously used school room proved too small, so Finney adapted his method and, with the crowded building making the "anxious seat" impracticable, he asked those seeking salvation to stand where they were for prayer. To Finney, from the pulpit, it seemed that on some occasions nearly everybody in the congregation rose to their feet.[56]

A question arises here, however. Finney's mission at the Tabernacle lasted for nine months and the building held between three and four thousand people.[57] If frequently hundreds, and seemingly on more than a few occasions over one thousand, responded to the appeal, were some responding more than once? Finney usually preached at both morning and evening services on the Sunday and several times during the week, and it was not uncommon for hundreds to be turned away because the building was full. This suggests that the make up of the congregation at any one service might vary considerably from that at the others. This is supported by a statement made by the minister of that church, John Campbell, to the effect that he did not recognize most of those in attendance. Indeed, Campbell indicates that a great deal of work had been done to attract new people to the Tabernacle to hear Finney. Apart from articles in the magazines he edited, Campbell had tens of thousands of leaflets distributed, advertising the meetings.[58] Yet, bearing in mind present experience, that those impressed by such gatherings usually attend not once but repeatedly, there still seems some justification for believing that some must have responded to the invitation more than once, some, perhaps, numerous times.

On his second British tour Finney again did not use the public invitation slavishly. He was inclined not to use it at the beginning of his mission in any one town, then, when he felt led, he suddenly introduced it.[59] In his campaign in Bolton, after preaching in churches of different denominations, it was decided to hold meetings in the Temperance Hall, which had a much larger seating capacity than any of the churches. Because it belonged to no particular denomination it also gave opportunity for the churches to work together. A massive publicity campaign was organized, including extensive house-to-house visitation. In this setting Finney began to issue an invitation for public response nightly. Many came forward, yet not as many were converted as Finney had come to expect from such large responses. He believed the lack was because of the Methodist practice of praying out loud as the inquirers came to the front and after. This, he felt, distracted the inquirers. After a couple of weeks of this, he gently suggested that the Methodists display a little more decorum, which they did, and, according to Finney, better results were seen. It was estimated that after three and a half months in Bolton there had been 2000 inquirers and 1200 converts.[60]

In addition to these visits by Americans, British clergy were also testing the new waters in America. Richard Reece, a Methodist, visited America in the 1820s, and upon his return began using the public invitation. In 1834 two Congregational ministers journeyed across the Altantic to investigate the "revivals" occurring there, and they were followed the next year by two Baptists on the same mission. On his return to England, Andrew Reed, one of the Congregationalists, began to advocate a limited use of the "anxious seat", though he was not uncritical of the new measures generally.[61]

English Independent Evangelists.

In the 1850s Reginald Radcliffe, a British independent evangelist, was regularly using the public invitation, and also employed personal workers to be on the lookout "for anxious ones". His normal method of delivering the invitation was, after a sermon, to invite those concerned about their salvation to go into an adjoining vestry for counseling. This practice seems to have been sufficiently familiar to his hearers that after one meeting over 50 walked into the vestry for counseling, even though they had not been invited to do so.[62]

Rough-hewn English evangelist Richard Weaver was converted in a field early one Saturday morning in 1852. Eight days later he attended his local Primitive Methodist Chapel, dragging along seven of his old drinking companions. His account runs:

> When the minister invited any who wished to be saved to come forward, I said to the one who sat by me: "Go up and be saved". He said: "I will go up if thou wilt". I spoke to another and got the same answer. I said: "Well, come along". They all followed. me, and all professed to find the Saviour.

Even allowing for the fact that Weaver's account was written some years after the event, there is a suggestion here that this practice was already familiar to him. (One of his brothers was a Primitive Methodist preacher, so he may have known of it through him). It was not long before he became an evangelist, and in the 1850s he himself was inviting "sinners" to come to the "penitent form" at the front of the church, or to a nearby vestry.[63]

In the early 1860s Weaver and Radcliffe united in a mission in Scotland. At the conclusion of one large open-air meeting they "invited the anxious" to follow the two preachers as they walked to the other side of the field to find a quiet spot for counseling. "Hundreds followed" them.[64] Yet, there were those in that period, particularly in Scotland, who were still unaware of such practices.[65]

In evangelistic campaigns in mid-Victorian Britain, it was common to have lay workers walking around the congregation after sermon "picking up the shot birds"[66] (i.e. ministering to those in distress). Further development in the use of lay workers for such purposes will be noted in the next chapter.

Summary

As far as can be established, then, the public invitation system did not originate in Britain, but seems to have been an American invention, indeed, in some British circles it was dubbed "the American Custom".[67] It was possibly being used by one or two Wesleyan Methodist preachers at the end of the eighteenth century, and the Primitive Methodists early in the next. It had become a fairly common practice in Britain in a variety of denominations by the 1860s, especially in the various streams of Methodism, though there was still considerable opposition to it. It was probably Moody's tour of the 1870s (see chapter eight) that sealed it as a regular part of British evangelical practice, though it does not seem to have ever been as popular in Britain as in America. This may indicate a greater reluctance amongst the British to accept religious innovations, and, generally speaking, their being less comfortable with public display.

Notes

[1] Dow, *Cosmopolite*, 76.

[2] Dow, *Cosmopolite*, 77.

[3] Dow, *Cosmopolite*, 267, 295-96.

[4] Dow, *Cosmopolite*, 289. Dow's Journal dates this the 14th, but as this entry appears between the 17th and the 19th, and there is an earlier entry for the 14th; presumably it should be the 18th.

[5] Peggy Dow, *The Journey of Life*, bound with Lorenzo Dow's *Cosmopolite*, 617.

[6] Peggy Dow, *Journey*, 617; Dow, *Cosmopolite*, 264.

[7] Dow, *Cosmopolite*, 257-59. Peggy Dow says that though their ship arrived at Liverpool in mid-December, they were not allowed to disembark until December 24 or 25, because of a yellow fever scare, and Lorenzo's first sermon there seems to have been soon after disembarkation, Peggy Dow, *Journey*, 613.

[8] *Methodist Magazine* 25-27 (May 1802- May 1804).

[9] Bourne, *Primitive Methodists*, 10-12; Thomas Church, *A History of the Primitive Methodists* (3rd ed. London: Bemrose, 1869) 98, 102; Kendall, *Primitive Methodist*, 1:56-61; John Kent, *Holding the Fort* (London: Epworth, 1978), 50; Petty, *Primitive Methodist*, 11-12, 15-18; Joseph Ritson, *The Romance of Primitive Methodism* (London: Dalton, 1909), 58.

[10] Kent, *Holding the Fort*, 50.

[11] Bourne, *Primitive Methodists*, 14-17, 23-24, 30-32; Kendall, *Primitive Methodist*, 1:62-69, 74, 77, 80-81; Petty, *Primitive Methodist*, 25-26. 35-36, Ritson, *Primitive Methodism*, 59-70. Dow speaks of an out-doors meeting held

in Ireland in June 1806 being called a "camp-meeting", but he preferred to call it a "field meeting", as there were no tents, and it only lasted one day, Dow, *Cosmopolite,* 267.

[12] Bourne, *Primitive Methodists,* 16-17.

[13] Kendall, *Primitive Methodist,* 1:513.

[14] Bourne, *Primitive Methodists,* 18-24; Kendall, *Primitive Methodist,* 1:77-79; Petty, *Primitive Methodist,* 30; Ritson, *Primitive Methodist,* 75-76.

[15] Bourne, *Primitive Methodists,* 45-46; Kendall, *Primitive Methodist,* 1:82-89, 99-103, 106-115, 132; Petty, *Primitive Methodist,* 33, 39-43, 49-51. The Primitive Methodist Church was officially formed in 1811, though that name was not taken till the following year, Kendall, 1:1, 132; Ritson, *Primitive Methodism,* 96-97.

[16] Bourne, *Primitive Methodists,* 62-63, 70; Kendall, *Primitive Methodist,* 1:507-9. Kendall states that Bourne had a "tendency to undervalue preaching", Kendall, 1:131.

[17] Kent, *Holding the Fort,* 55-56.

[18] Bourne, *Primitive Methodists,* 70; Kendall, *Primitive Methodist,* 2: 87.

[19] Bourne, *Primitive Methodists,* 70. Though Bourne does not date this practice, the note which details it accompanies a reference to a meeting on 30 July 1820. Petty states that the "praying companies" were in use by 1820, Petty, *Primitive Methodist,* 109, 122.

[20] Johnson, *Camp Meeting,* 133-34.

[21] Kent, *Holding the Fort,* 56.

[22] Kendall, *Primitive Methodist,* 1:198; Kent, *Holding the Fort,* 51-52; Petty, *Primitive Methodist,* 15-18.

[23] Petty, *Primitive Methodist,* 137, 177-78, 186.

[24] Petty, *Primitive Methodist,* 207-8.

[25] Kendall, *Primitive Methodist,* 2:185-86; James Paterson (ed.) *Richard Weaver's Life Story* (London: Morgan & Scott, c. 1898), 92, 127.

[26] Hugh T. Kerr and John M. Mulder (eds) *Famous Conversions* (Grand Rapids: Eerdmans, 1983), 129-132.

[27] Ritson, *Primitive Methodism,* 126.

[28] Kent, *Holding the Fort,* 25-26. General William Booth was another who claimed that Bramwell (and others) used such devices as after service prayer meetings and penitent forms, letter to Catherine Mumford (Booth), 17 Nov. 1852 (some recent research suggests that this letter should be dated 23 Dec. 1852), Harold Begbie, *Life of William Booth* (2 vols. London: Macmillan, 1920), 1:158. The Booths named their first son William Bramwell Booth after Bramwell.

[29] Kent, *Holding the Fort,* 25.

[30] Thomas Harris, *A Memoir of the Rev. William Bramwell* (London: Kelly, c. 1900), 27-29; James Sigston, *Memoir of the Life and Ministry of William Bramwell* (NY: Hunt & Eaton, 1820), 47.

[31] The main source on Shadford is his mini-autobiography, which was originally written in 1785, and appeared in the *Arminian Magazine* in 1790, so it makes no reference to his practice in the last 25 or so years of his life,

Telford, *Wesley's Veterans*, 2:169, 212. Incidental references to him are also found in several other publications, such as Wesley's *Works* and Asbury's *Journal*.
[32] Bangs, *Methodist*, 1:123-24; Jackson, *Methodist Preachers*, 5:185; Sweet, *Revivalism*, 101; Telford, *Wesley's Veterans*, 2:207-211.
[33] Sigston, *Bramwell*, 47.
[34] William Bramwell, letter to George Marsden, 1795, Sigston, *Bramwell*, 129.
[35] William Bramwell, letter to Miss Barrett, 17 Nov. 1801, Sigston, *Bramwell*, 184 (emphasis in original).
[36] Sigston, *Bramwell*, 155.
[37] Carwardine, *Transatlantic*, 28-29, 32-39; McBeth, *Baptist Heritage*, 211-12.
[38] Carwardine, *Transatlantic*, 67.
[39] Colton, *American Revivals*, 95-98. Colton sympathies were mainly with the New England scene, and he was uneasy about the extravagancies in the western and southern states where the altar was most used, 128-135. See also Kent, *Holding the Fort*, 19-20.
[40] Colton, *American Revivals*, 77, 83.
[41] Carwardine, *Transatlantic*, 73-74, quoting David O. Mears, *Life of Edward Norris Kirk, D.D.* (Edinburgh: 1888), 44-45, 63-74, 95, 98; Carwardine, *Transatlantic*, 90-91, quoting B.W. Chidlaw, *The Story of My Life* (Philadelphia: 1890), 94-100. Chidlaw was born in Wales but went to America as a child.
[42] Carwardine, *Transatlantic*, 107-120.
[43] Begbie, *Booth*, 1:10-13, quoting from an unnamed journalist, reporting on Caughey's campaign in Nottingham; Carwardine, *Transatlantic*, 120.
[44] Carwardine, *Transatlantic*, 118-19, quoting from J. Caughey, *A Voice From America* (2nd Ed. Manchester: 1847), 5-14.
[45] Carwardine, *Transatlantic*, 120-121, 125.
[46] Carwardine, *Transatlantic*, xiv, 83-84, 89-90; Hardman, *Finney*, 276-77, 398-99.
[47] Carwardine, *Transatlantic*, 98-99; Finney, *Memoirs*, 590-91ns3-6; Hardman, *Finney*, 436.
[48] Briggs, *Nineteenth Century*, 296; Richard Carwardine, "The Evangelist System: Charles Roe, Thomas Pulford and the Baptist Home Missionary Society" *Baptist Quarterly* 28: 5 (Jan. 1980): 211-13; Hardman, *Finney*, 402-3.
[49] Carwardine, *Transatlantic*, 73; Carwardine, "Evangelist System": 215-225.
[50] Carwardine, *Transatlantic*, 97-99; Finney, *Memoirs*, 590-91ns3-6; Hardman, *Finney*, 436.
[51] Murray, *Revival*, 393, quoting R.W. Dale, *Life and Letters of J.A. James*, 420. James had written an introduction to a British edition of Finney's *Lectures on Revival*, and had supported his campaign in Birmingham, even though he had some reservations about Finney's teachings, but he later became more critical, Finney, *Memoirs*, 486-87 (NB n41); Murray, *Revival*, 392-93. See also

Hardman, *Finney,* 402-3.

[52] St. John Ervine, *God's Soldier: General William Booth* (2 vols. London: Heinemann, 1934), 1:363-66. The Booths' grand daughter says that Catherine read Finney's "writings" when bed-ridden as a fourteen-year-old for a lengthy period in 1843. Though she mentions specifically Finney's "lectures on theology", as this was not published at that date it was presumably *Lectures on Revivals* that the young Catherine Mumford avidly devoured, Catherine Bramwell-Booth, *Catherine Booth* (abr. ed. London: Hodder, 1973), 26.

[53] Begbie, *Booth,* 1:9-13; Norman H. Murdoch, *Origins of the Salvation Army* (Knoxville: Uni. of Tennessee Press, 1994), 12. In chapter ten the results of a survey conducted in a number of Australian denominations about their use of the public invitation will be noted. The Salvation Army was one of the denominations where all respondents reported that they used the system.

[54] Carwardine, *Transatlantic,* 85-89, 91-93; Hambrick-Stowe, *Finney,* 229; Hardman, *Finney,* 399; Garth Rosell, "Sailing for the Kingdom", *Christian History* 7: 4 (Issue 20): 22.

[55] This point seems to be tentatively accepted by Rosell, who while calling some of the response to Finney's preaching in Britain "remarkable", can still say that "it may be true that, in the long run, Finney's writings have had a more profound impact upon the British churches than did his actual ministry there." "Sailing for the Kingdom": 23.

[56] Carwardine, *Transatlantic,* 144-45; Finney, *Memoirs,* 489, 503-7; Hardman, *Finney,* 411-13; Rosell, "Sailing for the Kingdom": 23.

[57] Finney, *Memoirs,* 502n11, 509n21.

[58] Finney, *Memoirs,* 503-9; Hambrick-Stowe, *Finney,* 246-48; Hardman, *Finney,* 413-14, 417. Hardman quotes a letter from Henry Ward Beecher, in which he states that on each of two occasions when he was present at the Tabernacle during Finney's ministry "more than a thousand" went to the inquiry room.

[59] Finney, *Memoirs,* 600-1.

[60] Finney, *Memoirs,* 601-3; Hardman, *Finney,* 439.

[61] Carwardine, *Transatlantic,* 68; Murray, *Revival,* 295, quoting Andrew Reed, *Visit to the American Churches,* 2:74-75.

[62] Jane Radcliffe, *Recollections of Reginald Radcliffe* (London: Morgan & Scott, c. 1896), 19, 41-43, 66-67.

[63] Paterson, *Weaver,* 47-50, 92, 111-12, 127. Much of this volume, including this quotation, is in Weaver's own words.

[64] Paterson, *Weaver,* 130.

[65] Radcliffe, *Recollections,* 66-67, 81.

[66] George E. Morgan, *R.C. Morgan: His Life and Times* (London: Morgan & Scott, 1909), 118n2.

[67] Carwardine, *Transatlantic,* 120.

Chapter 8

Further Development

Further development in the system took place in the second half of the nineteenth century. This development will first be noted in the influence of the Plymouth Brethren during this period, and then in the career of revivalist D.L. Moody.

The Brethren

The Christian (Plymouth) Brethren emerged in Britain early in the nineteenth century, and it has been suggested that, as their theology took shape, it began to advocate a concept of conversion which understood faith as primarily intellectual belief about Christ, largely neglecting the idea of faith actually in Christ. (This concept was also noted in chapter five as being characteristic of Alexander Campbell of the Disciples of Christ.) It is also said that the Brethren stressed the concept of "receiving" Christ, thought of feelings as being irrelevant in conversion, and downplayed repentance and, in assurance at least, the role of the Holy Spirit.

Phyllis Airhart details these charges in relating the story of a dispute over the nature of conversion between the Brethren and the Canadian Methodists in the late nineteenth century.[1] One Methodist minister charged that the Brethren evangelists told seekers to believe "not on the person of Christ, but - in the fact that Christ 'paid [the seeker's] debt' and 'blotted out' his sins", thus reducing faith to belief in certain facts.[2] Indeed, he boiled down Brethren belief on conversion to: "You are saved because you believe you are saved." Often in the counseling rooms the inquirer was just asked, "Do you accept Jesus as your Savior?", and when the person said "Yes!", as most did, that individual was immediately regarded as converted. One Methodist critic dubbed such conversions as "a sort of hold-up-your-hand conversion",[3] presumably in reference to inquirers being asked to raise their hands as an indication of an interest in the gospel. Nathanael Burwash, the leading theologian of Canadian Methodism at that time, said that the Brethren lost sight of the work of the Spirit in the new birth. The Methodists also frequently observed that the Brethren neglected repentance.[4]

Not that the Methodists were alone in their concerns. James Duncan, a minister in the Presbyterian Free Church, said that with the Brethren's understanding of conversion the Holy Spirit might just as well not exist. The Brethren in return criticized the Methodists for stressing the emotional side of conversion. This opposition towards emotion in religion, which appears to have been general amongst the Brethren, seems to have been an over reaction against the excessive emotionalism of some revivalists.[5]

What should be made of these observations about the Brethren? There seems to be some truth in them, though, as shall be seen, they are not the complete picture.

In 1841 George Muller, a major Brethren leader and teacher, answered a number of questions on conversion in his journal. He wrote,

> I. **Question.** How may I obtain the knowledge that I ... have everlasting life?
> **Answer.** Not by my feelings, not by a dream, not by my experience being like this or that one's ... but this matter is entirely to be settled ... by *the revealed will of God*, the written word of God...
> II. **Question.** By what passages, then ... may I make out that I am ... born again?
> **Answer. 1,** In 1 John V. 1, it is written: "Whosoever believeth that Jesus is the Christ is born of God." The meaning of these words is evidently this, that every one ... who believes that ... Jesus of Nazareth ... was the promised Christ or Messiah, such a one is no longer in his natural state, but is born again... The question therefore is, Do you believe that Jesus ... is the promised Saviour...? If so you are a child of God, else you would not believe it. It is *given* unto you to believe it...

Then later he states that the NT teaches that "you must believe that Jesus ... is *the* Christ, *the* Saviour; and if you believe that, you have a right to look upon him as *your* Saviour."[6] Two points should be noted here that correspond to the claims made above, first, that "feelings" are discounted. Secondly, that, seemingly, simply a belief in a number of facts about the person and work of Christ is sufficient for salvation.

But Muller does make clear that this belief is *"given"*, and later states that if one trusts in and depends upon "the Lord Jesus for salvation", then one "shall have everlasting life,"[7] though faith in the sense of trust seems to play a minor role in his understanding. There is not a hint in Muller's words in this section of repentance, nor is there mention of any ethical outworking following conversion, and, though assurance is a major subject of this portion, the "Holy Ghost" is mentioned only once, but that as a comforter.[8] Apart from his more famous orphanages, Muller also founded the "Scriptural Knowledge Institute" in 1834, part of the task of which was to establish new "Day-Schools, Sunday-Schools and Adult-Schools, in which instruction [was] given upon *scriptural principles"*,[9] presumably including such teachings as indicated above.

George Soltau, another Brethren teacher, seems to have been an early advocate of the "carnal Christian" idea, i.e., that a person can be a Christian, even though there is little, or even no clear, evidence of it in the individual's behavior. In Soltau's terms such a person is an "ungrown Christian" who exhibits "carnal" features, such as "acting as human beings who have no Divine life".[10] This teaching devalues repentance, suggesting, as it does, that a conversion experience (of which repentance is an integral part) may do little or nothing to change a person's life.

However, Soltau did regard the Spirit as active in convicting of sin and in the new birth, though such activity was subordinate to the human will. Another Brethren teacher, "C.H.M.", said that conversion was produced by "the word of God brought home [by] the mighty power of the Holy Ghost". Also, in 1878, J.N. Darby said that, "the Spirit ... gives the assurance of salvation..."[11] Whilst on another occasion when speaking of assurance he said, "I was in Christ united to Him by the Holy Ghost."[12] Another early Brethren leader, A.N. Groves, could also speak of the basis of Brethren fellowship being "life in the Christ of Scripture, rather than Light in the teaching of the Scriptures,"[13] indicating his belief that relating to Christ was more than just an intellectual acceptance of his claims.

So it can be seen that though the charges are not completely true, they do have some substance. The view of conversion held by at least some brethren was different from those that commonly preceded it, particularly the Methodist.

The Brethren split into two groups in the late 1840s over doctrinal differences, but the matters being considered here do not seem to have been part of the problem.[14] J.N. Darby, perhaps the major Brethren figure prior to the division, became leader of the exclusive section, but remained very influential and traveled widely, making a number of trips to various European countries, and visiting North America (USA and Canada) on seven occasions between 1862 and 1877.[15]

The Brethren had numerous itinerant evangelists in the second half of the nineteenth century, and it is clear that Brethren teachers influenced a number of other leading evangelists and teachers, including D.L. Moody, R.A. Torrey, D.W. Whittle, L.S. Chafer, and C.I. Scofield.[16] For example, Brethren preacher Henry ("Harry") Moorhouse, who made numerous visits to America, was a major influence upon Moody, and Moody also engaged in Bible studies with Brethren leaders and purchased Brethren commentaries.[17] Moorhouse's counseling practice did have an emphasis upon an intellectual acceptance of rational facts, while heart experience of God in conversion and assurance seems to have been downplayed.[18]

Some Brethren teachers were openly critical of emotion in and prior to conversion, and their rejection of such feeling even led some of them to reject inviting people forward.[19] Moorhouse, though, appears to have been one who did use the public invitation. Certainly he saw it used in 1867, and used a form of it in America in 1874, when on one occasion he saw a whole congregation stand to his invitation. He definitely made frequent use of inquiry rooms.[20] His use of inquiry rooms might imply that he frequently used the altar call, though the two are not inseparably linked, as has already been noted.

In addition, a number of Brethren evangelists visited Australia in the last thirty-five years of the nineteenth century, some of them eventually staying there.[21] Brethren missionaries also ministered in Africa and Asia from the second quarter of the nineteenth century.[22] So the influence of this relatively small group was widespread.

It would seem significant that many of the emphases in modern evangelism are the same as those credited to the early Brethren. For example, it is often stated today that one should not trust one's feelings. Indeed, people are often told that the Bible says we are saved because we have "believed" and even if we do not "feel" saved that does not matter. While it needs to be admitted that feelings can certainly be over stressed, the emotions are an essential part of life, and the new life, and they have their part to play in the conversion process. In addition, the undervaluing of repentance is also a feature of much of modern evangelism.

D.L. Moody

Dwight Lyman Moody was a poorly educated but successful salesman turned preacher, who established a major church in Chicago in the 1860s. He left America with the singer Ira Sankey to evangelize Britain, where he had previously been little known. To make matters more difficult, two of his main British supporters died shortly before his arrival. But the two evangelists, beginning in a very small way in York, in June 1873, proved so successful that 21 months later, by God's blessing, they did the impossible and took London by storm.[23] Their return to America met with like success there.

Moody was the first to use modern mass evangelism, that is a highly organized campaign, in which the evangelists move from town to town, holding meetings in large venues, attracting thousands of people, receiving support from a wide variety of denominations, and using some form of the public invitation. Wesley and Whitefield had preached to ten thousand or more at a time, in large, but usually open-air venues. Whitefield and Finney had been backed by a variety of denominations. Finney, but not Wesley and Whitefield, had used the public invitation. All three had traveled from place to place, and all three, to some degree had organized their evangelistic strategy, but no one before Moody had used all these components which typify the modern "crusade". Moody was an experienced and able businessman and, as William McLoughlin claims, "Moody applied the techniques of corporate business enterprise to evangelism".[24] To some degree, as was noted in chapter three, business had now entered the world of evangelism and evangelism had entered the world of business. Not that all this was something he had sat down to plan, rather it developed as his ministry became more successful. Moody, as the *Chicago Tribune* colorfully put it, was said to have "traveled nearly a million miles, spoke to more than 100 million people and reduced the population of hell by one million souls."[25]

There were two major incidents in his life that affected his theology and ministry style. The first was his meeting with Henry Moorhouse. In his early days Moody was a hell-fire preacher, then he heard Moorhouse preach a series of sermons in Moody's church on "For God so loved the world...." From that time Moody's emphasis changed from God's judgment to his love.[26]

The second incident was the terrible Chicago fire, which was the catalyst for his insistence on bringing people to an immediate decision. On the evening of that black Sunday in October 1871, he preached on "What shall I do with Jesus?" He concluded his sermon by saying,

"Now, I want you to take that question with you and think over it, and next Sunday I want you to come back and tell me what you are going to do with it." After Moody's sermon Sankey sang, "Today the Savior calls". Before twelve hours had passed much of Chicago had been destroyed by fire, including his own church, up to three hundred had been killed, tens of thousands made homeless, and, in a sense, "next Sunday" never came. He vowed that he would never again give a congregation a week to think over their need of salvation.[27]

Whilst considering influences upon Moody, it is surprising to note that, according to Stanley Gundry and W.O. Thompson, Finney was probably not one of them. It is unlikely that Moody ever heard Finney speak or that they ever met or communicated with each other, even though their lives overlapped by about 38 years. Nor is there any evidence that Moody ever read any of the older evangelist's books.[28] Any influence Finney had upon Moody would seem to have been indirect rather than direct.

It is difficult to pin down precisely where Moody stood on the calvinist/arminian spectrum. It would seem that he regarded himself as a calvinist of sorts, as did some of those that observed him. This for a while, was a barrier to his gaining the support of the English Methodists.[29] Yet his sermons contain numerous statements of an arminian, or probably more accurately a semi-pelagian, nature.[30] Gundry notes that he could be preaching like a calvinist, and then proclaim a "universal remedy", for, he would say, salvation "is for all, all!" His view on the human will was much in the mold of Finney, for he pressed his hearers to decide for Christ with such phrases as, "You can if you will", and "Every creature can be saved if he will."[31] He also argued with J.N. Darby against the latter's calvinism.[32] One is justified in regarding Moody's theology as confused, but it must be remembered that his education, general and theological, was limited and largely informal, though he had a great willingness to learn. To him, evangelists were "just to proclaim the gospel"; deep thinking and doctrinal preaching was not their role, and certainly not his.[33]

But that is not to say that Moody had no theology, for he did, albeit a simple one. His theology he summed up in the three Rs: "*Ruined* by the fall; *redeemed* by the blood; and *regenerated* by the Holy Spirit."[34] In the latter he can be seen as having a wider understanding of the Holy Spirit's role in the conversion process than did Finney, believing, differently from Finney, that the work of conversion was "supernatural", and the work of the Spirit in it more than just persuasion.[35]

What were Moody's methods? Back in the 1860s in Chicago, he

would often roam around his congregation asking anyone who looked concerned after the just-preached message, if they were Christians or not. If the reply was hesitant or negative, Moody, who was a big man, would ask, "Do you want to be saved? Do you want to be saved now?" Often not waiting for an answer, he would urge the man or woman to kneel, then kneel down beside them and plead the Savior's cause. Under these circumstances, in the words of W.H. Daniels, an American Methodist minister, the seeker "would generally give himself to the Lord." He did not usually in this period make a formal appeal for a public response, but after-service inquiry meetings were already a common part of his ministry.[36] Later his methods were somewhat less aggressive.

On 28 December 1873 he held a massive meeting for men in the Edinburgh Corn Exchange. At the close of the service, Moody invited all those concerned about their souls to follow him to the nearby Free Church Assembly Hall where an inquiry meeting was already in progress, the result of a separate meeting for women held in the Assembly Hall. It is estimated that over 600 followed Moody to the hall, where they were counseled collectively because of the vast numbers.[37] If not quite in the modern mold, this was a public invitation.

At his final meeting in London on 11 July 1875, Daniels says that near the end of his address, Moody called out, "Who will accept Christ tonight?" Immediately calls of "I will!" were heard coming from various parts of the Camberwell Hall. Then Moody instructed those who wanted to be Christians to stand, and, according to Daniels, about one thousand did. The year before Moody had also instructed inquirers to stand at the end of a meeting in Birmingham. The meeting then concluded with the benediction and the remainder of the congregation was dismissed whilst those who had stood were then directed to the inquiry room(s).[38] At a meeting in Louisville, the date of which has been lost (but certainly after the two just mentioned), Moody again asked those requiring prayer to stand. About 80 did, and were later led to the inquiry room.[39] In 1887, however, he was negative in his response to a student who asked whether it was a good idea to ask prospective converts to stand in public commitment to Christ, but this may have been more to do with the way it was done than the method itself.[40]

In November 1882 Moody and Sankey went to Cambridge. On Guy Fawkes Day they spoke and sang to a large, explosive crowd of students from the university who did their best to upset proceedings. The next two nights the evangelists addressed much smaller, but more orderly gatherings, with little result. The following night the

congregation was larger, and Moody made a public appeal, which not
only shows clearly one of his methods, but also a little of the rationale
behind his invitations. He said:

> I have not yet held an inquiry meeting for you gentlemen, but I feel
> sure many of you are ready and yearning to know Christ. When you are
> in difficulties over mathematics and classics you do not hesitate to
> consult your tutors. Would it be unreasonable for you to bring your
> soul-trouble to those who may be of help to you? Mr. Sankey and I will
> converse with any who will go up to the empty gallery yonder.

This appeal was followed by silence and stillness. According to
cricketer, Kynaston Studd, one of the organizers of the gathering,
"There was no response until the third or fourth appeal", then one
student, "half hiding his face in his gown, bounded up the stairs two at
a time." The ice broken, a further fifty-one followed him.[41] It is an
intriguing thought that so many students, who would have been far
better educated than the evangelists, could see them as "tutors", albeit it
for Christ. Also it should be noted, assuming Studd is correct, that
Moody was not afraid to repeat his invitation, when there was no initial
response. The request for seekers to walk towards a specific meeting
point, in view of the rest of the congregation, was one of several
methods Moody used to gather inquirers together for counseling.[42]
    Carwardine says that Moody never used the "anxious seat" as
such,[43] but this is not strictly true. Moody was always prepared to use
what he considered to be the best method to suit the circumstances, and
was no slave to any set procedure, and he did use it on at least one
occasion, seemingly on the spur of the moment. At the conclusion of
one address in Oxford, he urged those sitting in the front seats of the
auditorium to vacate them, so that those concerned about their souls
should come forward and occupy them. The seats emptied; the seats
filled again.[44] It must be said, though, that generally he preferred the
comparative privacy of the inquiry room for counseling.
    It is instructive to note the wording in some of Moody's sermons
and appeals. He would say: "The way to be saved is not to delay, but to
come and take, t-a-k-e. TAKE."[45] "Decide for Christ now, with Calvary
in sight. Choose ye this day whom ye will serve." "Settle it this
morning, my friends, once for all. Begin now to confess your sins, and
to pray the Lord to 'remember you when He cometh into His
kingdom.'" "If you give yourselves to God tonight, everything will date
afresh from now and you will become a citizen of a better world." "It
don't take time; it takes decision."[46] It can be noted from this small
selection that to Moody, gaining salvation was simple, something that

could be immediately received, and a major facet of it was human decision. These first and last points indicate a definite shift from the evangelism of a century before, though they were not original to Moody.

Much of his work took place away from the churches, but usually with the support of a variety of denominations. Yet he was very conscious of the importance of the church, and advocated that his "converts" join a local congregation. The primary criterion for deciding which church was not the particular denomination, but where they would be able to work most successfully for God. He was also very aware of the local church's important role in nurturing believers.[47]

What, apart from the modern crusade with its apparently mandatory concluding "appeal", did Moody contribute to the public invitation system? Some have attributed the introduction of the inquiry room to Moody, which we have seen was an essential part of his methods, and he certainly believed this device to be extremely important and biblically justified.[48] We have also noticed that the various ways he assembled the seekers for the inquiry room fits in with our definition of the public invitation system, in that it was usually public, and was to some degree systematic, though not rigid. His son, William, regarded the inquiry room as the most "original feature" of the elder Moody's work.[49] Yet the inquiry room, if not always called that, had been in use even before the public invitation, in that preachers as far back as Edwards, John Wesley and Whitefield would often meet seekers in a separate room, sometimes in a church, at others in someone's home, either soon after sermon, or a day or two later. These meetings, though, were by private appointment rather than public appeal. Asahel Nettleton was a regular user and an advocate of inquiry meetings, fifty and more years before Moody's ministry.[50] Significantly, Moody seems to have learned of the use of such rooms on a private trip to Britain, six years before his first evangelistic tour. Even so the inquiry room was new to some, and at times opposed.[51] It would seem, however, that Moody introduced one new feature into the inquiry room (possibly learned from others). It was the common refusal to deal with inquirers' problems and difficulties. Rather, the preferred method was to direct them quickly to Scripture and to Christ, ignoring any personal problems they may raise.[52] This also has become a common feature of modern evangelistic counseling.

Nor does it seem necessary to draw any great distinction between the "mourners' bench", the "anxious seat", the "altar", and the "inquiry room" when used with the public invitation. The only real difference was that while the last two were fairly private, the "bench" and the "seat" were open to public view, thus making a public invitation even more public. Certainly, the purposes of them all were really the same, and they had all been in use long before Moody. But having said all this, it is true to say that Moody's advocacy of the inquiry room did further increase its usage. Because of his widespread popularity, it was brought to the attention of many whom had not previously used it.

Two other features of the invitation system can be regarded as having been popularized by Moody, perhaps even introduced by him. First, there was the use of a soloist working alongside the preacher, in Moody's case, usually, Ira D. Sankey; secondly, was organized and regular counseling by trained lay people.

The use of music in evangelism was not by any means new. Singing has been part of Christian worship from the beginning. Wesley and his helpers often sang at the commencement of their outdoor gatherings. Simple songs and choruses were an integral part of the camp-meeting scene in frontier America. Finney used choirs and employed a musical co-worker.[53] Congregational singing allied with a preacher's invitation or exhortation was common enough before.[54] But to have a soloist sing at various points in an evangelistic service, and even after the sermon to augment the invitation, if not necessarily unique, was certainly rare. Philip Phillips and Philip Bliss were noted gospel singers of this period, but up until this time their work was more often in the form of Christian concerts.[55]

But Sankey's job was quite deliberately to sing the gospel in partnership with Moody the preacher. Sankey would usually have his small harmonium transported from venue to venue, and he would take the dual role of instrumentalist and singer.[56] Accusations were made about bringing the Music Hall into the church. One publication noted that the tunes of Sankey's "Sacred Songs" commonly included the features of "many secular contrivances".[57] Certainly, the songs Sankey and his congregations sang, with their simple, easy-to-sing tunes, and frequently with very sentimental words, were similar in style to the songs sung in the Music Halls. In addition harmoniums were often used in Music Halls, thus presenting another similarity.[58] Not that Moody and Sankey were the first to use such songs. William Booth in the early days of the Christian Mission (later the Salvation Army), and even in his days as a Methodist minister, had quite deliberately set Christian words to popular tunes which previously had only secular associations, and these were often of the Music Hall type.[59]

The vast numbers filling the inquiry rooms at Moody's campaigns frequently presented a major problem: there were too few clergy and other experienced workers to counsel those in need. Moody had on occasions enlisted the aid of theological students to help with this, but at times, especially in the early days, individual counseling was not possible because inquirers frequently greatly outnumbered counselors. In such cases Moody usually gave some general words of counsel to them collectively. At other times, personal workers counseled the inquirers in small groups.[60] The Chicago Evangelization Society, set up by Moody and his associates in 1887, began the work of training the laity for evangelism to help fill such needs. But it was felt that this was not enough, and so it was decided to set up a short-term school to do the work more effectively, and so in 1889 the Chicago Bible Institute was established. Later, after Moody's death, it became the Moody Bible Institute.[61]

Summary

Mainly through the work of a new denomination and a major evangelist there were a number of changes to the public invitation system in the last sixty years of the nineteenth century. The theological understanding of conversion held by at least some Brethren teachers seems to have had a major influence upon evangelistic counseling generally, but particularly in public invitation evangelism. Moody, who was certainly influenced by the Brethren, developed the modern crusade and encouraged the use of lay counselors and soloists at major campaigns.

Notes

[1] Phyllis D. Airhart, *Serving the Present Age: Revivalism, Progressivism, and the Methodist Tradition in Canada* (Montreal & Kingston: McGill-Queen's Uni. Press, 1992), 41-48; Phyllis D. Airhart, "'What Must I Do to be Saved?' Two Paths to Evangelical Conversion in Late Victorian Canada". *Church History* 59: 3 (Sept. 1990): 376-380.

[2] Airhart, "'What Must I Do?'" 377.

[3] Airhart, *Serving*, 69-70.

[4] Airhart, *Serving*, 43-47; Airhart, "'What Must I Do?'" 376, 378-79.

[5] Airhart, *Serving*, 45, 47; Airhart, "'What Must I Do?'" 380; Roy Coad, *A History of the Brethren Movement* (Exeter: Paternoster, 1976), 279.

[6] George Muller, *A Narrative of Some of the Lord's Dealings with George Muller* (3rd. ed. London: Nisbet, 1845), 409, 412 (emphasis in original).

[7] Muller, *Narrative*, 413.

⁸ See the whole extract, Muller, *Narrative*, 408-415.

⁹ Muller, *Narrative* 109-115 (emphasis in original). See also Robert Baylis, *My People: The Story of those Christians Sometimes Called Plymouth Brethren* (Wheaton: Shaw, 1995), 69; Harold H. Rowdon, *The Origins of the Brethren: 1825-1850* (London: Pickering & Inglis, 1967), 129-130, 134-35.

¹⁰ George Soltau, *The Person and Mission of the Holy Spirit* (London: Roberts, c. 1890), 36-37.

¹¹ Soltau, *Person and Mission*, 33-34; C.H.M. *The Miscellaneous Writings of C.H.M. Conversion What is it?* London: Morrish, n.d., 27; H.A. Ironside, *A Historical Sketch of the Brethren Movement* (Grand Rapids: Zondervan, 1942), 194.

¹² H.A. Ironside, *A Historical Sketch of the Brethren Movement* (rev. ed. Neptune: Loizeaux Bros., 1985), Appendix B, 189-190.

¹³ Nathan Delyn Smith, *Roots, Renewal and the Brethren* (Pasadena: Hope, 1986), 10.

¹⁴ Bayliss, *My People*, 45-50; Rowdon, *Brethren*, 236-252, 258-264. To pin down precisely what the Brethren believed on particular issues can be difficult, as they did not draw up or conform to any particular creed, Rowdon, *Brethren* 270-71, 289.

¹⁵ Airhart, "'What Must I do?'": 374; Rowdon, *Brethren*, 204-214.

¹⁶ Ahlstrom, *Religious History*, 809; Airhart, "'What Must I do?'": 380; Arnold Ehlert, *Brethren Writers: A Checklist with an Introduction Essay and Additional Lists* (Grand Rapids: Baker, 1969), 36-37; Ironside, *Brethren Movement* (1942), 71, 82; McLoughlin, *Modern Revivalism*, 177, 257-58.

¹⁷ Baylis, *My People*, 62-65; Ehlert, *Brethren Writers*, 36; John MacPherson, *Henry Moorhouse: The English Evangelist* (Kilmarnock, Ritchie, n.d.), 65-68; Hy Pickering, *Chief Among the Brethren: One Hundred Records and Photos* (London: Pickering & Inglis, 1931), 91; Pollock, *Moody*, 68-74.How much influence Darby himself had on Moody may be debated. Darby conducted a series of Bible readings in Chicago's Farwell Hall, at Moody's invitation, so they certainly had contact with each other, but the series was cut short because the two argued over Darby's calvinism, Ironside, *Brethren Movement* (1942), 81-82; Weremchuk, *Darby*, 143.

¹⁸ MacPherson, *Moorhouse*, 59-61, 68, 101.

¹⁹ Airhart, "What must I do?" 378-380. See also C.H.M. *Writings, Conversion*, 20, 27, and *Papers on Evangelization*, 23.

²⁰ MacPherson, *Moorhouse*, 56, 68, 74, 81.

²¹ K.J. Newton, "A History of the Brethren in Australia with Particular Reference to the Open Brethren". (Ph.D., Fuller Theological Seminary, 1990), 39-59; Pickering, *Chief Among*, 102, 165.

²² Baylis, *My People*, 65-68; Rowdon, *Brethren*, 195-99.

²³ W.H. Daniels, *D.L. Moody and His Work* (London: Hodder, 1875), 240-45, 353-381; D.L. Moody *et al*, *Addresses and Lectures of D.L. Moody, with a Narrative of the Awakening in Liverpool and London* (NY: Randolph, 1875), 22-24; Pollock, *Moody*, 99-102, 136-152.

²⁴ McLoughlin, *Modern Revivalism*, 166.

[25] "When Brother Moody preached, the city and the world listened", *Chicago Tribune* (Aug 8 1987). According to Gundry, that estimate of his auditory may well be conservative, Stanley N. Gundry, *Love Them In* (Chicago: Moody, 1976), 10.

[26] Daniels, *Moody*, 176-78; Gundry, *Love Them*, 45-46; McLoughlin, *Modern Revivalism*, 247; Pollock, *Moody*, 72-73. This does not mean that Moody never spoke on judgment or hell, rather that they were usually mentioned in passing, not emphasized, Gundry, *Love Them*, 96-101; in this he was quite different from Finney, who had a much greater emphasis on God's judgment, McLoughlin, *Modern Revivalism*, 89-90.

[27] Daniels, *Moody*, 237; Pollock, *Moody*, 84-86; Walter Rue, "The Legend of Mrs O'Leary's Cow", *Seattle Post Intelligencer* (Aug 20 1966); Alex Small, "Old Chicago had Charm and Character", *Chicago Tribune* (Oct 4 1964); Thompson, "Public Invitation", 127-28.

[28] Gundry, *Love Them*, 77-78; Thompson, "Public Invitation", 138-39.

[29] Daniels, *Moody*, 107, 249; Gundry, *Love Them*, 46; Iain Murray, *The Forgotten Spurgeon* (London: Banner of Truth, 1973), 172-73.

[30] Daniels, *Moody*, 407, 418, 423, 438-39 (these pages contain some of Moody's sermons, which include such phrases as, "Christ wants to [take into heaven] every sinner here"); Gundry, *Love Them*, 135-36; Weisberger, *Gathered*, 211. Gundry says that Moody's sermons often underwent considerable editing before being published, because of his poor English (Gundry, *Love Them*, 9), but there seems no good reason to believe that his theology experienced any apparent change as a result of the editor's blue pencil.

[31] Gundry, *Love Them*, 123-26; quoting from Moody's sermon on the "New Birth",135-6.

[32] Ironside, *Brethren Movement*, 81-82; Weremchuk, *Darby*, 143.

[33] Gundry, *Love Them*, 19-23, 39-45, 94-95; Weisberger, *They Gathered*, 209-210.

[34] Gundry, *Love Them*, 87-88, quoting from D.L. Moody, *The Way and the Word* (Chicago: Revell, 1877), iii, (emphasis in the original). The same three points, with slightly different wording, are on the memorial tablet to English evangelist Henry Varley (Henry Varley Jr., *Henry Varley's Life Story* [London: Holness, c. 1913], 281), who it is known had been another influence upon Moody (Pollock, *Moody*, 68-69, 94).

[35] Gundry, *Love Them*, 84-85, 87, 121-25.

[36] Daniels, *Moody*, 135-36, 154-55.

[37] Daniels, *Moody*, 285-86.

[38] Daniels, *Moody*, 464; Thompson, "Public Invitation", 131-32.

[39] Olive, "Evangelistic Invitation", 45, quoting from an undated article in the *Courier-Journal*.

[40] Gundry, *Love Them*, 83.

[41] G.E. Morgan, *R.C. Morgan*, 210-11 (the author of this book was an undergraduate at Cambridge at this time and was involved in these meetings); Pollock, *Moody*, 203-5.

[42] Pollock, *Moody,* 250.

[43] Carwardine, *Transatlantic,* 17.

[44] G.E. Morgan, *R.C. Morgan,* 217-18.

[45] Weisberger, *Gathered,* 211.

[46] Daniels, *Moody,* 407 (emphasis in the original), 423, 427, 442.

[47] Gundry, *Love Them,* 164-66.

[48] Thompson, "Public Invitation", 130-31.

[49] Thompson, "Public Invitation", 128.

[50] Thornbury, *Revival,* 81, 110-15. See also Alvan Hyde, letter dated 22 Mar. 1832, and Noah Porter, letter dated 12 Mar.1832, in Sprague, *Revivals,* Appendix, 51-52, 71-73.

[51] G.E. Morgan, *R.C. Morgan,* 173; Pollock, *Moody,* 109; Thompson, "Public Invitation", 129-130.

[52] Kent, *Holding the Fort,* 211.

[53] Bruce, *Hallelujah,* 96-122; Hardman, *Finney,* 253; McLoughlin, *Modern Revivalism,* 99.

[54] Bruce, *Hallelujah,* 80-81, 96-97; James Caughey, *Earnest Christianity: Selections from the Journal of James Caughey* (ed. Daniel Wise, Boston: Magee, 1855), 274, 306-7; G.W. Hervey, *Manual of Revivals* (NY: Funk & Wagnalls, 1884), 53-55, 80; Johnson, *Camp Meeting,* 197-99.

[55] Norman Mable, *Popular Hymns and their Writers* (London: Independent, 1945), 40-42; McLoughlin, *Modern Revivalism,* 178; Pollock, *Moody,* 75-76, 97. Bliss did later team with the preacher D.W. Whittle, Pollock, *Moody,* 117, 157, 167.

[56] Daniels, *Moody,* 234-37, 244, 267-69; Pollock, *Moody,* 75-77, 103-8, 122-27; Thompson, "Public Invitation", 134. Hervey says that Orson Parker used his two singing daughters to support his evangelistic labors, presumably in duet, before Sankey appeared on the scene, but gives no details, Hervey, *Revivals,* 53-54.

[57] McLoughlin, *Modern Revivalism,* 234.

[58] Nicholas Bentley, *The Victorian Scene: 1837-1901* (London: Weidenfeld, 1968), 288; Eric De Mare, *The London Dore Saw: A Victorian Evocation* (London: Allen Lane, 1973), 193; McLoughlin, *Modern Revivalism,* 233-39.

[59] Murdoch, *Salvation Army,* 62-64.

[60] Will Houghton & Chas. T Cook, *Tell me about Moody* (London: Marshall, Morgan & Scott, 1936), 123-24; Pollock, *Moody,* 95, 110, 166; Thompson, "Public Invitation", 132, quoting from Arthur T. Pierson, "D.L. Moody, the Evangelist", *The Missionary Review of the World* 10 (Jan.-Dec. 1900): 90.

[61] Gundry, *Love Them,* 55-56; Houghton & Cook, *Moody* 56-66; Pollock, *Moody,* 226-232, 244.

Chapter 9

The Altar Call in Australia

The Coming of Christianity

Because of the late arrival of Christianity to Australia and the nature of early European settlement, it would appear that the use of the public invitation commenced later in the Australian colonies than in America or Britain. Christianity could be said to have arrived in Australia with the arrival of the First Fleet in 1788. Amongst the disembarkees were an evangelical Anglican minister, Richard Johnson, his wife, and their collection of Bibles, New Testaments, and other Christian books and tracts.[1] But it is almost certain that Johnson (who was dubbed a "Methodist")[2] had never seen, far less practiced, the public invitation, for, probably no instances of it had occurred in Britain at this time. However, some of the marines in the party had previously been to America, so it is possible that some had seen the public invitation used. But as the practice was only just beginning in the USA in the 1780s this would seem unlikely.

It would appear from contemporary sources that the main users of the public invitation in Australia during the period under consideration were the various branches of Methodism, so most attention will be paid to the different branches of that denomination.

The Wesleyan Methodist Church commenced in New South Wales (NSW) in the second decade of the nineteenth century. A Thomas Bowden held the first Australian Methodist class meeting on 6 March 1812,[3] and in November 1813 the missionary society of the Wesleyan Methodist Church in England decided to send two missionaries to the young colony. The first of these, Samuel Leigh, arrived in August

1815. But until the 1830s progress was very slow.[4] The first Methodist service held in South Australia was conducted by a Wesleyan layman shortly after the colony's foundation in 1836, and the first minister arrived there two years later.[5]

Joseph Bennett appears to have been the first Primitive Methodist lay-preacher to arrive in NSW, some time in the early 1840s.[6] But his arrival seems to have been preceded by some Primitives in South Australia, who held their first open-air service on 26 July 1840 and their first Quarterly Meeting in March 1841.[7] The first Primitive Methodist minister to be sent from England arrived in Adelaide in October 1844. They did not commence work in Queensland until 1859.[8]

By 1851 there were nearly 19 000 Methodists of all types in NSW, Victoria and Tasmania, 5.63% of the population. Twenty years later there was more than ten times that many in those three states plus Queensland, 11.77% of the population.[9] It is clear from that percentage increase, that the additions could only partly be attributed to immigration, which boomed during the gold rushes. The other reason for it was that Methodism was vigorously and successfully evangelistic.[10]

The first Presbyterian ministers arrived at the end of 1822 and in 1823,[11] the first Baptist pastors in 1834,[12] whilst the first Congregationalists, in the form of LMS missionaries, arrived as early as 1798.[13] The Churches of Christ did not arrive until 1846/7.[14]

The Altar Call Australian Style

Undoubtedly, part of the evangelistic methodology used by the Wesleyan Methodists from quite early on was various forms of the public invitation. Joseph Orton, sent to Australia by the Wesleyan Missionary Committee in London in 1831, would appear to have been amongst the first, perhaps even the first, to use the public invitation in Australia. At a Love Feast at Princes Street Chapel, Sydney, on 15 January 1835, the mood was rather "dull", but the spiritual temperature rose, and Orton

> requested that those who were really seeking the forgiveness of their sins, would simply express their feelings, and many were led to do so. The expression of feeling so much increased, and it was getting late, I concluded the public service and requested as many as thought proper to remain. The penitents were collected near to the pulpit, and we recommenced our supplications... Six persons found the pardoning

mercy of God.[15]

The collecting of "The penitents" around the pulpit seems to have been to some degree public, and, certainly, Orton's earlier invitation to them to respond vocally before the remainder of the congregation was a public invitation as has been defined. Whether this was Orton's regular practice or just a device he used occasionally is unclear. It may be pertinent to note that a family by the name of Wilkinson, which had attended a Methodist church in Sunderland, England at about the time William Bramwell was minister there, later befriended Orton in London.[16] It is possible that the Wilkinsons spoke of Bramwell and his methods, and Orton decided to follow the example of that prominent Wesleyan.

James Colwell seems to confirm that Orton did use the public invitation. Indeed, he describes Orton's "appeals" as being "very pointed". For example, Orton would say, "I want ten of you, twenty of you to come to Christ to-night. You men and women sitting on the last form there, and that soldier in the corner."[17] Presumably, by "appeals" Colwell meant what we have called the public invitation; certainly "giving an appeal" is the common English term for the altar call. Though Colwell does not date this practice, it could not be later than 1842, as Orton died at sea at the end of April that year.[18] As Orton was the leading figure in Australian Methodism in those days (he had been appointed in England as Superintendent of the South Seas Mission), his use of the public invitation was, no doubt, an example for others to use it too. He served in New South Wales, Tasmania and Victoria, and spent a few months of 1840 in New Zealand,[19] which suggests he might have also been the first to use the public invitation in that land.

John Watsford, the Australian-born Wesleyan Methodist evangelist, recalled a service in Parramatta in 1840, in which the Rev. William Walker was preaching. Watsford wrote that after the sermon "people flocked to the prayer-meeting, till the schoolroom was filled".[20] Watsford gives no indication as to whether the inquirers were actually publicly invited to the schoolroom, and as after sermon prayer meetings for inquirers had been common in Britain for some time (Walker was born and trained in England), and were a regular practice in many churches in the early decades of Australian Methodism,[21] it is possible that no public invitation was given, but more likely that one was.

The following year Watsford went to Windsor, and he tells of concluding one session of Sunday School there by asking "those who wished to decide for Jesus to remain." According to Watsford about 70 children stayed behind and "gathered in great distress around the

Superintendent of the school and" himself.[22] After one of Watsford's sermons in the Goulburn circuit in 1857, the "Chief Constable" went forward to the penitent form, and a lay preacher then called out, "Who won't follow the Chief Constable to Jesus?" and it was recorded that "many did follow".[23] On another occasion Watsford preached at Bourke Street Methodist Church in 1860, and saw so many penitents come forward at the end of one service, that they were unable to be counted. He estimated it was over 200. On 25 June 1869, Watsford invited "those who were determined to consecrate themselves fully to God to come forward", and by his estimate about 50 came.[24] It is highly probable that these incidents were just a few of the many times that Watsford used the public invitation.

Thomas Camm, a member of the Chilwell Methodist Church, Geelong, recorded in his diary that after a service in May 1859 "the penitent rail was crowded with sinners calling for mercy." Camm also related that after one sermon by his minister the following year, twelve came forward.[25]

Camp-meetings were also held in the early days of Australian Methodism, though, apparently, more in the British mode than the American, occupying, generally, just one day.[26] At Newtown in 1849 the Methodists held a camp-meeting on Good Friday. At the end of it one class leader led his wife to "the penitent form". She had been a Methodist for a long time, but had never before "obtained a sense of her acceptance with God". In today's terms this lady would presumably have been regarded as going forward for "assurance". At the same gathering, another class leader led a young man to the penitent form who had only recently begun to attend class meetings.[27] It would seem, then, that in some churches class leaders took an active role in leading people forward or in encouraging them to take such a step, in a similar way to that used by the exhorters of the American frontier. In December 1859 a camp-meeting was held just outside Brisbane. At its conclusion the campers went to the "Valley" Chapel, where Rev S. Wilkinson urged his hearers "to an immediate consecration of themselves to God, then invited all those who were earnestly seeking the Lord ... to leave their seats and come up to the 'penitent form.'" A number of people came forward including some children.[28] Colwell also mentions camp-meetings being held in the Goulburn Methodist District in the mid-1850s, though whether the public invitation was used is not indicated.[29] Tom Brown, one of the Methodist preachers of the Goulburn circuit, also made use of "the penitent form" in the late-1850s.[30] It is important to note the use of the terms "penitent form" and "penitent rail"; these imply regular and predetermined use of the altar call.

Early in 1860, the Methodists in Drysdale, Victoria, placed a form near the front of the church during a revival, specifically for those "under concern for their soul". "Night after night ... penitents flocked to" it.[31] In Kiama, NSW, in 1864 the preaching of Thomas Angwin resulted in the communion rail being "crowded with seekers,"[32] presumably called forth by the preacher.

Richard Fitcher, a Wesleyan Methodist minister, was using the method in Victoria in the 1860s. Alexander Edgar, later a leading figure in Methodist circles in Melbourne, was converted through Fitcher's ministry in 1867 in St. Arnaud. The teenage Edgar took a peep into a chapel where Fitcher was preaching, and saw a number of people kneeling at the communion rail, having, presumably, just come forward at Fitcher's invitation. Edgar vowed that he would never make such a fool of himself as those folk. He later went to one of Fitcher's meetings, and the preacher, coming down from the pulpit, confronted Edgar and urged him to make his peace with God. The confused Edgar asked the evangelist if it was possible to make peace with God without moving forward to the rail, to which Fitcher responded, "I do not say that you cannot find peace where you are, but if that is what is holding you back from God, I doubt whether you will." At that Edgar went forward.[33] Edgar soon became a preacher and used the public invitation from early in his ministry.[34] Clearly the practice was being used quite widely in Australian Methodist circles in the mid-nineteenth century, and it gathered momentum from those converted through the method entering ministry and then using it themselves.

But if the practice began in Australia under the influence of the British and their descendants, American Christianity did have its input. William "California" Taylor of the California Methodist conference campaigned in Australia from 1863-1866 and again in 1869-1870. He had inquirers coming to the front in droves. He was probably the first American mass-evangelist to preach in Australia, and at one open-air service in South Australia had about 5000 in attendance, and 10 000 at another in Sydney. He was described as using methods "all his own", and certainly regularly invited people forward to the "altar".[35] How successful his work was in the long term is debated. Methodist preacher, D.J. Draper, an early supporter of Taylor, later expressed doubts about the long-term success of his work.[36] Yet some converts did last and became effective Christians. The Wesleyans had a net increase of 21 000 members over the seven years covered by Taylor's two visits,[37] which must have owed something to his efforts.

A namesake of the above, William G. Taylor, was fresh from

England in 1871, indeed, a "'chum' preacher", whose first major appointment was to Brisbane. He spoke of the communion rail of the South Brisbane Methodist Church being "filled with penitents at almost every Sunday-night service",[38] presumably assembled by a public invitation. (His own conversion had taken place in a Methodist class meeting in 1857, and was triggered by a most direct and public challenge.)[39] He moved to Warwick in 1873, where Methodism was in a poor state and immediately dramatic events took place. At the first evening service eleven "came forward as seekers of salvation, amongst these being the two circuit stewards ... and several other leading members of the church." We can do no better than guess at whether these "leading members" where going forward for what nowadays might be considered rededication, but Taylor seems to have had no doubt that this was an initial work of salvation. Taylor goes on to say "This was a new thing in Warwick", so presumably the altar call had not been used there before. He also appears to have used another method of invitation. In his church in Taree, NSW, in 1879, he spoke of 32 people rising to ask "for the prayers of the congregation",[40] presumably in response to an invitation to do so.

It is probable, though the proof has not yet been found, that the early Australian Primitive Methodists used the public invitation in some form or another, soon after their arrival in the early 1840s. The earliest recorded use by them so far discovered, however, was at Kent Street Chapel in Sydney on Easter Monday, 2 April 1866, where it seemed to have had more to do with signing the "temperance pledge" than conversion.[41]

The Bible Christians were a breakaway Methodist group that became very strong in the south-western counties of England early in the nineteenth century. It became quite a large group in South Australia in the 1860s-80s, and was also active in Victoria. Bible Christian preachers were also using the public invitation in South Australia in the 1860s. In the middle of 1867 a series of meetings were held in Myrtle Grove during which "several came to the penitents' pew, crying for mercy", as did others at Middleton later that year. In the following year a woman of 62 years of age went forward to the "penitent form" at the Bible Christian Chapel in Virginia.[42] In Moonta, a mining district in South Australia, in 1875, people were said to be coming to Christ practically every night, apparently through the use of the public invitation. One young man urged to go forward, cried out, "I cannot, I cannot, the Devil has got me chained to the seat, but by God's help will snap the chain asunder, as I am determined to find Christ." Seemingly, the chains were snapped and he moved forward to "The penitent form" which "was soon crowded with anxious ones." There is here the sound of the belief that conversion was dependent on going forward. On a later occasion "many" went forward to "the penitents' pew", nine of whom "professed to find peace."[43] According to Arnold Hunt, the Bible Christians did not have a communion rail, the elements being brought around to the communicants at the Lord's Supper in that denomination,[44] hence the necessity of a specific "penitent form" or "pew".

The Salvation Army, another church of Methodist origins, arrived in Australia in 1880, and (as was seen in chapter seven) the public invitation was an integral part of Salvationist worship, though not always ministered with decorum. An early example of this was the method of Adelaide Sutherland (known before her marriage as "Hot" Milner). She arrived, appropriately, in Adelaide with her husband in 1881. The London *War Cry* declared that at times she would actually clamber over the seats to reach those who appeared penitent and "order [them] out to the penitent-form".[45]

The Baptists do not seem to have used the public invitation in Australia at a significantly early date for two main reasons: first, their arrival in this country, as has been seen, was fairly late (mid to late-1830s) and it took them a while to become firmly established. Secondly, most of the early Australian Baptists came from Britain, where that denomination was rarely using the public appeal at that time, unlike their American counterparts. It would appear not to have been used by British Baptists before the publication of Finney's *Lectures on Revivals* in Britain (1837), and even then only in a limited way, and at first, probably, only by full-time evangelists. It was noted in chapter seven that some preachers of the British Home Missionary Society used a modified form of the public invitation, probably from the late-1830s.[46] At least one of the early Baptist ministers arriving in Australia was sent by that Society, and thus may well have used its methods. He was the Rev G. Slade, who served in Geelong for the best part of two decades from 1858, became the Victorian "Pioneer Home Missionary" in Kerang from 1877-81, and then spent four years in Rockhampton in Queensland.[47] Prior to Slade's arrival in Rockhampton, the Baptist Church there posted two laymen at the church on specific weekdays to hold conversations "on religious matters with any persons who might desire it", which might suggest that public invitations were not given at that time (1871-2) in that church. This same practice was used in the Jireh (Brisbane) and the South Brisbane churches.[48]

Of Brunswick Baptist Church, Victoria, it was recorded that early in

1877 "Many old and young [were] still coming forward and professing themselves on the Lord's side",[49] though this may refer to baptism rather than responses to public invitations.

The public invitation was definitely used in Australian Baptist churches in 1881 by two evangelists, named Harrison and Isaac, from Spurgeon's College, London. They preached at numerous churches in south-east Queensland including nineteen services in the Jireh Church, at which "between 200 & 300 retired to the vestries" for counseling.[50] The method of invitation at Jireh is not stated, but at South Brisbane the pastor reported about 30 "had come forward ... as enquirers" after the preaching of these visitors. Another "60-70 responded to the invitation" at Petrie Terrace.[51] Though South Brisbane and Petrie Terrace had an arminian theology, it should be noted that Jireh was distinctly calvinistic,[52] so the evangelists may have modified their methods at that church. *The Queensland Freeman* reported in its editorial for November that there was an expected total addition of about 150 members to the churches hosting the two evangelists, but showed no surprise nor made any criticism or affirmation about the method of evangelism,[53] which might suggest that the practice was already familiar to Queensland Baptists. Jireh recorded the addition of 33 members by baptism in November and December that year,[54] presumably most, if not all, of these were amongst the more than 200 counseled in the vestries.

The Churches of Christ were established in Australia by British Christians, and most of the early influence upon that denomination was from Britain. It does not seem that the public invitation was used in the early period in Australia (1846-63), but when a number of American Churches of Christ evangelists arrived in 1864 and soon after, the practice was introduced and popularized by them.[55]

The only usage of the public invitation discovered in an Australian Congregational church in the period under consideration was during an eight-day mission at Pyrmont Centenary Church in New South Wales in 1889. The preaching was shared by the minister, Rev J. Buchan, and a guest preacher, Mr. B. Short. It would appear that during this campaign, Short invited "those who accepted Christ to stand up," and on one night "at least ten responded," and others on subsequent evenings.[56]

No specific trace has been found of the use of the public invitation by Australian Presbyterians in this period. However, a Scottish Presbyterian evangelist named Alexander Somerville visited Australia in 1877. He had been associated with Moody and Sankey in Britain, and his methods were based on theirs. He brought with him his son to lead the musical side of the work, used the public invitation, and sought and received backing from various denominations, and thus was probably the first to conduct a modern evangelistic crusade as such in Australia. C.A. White notes that Somerville's mission was of particular benefit to Presbyterian "sabbath schools".[57]

Matthew Burnett, a Methodist of English origins, preached a mixture of Christian gospel and teetotalism in Victoria and South Australia in the 1870s and early 1880s. Those indicating acceptance of his message were expected to sign the pledge. Arnold Hunt said that with such as Burnett "it was impossible to distinguish between deciding for Christ and deciding for abstinence." In one of his Adelaide meetings, as people came forward to take the pledge, the choir sang "Men of Harlech".[58] Burnett, however, was just one of a number with this twin agenda. William Noble, a visiting English speaker, saw himself as an evangelist first and a temperance advocate second, but according to Phillips the emphasis in his preaching generally reversed this. At one meeting Noble asked his large audience to stand. Everybody did. He then told all the abstainers to sit, which left only about twenty standing, and these were immediately given pledge cards.[59] Henry Varley and Dr. Harry Grattan Guinness both came from Britain to Australia to preach a twin agenda in the late-1870s and 1880s, though in their case sexual morality was the companion to the gospel of Christ. Both expected and received a public response.[60]

Summary

The public invitation was first used in Australia by the Wesleyan Methodists, then later by other Methodist denominations. The Methodists seem to have been its only regular users until the 1870s. From then it was promoted to a wider audience by various itinerant evangelists, but there is little evidence of it being widely used in denominations of non-Methodist origins in the period under consideration.

Notes

[1]   Barry Chant, "Australia's Destiny in God" *Understanding Our Christian Heritage* 2 (1989): 7; Richard Johnson, *Some Letters of Rev. Richard Johnson, B.A. First Chaplain of NSW* (ed. George Mackaness, 2 vols. Dubbo: Review [1954] 1978), 1:6-8; Iain Murray, *Australian Christian Life From 1788: An Introduction and an Anthology* (Edinburgh: Banner of Truth, 1988), 3-4; Jim

Stebbins, "Historical Models for Christianity in Australia", *Zadok Papers* (Series 1: S 19): 1-2.

[2]   Johnson, Letter to Henry Fricker 4 Oct. 1791, *Letters of Johnson*, 1:39; Murray, *Australian*, 3, 14. Any evangelical Anglican of that time might be thought of by others as a Methodist, whilst not necessarily being such. John Wesley did not die until 1791, and the Methodists were still considered, by him at least, as part of the Church of England.

[3]   R.B. Walker, "The Growth and Typology of the Wesleyan Methodist Church in NSW, 1812-1901", *Journal of Religious History* 6: 4 (Dec. 1971): 331; Don Wright & Eric Clancy, *The Methodists: A History of Methodism in NSW* (St Leonards: Allen & Unwin, 1993), 3.

[4]   J.D. Bollen, "A Time of Small Things: The Methodist Mission in NSW, 1815-1836", *Journal of Religious History* 7: 3 (June, 1973): 226; James Colwell, *Illustrated History of Methodism: Australia: 1812 to 1855, NSW and Polynesia: 1856 to 1902* (Sydney: Brooks, 1904), 52; Murray, *Australian* 54; Stuart Piggin, *Evangelical Christianity in Australia: Spirit, word and world* (Melbourne: Oxford, 1996), 8, 20, 40; R.D. Pretyman, *A Chronicle of Methodism in Van Diemen's Land* (Melbourne: Spectator, 1970), 7; Wright & Clancy, *Methodists*, 4, 16.

[5]   Arnold D. Hunt, *This Side of Heaven: A History of Methodism in South Australia* (Adelaide: Lutheran, 1985), 25-27.

[6]   Wright & Clancy, *Methodists*, 25.

[7]   Eric C. Clancy, "The Primitive Methodist Church in NSW 1845-1902", (M.A., School of Historical, Philosophical and Political Studies, 1985): 32; Hunt, *This Side* 17, 58; R.B. Walker, "Methodism in the 'Paradise of Dissent', 1837-1900" *Journal of Religious History*, 5: 4 (Dec 1969): 333.

[8]   Clancy, "Primitive Methodist", 32-33; R.S.C. Dingle, *Annals of Achievement: A Review of Queensland Methodism 1847-1947* (Brisbane: QBD, 1947), 67.

[9]   Hans Mol, *Religion in Australia, A Sociological Investigation* (Melbourne: Nelson, 1971), 5. These are census figures, so actual membership statistics were less. An official membership figure from the Australasian Methodist Conference of 1855 was 19 897, but this included New Zealand, "Feejee", etc., see Dingle, *Annals*, 41.

[10]   Barry Chant, "The Nineteenth and Early Twentieth Century Origins of the Australian Pentecostal Movement", Mark Hutchinson, Edmund Campion, & Stuart Piggin (eds.) *Reviving Australia: Essays on the History and Experience of Revival and Revivalism in Australian Christianity* (Sydney: CSAC, 1994), 97-98; Murray, *Australian*, 58-69, 213-14, 291-95; Stebbins, "Christianity in Australia": 5-6; Walker, "Growth and Typology": 333-36; Walker, "'Paradise of Dissent'": 331-341.

[11]   Murray, *Australian*, 74-75, 111; Rowland S. Ward, *The Bush Still Burns* (Wantirna: Ward, 1989), 33.

[12]   L.J. Ball, "Baptist Heritage" in David Parker, *Baptists in Queensland* (Brisbane: Bapt. Hist. Soc., 1994), 25; L.J. Ball, "Queensland Baptists in the Nineteenth Century: The Historical Development of a Denominational

Identity", (Ph.D., University of Queensland, 1994), 62; F.J. Wilkin, *Baptists in Victoria: Our First Century 1838-1938* (Melbourne: Baptist Union, 1939), 52.
  ¹³ Geoffrey L. Barnes, "Liberalism and the Decline of Evangelical Theology in the Congregational Churches of Australia", *Church Heritage* 10:1 (Mar. 1997) 3; Piggin, *Evangelical,* 17-18; G.G. Howden, "The Congregational Churches of New South Wales", *Report of the Intercolonial Conference Held in Pitt Street Church,Sydney, May 15th to 23rd, 1883 (Under the Auspices of the NSW Congregational Union)* (Sydney: Lee & Ross, 1883), 19.
  ¹⁴ Taylor, *Churches of Christ,* 1-7.
  ¹⁵ Trish Orton, "Reverend Joseph Orton: The Wesleyan Methodist Missionary Known as 'The John Wesley of Australia'", *Understanding Our Christian Heritage* 2 (1989): 95. This account is taken from Orton's own record of the occasion, written the same evening.
  ¹⁶ Orton, "Joseph Orton": 90. Ms. Orton makes no mention of Bramwell, nor the precise dates of the Wilkinsons' time in Sunderland, though one of their children was born there in 1799. Bramwell's Sunderland ministry occupied the years 1806-1810, therefore the link is possible, rather than probable.
  ¹⁷ Colwell, *Methodism,* 336n2.
  ¹⁸ Colwell, *Methodism,* 233-34; *Methodist Magazine* 3ʳᵈ. series 21 (Oct. 1842): 869.
  ¹⁹ Colwell, *Methodism,* 217-233; Pretyman, *Van Diemen's Land,* 84-97, 114-16, 121.
  ²⁰ John Watsford, *Glorious Gospel Triumphs* (London: Kelly, 1900), 22. See also Murray, *Australian,* 152-53; Stuart Piggin, "The History of Revival in Australia", Mark Hutchinson & Edmund Campion (eds.) *Re-Visioning Australian Colonial History: New Essays in the Australian Christian Experience 1788-1900* (Sydney: CSAC, 1994), 180-81.
  ²¹ Hunt, *This Side,* 151; letter from a Mr Simpson of Hobart, 8 Aug. 1831, *Methodist Magazine* 3ʳᵈ. series 11 (Mar. 1832) 216-17; W.G. Taylor, *The Life-story of an Australian Evangelist* (London: Epworth, 1920), 50, 67; Watsford, *Gospel Triumphs,* 138.
  ²² Murray, *Australian,* 154, quoting Watsford, *Gospel Triumphs.*
  ²³ Watsford, *Gospel Triumphs* 119.
  ²⁴ Watsford, *Gospel Triumphs,* 123, 152. See also Piggin, "Revival in Australia", *Re-Visioning Australia,* 181.
  ²⁵ Walter Phillips, "The piety of a young Methodist in Colonial Victoria: The diary of Thomas Cornelius Camm", *Re-Visioning Australia,* 104-5.
  ²⁶ Colwell, *Methodism,* 370-71; Watsford, *Gospel Triumphs,* 152.
  ²⁷ Colwell, *Methodism,* 371.
  ²⁸ *Christian Advocate and Wesleyan Record* 2 (19 Jan. 1860): 21.
  ²⁹ Colwell, *Methodism,* 280.
  ³⁰ Colwell, *Methodism,* 280, 282. The second incident is mentioned in a letter from Brown to John Watsford in October 1858.
  ³¹ *Christian Advocate* 2 (29 Mar. 1860): 83.
  ³² Piggin, "Revival in Australia", *Re-Visioning Australia,* 179-180, quoting from J.E. Carruthers, *Memories of an Australian Ministry* (1922), 32.

[33] W.J. Palamountain, *A.R. Edgar: A Methodist Greatheart* (Melbourne: Spectator, 1933), 25-26.

[34] Palamountain, *Edgar*, 72-73, 107.

[35] Eric G. Clancy, "William 'California' Taylor: First Overseas Evangelist to Australia", *Church Heritage* 6: 3 (Mar. 1990): 45, 56, 78; Colwell, *Methodism*, 408-9; Hunt, *This Side*, 92; William Taylor, *Christian Adventures in South Africa* (London: Jackson, Walford & Hodder, 1867), 1-9, 36, 42-44, 57-60; (the first chapter of Taylor's book deals with his first visit to Australia; Watsford, *Gospel Triumphs*, 140.

[36] Murray, *Australian*, 136, quoting from John C. Symons, *Life of Daniel J. Draper* (1870), 267.

[37] Clancy, "William 'California' Taylor": 55; Colwell, *Methodism*, 409.

[38] Taylor, *Australian Evangelist*, 85; See Murray, *Australian*, 297; Dingle, *Annals*, 81.

[39] Taylor, *Australian Evangelist*, 29-30.

[40] Taylor, *Australian Evangelist*, 100, 116.

[41] *New South Wales Primitive Methodist Messenger* 1: 10 (July 1866) 242-23. According to Eric Clancy, archival material on the Australian Primitives is neither plentiful nor, in some cases, orderly, hence the paucity of references, Eric Clancy (retired Uniting Church archivist) conversation, 29 Apl. 1997.

[42] *Bible Christian Magazine* 47: 2 (Feb. 1868): 94; *Bible Christian Magazine* 47: 6 (June 1868): 288-89.

[43] Hunt, *This Side*, 124-55, quoting from the *Bible Christian Magazine* (Aug. & Nov. 1875).

[44] Hunt, *This Side*, 151.

[45] Barbara Bolton, *Booth's Drum: The Salvation Army in Australia 1880-1980* (Sydney: Hodder, 1980) 10-11.

[46] Carwardine, "Evangelist System": 211-17.

[47] *Australasian Baptist Magazine, The* 1 (July 1858): 18; *Queensland Freeman* 1: 8 (Aug. 1881); Wilkin, *Baptists in Victoria*, 49-50, opp. 81, 84-85, 200.

[48] Ball, "Queensland Baptists", 156, quoting the minutes of Rockhampton Tabernacle, 30 Nov. 1871 and 1872 (passim), Jireh Church, 20 Aug. 1867, and South Brisbane Church 22 June 1874.

[49] *Victorian Freeman* 1: 4 (Mar. 1877): 63.

[50] Minutes of Jireh Baptist Church, additional minute 15 Sept. 1881; *Queensland Freeman* 1: 10 (Oct. 1881) 149.

[51] Ball, "Queensland Baptists", 165-66, quoting the minutes of South Brisbane Church, 24 Aug. 1881; *Queensland Freeman* 1: 9 (Sept. 1881) 130.

[52] Ball, "Queensland Baptists", 86-89; P.J. O'Leary, "Queensland Baptists: The Development of Baptist Evangelicalism, 1846-1926", (M.A., University of Queensland, 1991), 40-43.

[53] *Queensland Freeman* 1: 11 (Nov. 1881) 161.

[54] Minutes of Jireh Baptist Church, various entries November and December, 1881.

[55] Graeme Chapman, *One Lord, One Faith, One Baptism: A History of the*

Churches of Christ in Australia (Box Hill: Vital, 1979), 41-2, 51-2 61-5, 69; Taylor, *Churches of Christ,* 1-7.

[56] *The Australian Independent* New Series 2: 10 (15 Oct. 1889): 198.

[57] Walter Phillips, *Defending "A Christian Country"* (Brisbane: UQP, 1981), 59-62; Joan Mansfield, "The Music of Revivalism, 1870-1910", Hutchinson, *Reviving Australia,* 125; C.A. White, *The Challenge of the Years: A History of the Presbyterian Church of Australia in the State of New South Wales* (Sydney: Angus & Robertson, 1951), 29.

[58] Hunt, *This Side,* 127-28; Phillips, *Defending,* 69.

[59] Phillips, *Defending,* 68-69.

[60] Phillips, *Defending,* 70-73; Varley, *Henry Varley,* 121-25, 135-36, 141-153.

Part Two

Chapter 10

Modern Usage

It is not intended to sketch a complete history of the public invitation system, so its use through most of the twentieth century will not be detailed. Biographies of major evangelists such as Billy Sunday and Billy Graham[1] can be consulted to gain an idea of how it has been used in that period. But it is intended to examine how it has been used in recent years. This will be done first through noting the responses to several surveys to determine the usage in local churches in America and Australia; secondly by looking at Festival '96 with Franklin Graham; and, more briefly, at the Billy Graham Global Mission to gain a picture of the way it is used in modern mass evangelism. It is recognized that calling people forward is used more than ever now for matters other than evangelism, particularly healing. This is most evident in charismatic churches. But this chapter will continue to focus primarily on the evangelistic usage of the practice.

Usage in America

W.O. Thompson gives the results of two surveys conducted in America on the use of the altar call. The first was amongst a thousand Southern Baptist Convention churches (521 responding) with a membership of over 300 each, and carried out in 1969. This showed that in the morning services 94.2% always gave a public invitation, and another 5.2% did so "almost always". In the evening services 77.1% always did so, whilst another 14.4 did so "almost always".

As the Southern Baptists had not conducted a similar survey since that time,[2] it was decided to approach a small number of Southern Baptist churches in October and November 1998 to ascertain whether there was any indication of a change in practice in that denomination during the intervening 29 years. Seventeen churches were surveyed from 17 different towns in 11 states. The churches ranged in size from a membership of 60 to that of over 4500. Fourteen of these had a membership of over 300.

Though the sampling was small, the similarity between the acquired data and that of the 1969 survey suggests that Southern Baptist practice in this area has changed very little. All 17 churches indicated that an altar call was given at every morning service. Of the 15 that had evening services, 12 stated that a call was given every time, two said on most occasions, and only the smallest of the churches surveyed indicated "A few Sundays". Fifteen of the churches reported that their frequency of giving invitations had remained about the same during the last 30 years, while two indicated that their frequency had declined a little. None said that the frequency had declined a lot or had increased. One difference, however, which was detectable concerned the reasons for giving altar calls. Ten of the churches indicated that they were more inclined now than before to give calls for other than evangelistic reasons, most notably for "call to mission".

The second survey was conducted by Thompson himself for his 1979 dissertation. It was carried out amongst 64 American denominations (53 responding). Eleven indicated that their congregations never used the invitation; these were mainly Lutheran and Reformed churches. Twenty-seven denominations said it was the "Usual Practice" of their churches; and the remaining 14 indicated that the practice was just used occasionally. Amongst the biggest users were the Southern Baptists, the Churches of Christ, the Nazarenes, the Assemblies of God, and the Salvation Army, all of which stated all or most of their local churches used it.[3] It is worth noting that with the exception of the Southern Baptists, these denominations did not come into being until after the altar call was systematized in the camp meetings at the beginning of the nineteenth century, so this is probably a factor in their widespread use of it. In some, if not all of these denominations, the altar call appears to have become an integral part of their public worship.

One highly influential and very evangelistic group that makes little use of the public invitation is Willow Creek. At their main church they do not usually make more than twelve evangelistic invitations to come forward a year, and in addition occasionally ask for people to raise their hands. It is not their normal practice to invite people forward for other reasons either, preferring to direct people to different ministry groups according to need. Their main evangelistic tool is the "seeker service", which is directed especially to those outside the faith, but interested in it, using as it does drama and modern music in an attempt to meet people with media with which they are familiar.[4]

Survey of Australian Churches

In July 1996 I undertook a survey to try to determine the usage of the public invitation in Australian Churches. Survey forms were sent to 477 churches of ten different denominations, in all six Australian states, but not the territories. The denominations were: Anglican, Assemblies of God, Baptist, Christian Outreach Center in New South Wales, Queensland, Tasmania and Western Australia and Christian Revival Crusade in South Australia and Victoria - these two appear as one on the table - Churches of Christ, Lutheran, Presbyterian, The Salvation Army, and the Uniting Church. About 80% of the distributed forms went to the capital cities, and most of the remainder to other major towns.

The response was remarkably good, 316 (66.2%) being returned. It was expected that those churches not using the system were less likely to reply, so it was deliberately made very simple for such to respond. In fact those not using the invitation had to answer no more than three questions. In spite of this the returns indicated that the four denominations that used the system least, also responded least, which suggests that the following figures show a bias towards the system. It should also be noted that the two largest denominations (Anglican and Uniting) were both under-represented in the survey, in an attempt to grant a substantial sampling to some of the smaller denominations. As these two large denominations leaned towards a "No" answer, this would also suggest a bias towards usage in the following figures. These biases must be recognized before drawing any conclusions from the following statistics.

Percentage returns varied quite widely from denomination to denomination, which was not unexpected. The Salvation Army had the highest rate of return (87.5%) and the Anglicans the lowest (54.5%). Other high return rates came from Baptists (76.7%) and the Christian Outreach Center/Christian Revival Crusade (75%). As already indicated churches in denominations indicating a high use of the system proved more likely to respond than others. The table on the following page indicates the percentage of responding churches that indicated that they did use the system, by state and denomination.

CHART OF AUSTRALIAN DENOMINATIONS
USING THE ALTAR CALL

STATE: DENOM	NSW	QLD	S.A.	TAS	VIC	W.A.	TOTAL
ANG	27.2	33.3	16.6	0	17.6	0	21.2
AOG	100	100	100	100	100	100	100
BAPT	64.3	87.5	83.3	66.7	30	75	64.4
CO/CR	100	100	100	-	100	100	100
Ch of Ch	100	100	100	-	100	100	100
LUTH	14.2	25	0	0	0	50	12.5
PRES	18	25	-	0	40	0	19.2
TSA	100	100	100	100	100	100	100
UCA	41	62.5	50	0	15.4	0	37.7
TOTAL	54.2	66.7	62.1	30.8	41.1	51.2	53.5

Key

State: NSW = New South Wales; QLD = Queensland; S.A. = South Australia; TAS = Tasmania; VIC = Victoria; W.A. = Western Australia

Denominations: ANG = Anglican; AOG = Assemblies of God; BAPT = Baptist; CO/CR = Christian Outreach Center and Christian Revival Crusade; Ch of Ch = Churches of Christ; LUTH = Lutheran; PRES = Presbyterian; TSA = Salvation Army; UCA = Uniting Church of Australia.

This table shows one highly significant factor. All the denominations that have been founded since the systematization of the public invitation in the early 1800s (Assemblies of God, Christian Outreach/Christian Revival Crusade, Churches of Christ, and Salvation Army) showed a 100% "Yes" response,[5] a similar situation to that in America. In the case of the Churches of Christ this was less emphatic than the others, in that one respondent said people were often invited forward if they had specific prayer needs, but "almost never" for evangelistic purposes. Another stated that it was used only "occasionally", and a third gave the impression it was done at least in part because it was expected. Churches of Christ usage was also generally less frequent than the other three. The Churches of Christ usage is also of particular interest because, as was indicated in chapter nine, they did not use the system in their early years in Australia.

In the denominations that did not use the system widely, there was a tendency for the individual churches that did use it to do so less frequently. Responses from all denominations indicated that though 53.3% use the system, a substantial number do so irregularly.

Though it was not requested quite a number who did not use the system gave reasons for not doing so. This was particularly evident amongst Anglicans from New South Wales (strongly evangelical) and Lutherans. These Anglicans often indicated that they preferred other methods of obtaining responses to evangelism, such as the filling in of response cards (three responses - three Anglican respondents from other states mentioned this too), an invitation to speak to a minister or other suitable person privately (one response), or by using the study booklet *Christianity Explained* (one response).

Though the Lutherans generally did not use the system, many of those responding made interesting and helpful comments. The most common observations they made were that opportunity to respond to Christ was inherent in the Lutheran liturgy, particularly during holy communion, therefore making the public invitation unnecessary, and even inappropriate (three responses), and that by its nature the public invitation centered the saving act upon human decision rather than God's saving act (two responses). This latter comment was also made by a few other respondents.

With regard to the frequency of usage, 72 said that they used it in "most" or "all services", 20 "at least once a month", 55 "a few times a year", and 4 "only when a visiting evangelist is preaching". Fourteen gave other responses, which included "occasionally" or similar phrase, (8), "very occasionally" or "once a year" (3).

A significant majority of responding Assemblies of God, Christian

Outreach, Christian Revival and Salvation Army churches use the public invitation at most services, thus these denominations not only have all responding churches using the system, but also have a very high frequency of usage. Only two Anglican, one Baptist, four Churches of Christ, and three Uniting churches use the altar call at "most services". Most churches that use the system in the four last named denominations do so only "a few times a year". Four of the five Presbyterian churches stating they used the system do so only "occasionally", whilst the other does so "a few times a year". Amongst the Lutherans, one answered "at least once a month", but the other two which used the system did so only "occasionally".

The survey did not ascertain the sizes of the various congregations, but a few hints did come through that smaller churches tended to use the public invitation less frequently.[6]

Summary

It is evident that the public invitation system is used widely in local churches in America and Australia, and in a variety of denominations. It is, however, used mostly in those denominations that have been established since the beginning of the nineteenth century. Those denominations in which all or most churches use it are also more inclined to use it frequently.

Festival '96 with Franklin Graham

The largest and probably most significant evangelistic campaigns ever held in Australia were the Billy Graham Crusades held in 1959, 1968, and 1979. All these had an impact upon Australian churches, and to some degree upon Australian society,[7] but as John Mavor successfully shows, using Sydney as an example, each successive crusade had less influence than the one that preceded it. For example, in 1959 in 26 days 980 000 people attended with an average attendance of 37 692. In 1979 the average was only 24 550 during that 20 day campaign, despite population growth. Though the average attendance in 1968 was the highest of the three, 46 333, as this crusade was conducted over only nine days, the total attendance was considerably less than half that in 1959. The concluding rallies of the three crusades showed a sharp decline in attendance, 150 000 (1959), 100 000 (1968) and 85 000 (1979).[8]

Jim Rawson, who was involved in all three of these campaigns, suggests that amongst the reasons for this decline was that with the first, as nothing on this scale had happened in Australia for many years, it had a "new" feel about it, which added to the excitement and expectancy. The second and third did not have that advantage. In addition, he says, the prayer support in 1959 was much greater than in the other two.[9]

Festival '96 in Australia was originally to have also featured Billy Graham, but he was taken ill so his son Franklin substituted. The following data is from the meetings held on 15-17 March 1996 at the Brisbane Exhibition Grounds.[10]

The style, particularly the musical content, of these meetings was more modern than one normally associates with this kind of gathering. The attendances were 25 000, 30 000, and 25 000 respectively. These figures come from estimates made by the Exhibition groundstaff, which were then rounded down by Festival '96 organizers. (By comparison, the total attendance at the three-day Billy Graham Crusade in Brisbane in 1968 was over 160 000, more than twice as many). Inquirers numbered 1100 on the first night, and 960 and 729 on the others, 2789 altogether. Of these approximately 1200 were for "salvation", 350 "assurance", 850 "rededication", 100 "enquiry", and 250 "other". "Other" included a variety of personal issues (marriage breakup, etc.) and those who came out for no apparent reason.[11]

Graham's sermons were much in the mold of his father, and included clear teaching on sin, God's judgment, and the human need of salvation. His invitations were fairly prolonged. The one on March 16 took over sixteen minutes from the end of the sermon until Graham began to give general counsel to, and prayed for the inquirers. This included the time when people were moving forward, during which a group was singing, but Graham was silent. As soon as the challenge to come forward had been made clear, there was almost a rush forward; many of those who moved early appeared to be carrying Bibles and small packages, and were, presumably, counselors. (The practice recommended to counselors for this crusade was that when they saw someone going forward of their own age and sex that they should rise and accompany them. It is probable that in the moments immediately after the appeal more than one counselor rose for some inquirers.)[12] I estimated that not less than 10% of the entire gathering eventually went forward, which would, of course, have included counselors. At the conclusion of the appeal there were numerous, long gaps in the stands, and the area on the oval previously crowded with people, was noticeably less so.[13]

Graham's appeal led fairly naturally from his sermon on the prodigal son, and was in three parts. The first (main) part ran:

Will you choose tonight? Will you come to Jesus Christ? Will you put
your faith and trust in him? ... Will you come to Christ tonight? Christ
died for you. You say, "But Franklin, why do I have to get up out of
my seat? Especially in front of this crowd of people?" Every person
that Jesus called, He called publicly. You see, He died on the cross
publicly. He shed His blood on a cross, in front of the whole world to
see. And if He was willing to go to the cross publicly for you, you
should be willing tonight to take a public stand for Him. That's why we
ask you to get out of your seat and come and stand here publicly,
because Christ died for you publicly, and I want you to take a stand for
Him tonight. I don't want you to come tonight if you don't mean it...
But if God is speaking to you tonight. You say, "Frank what do you
mean 'Is God speaking to me'? What does that mean?" As I've been
speaking tonight, if there's been a little voice saying, "This is what you
need to do. That's me; that's my life. I'm in that pigpen. I'm a sinner
and I'm not sure I'm forgiven." If there's been a little voice saying this
is what you need to do, you see that is the Holy Spirit of God calling
you tonight. And you come! You come! You've got a choice tonight: to
accept Christ or to reject Him. God is waiting to receive you. He is
wanting to forgive you, but Jesus said, "I am the way, the truth and the
life, no man comes unto the Father but by me." Friends, there's no
other way. Listen, there's no other way to Almighty God except
through Jesus Christ. And that's what I want you to do right now;
wherever you are just get up out of your seat, right now. Make your
way toward aisles, and come stand here, and I'm gonner lead you in a
prayer to invite Christ into your heart. You can experience God's
forgiveness right now; you can be cleansed of your sin and leave here
tonight knowing that you're forgiven, knowing that you're going to go
to heaven. You can settle this once and for all. God's going to win in
your life, whether you like it or not. It's going to be heaven or hell, but
you choose. It's your choice. This boy had to choose. He chose to come
home. That's what I'm asking you to do right now, is to come home to
your Father in heaven. Wherever you are, right now, get out of you
seat, and come stand here, and I'm gonner lead you in a prayer. You
come! God bless you. Come on![14]

It can be fairly said that this is typical of such appeals. The theology
is very arminian (some might say pelagian). The emphasis is upon
human decision: the eternal choice is being urged upon the listener.
Going forward is seen as following the example of other believers and,
especially, Christ. This act is viewed as a "stand" or witness for Christ.
Yet, no one really knows why any other individual is going forward.
The reasons people go forward are many and varied, as is evidenced by
the breakdown of inquirers into four specific groups and a fifth
designated "other" (see above). That "other" can embrace almost

anything.

In one of the closing phrases, "That's what I'm asking you to do right now, is to come home to your father in heaven", there is also a hint of confusing the outer act of going forward with the inner reality of conversion. In the context of "come forward", "come home" sounds almost a synonym.[15] There were, also, at least four comments during the night, two at the stadium and two on the radio commentary, which could have given the impression that going forward equaled conversion. Singer, Steve Grace said, "We have seen hundreds of people come out to make a decision in their lives." (In modern evangelical parlance "a decision" most often means conversion). Wayne Alcorn, one of the organizing committee, said that it was wonderful last night "to see hundreds and hundreds of boys and girls, and men and women coming to Jesus." On the radio, Leanne McDougall said, "All the people coming forward, and you think, 'O, yeah, that's great; they're making decisions'", whilst Dennis Agajanian said, "Right now, people are coming forward to know Christ ... Hundreds of people are coming forward right now to respond to the gospel."[16]

Another key point is the prayer of acceptance, its introduction and following declaration; here Graham said:[17]

> I want to say a word to those of you who have come this afternoon... Coming today, you're saying to God, "I have sinned, and I am sorry. I want your forgiveness. I want the debt canceled. I want to be set free. And I believe that Jesus Christ your Son died on a cross for my sins; shed His blood for my sins. That He was buried and that you raised Him from the dead." And, my friends, that Jesus Christ is alive; He is at the right hand of God the Father, and one day He's going to return. And one day He's going to judge sin. And right now I'm going to lead you in a prayer to invite Christ into your heart by faith, and experience right now His forgiveness, His cleansing, and to have the debt of sin canceled. And I want you to repeat this prayer after me... Let's just bow our head and close our eyes. "Dear Lord Jesus, I am a sinner. I need your forgiveness. I am sorry for my sins. I believe that you died for me. I want to turn from my sinful life. I now invite you to come into my heart. I want to trust you as my Savior. I want to follow you as my Lord. Amen."

Then he continued,

> If you prayed that prayer, and meant it... God has just forgiven you. He has just canceled the debt. He's just washed the slate clean... He's dumped your file... He cannot even recall it, if He wants. The debt's

canceled. And right now at 4.39 on 17 March, this is your spiritual
birthday. This is the day that you've been born again. This is the day
where God canceled the debt. This is where you've been set free from
the bondage of sin... You will never stand in front of God for judgment
of sin. You've been forgiven... This is a moment to rejoice. The Bible
says, if one sinner repents all the angels ... in heaven are rejoicing. Over
just one, and this afternoon there has been hundreds who've said to
God "I'm sorry." And if heaven's rejoicing, let all of Brisbane be
rejoicing.[18]

This, once more, can be fairly described as typical of such
acceptance prayers, and the remarks attached to them. It should be first
noted that all who came forward are addressed as one "category"
(desiring salvation), even though, as has already been suggested, no-
one really knows the motivation of any of those who have come
forward at this stage, and in any such large number there are always
bound to be different reasons for responding. (Sometimes evangelists
pray more than one prayer, and ask those responding to pray the one
appropriate for them. This method may not be used more often because
of problems in dealing with large crowds and time considerations.)
    If the prayer was "meant" ("sincere" is often used), then it is
generally assumed that that person has become a Christian. The
possible, indeed, probable, likelihood of many of those who have
responded praying sincerely but completely misunderstanding what is
going on is frequently not considered. Salvation is seen largely in terms
of confession of sin and the resulting forgiveness of God. This could be
considered an earned salvation - we confess our sin, therefore God
saves us. On the terms of the prayer, the subsequent interview by a
counselor becomes, theoretically, post-conversion counseling.
    There were four types of counselors:

    1/ teenage and adult;
    2/ children's;
    3/ special needs; and
    4/ special language.

These were all supervised by a team of ministers and other experienced
Christians.[19] There was a shortage of children's counselors, and some
had to counsel more than one child at a time; in addition, some
"teenagers and adult" counselors had to counsel children.[20] Counseling
sessions normally took 10-15 minutes, though some went for longer.[21]
Many sessions appear to have progressed satisfactorily and the
counselors reflected on them with joy, and could often write with

obvious enthusiasm of following up the counselee, usually by phone. But numerous counselors spoke of problems with noise, shortage of time, and the inquirers (especially children) being concerned about meeting up with family or friends afterwards, all of which interrupted the counseling process. It seemed that some "inquirers" (a small but noticeable number) had come forward for reasons no more important than idle curiosity, or because it was what their friends were doing. A few counselors spoke of some inquirers having an apparent lack of interest in spiritual matters, either being reluctant, or even refusing to speak of Christian things. One counselor who dealt with a child who had come forward on Friday, apparently "for no reason at all", spotted her among the inquirers again on Saturday.[22] It was evident in many of the counselor reports that in spite of the excellent organization (commented on by many) there was considerable confusion in the counseling situation (noise, distractions, inquirers that did not quite "fit"). This is probably inevitable when dealing with large groups of people, yet it would seem to be a problem inherent in the invitation system, at least in major meetings.

The counselor training was based around the *Christian Life and Witness Course (CLWC).*[23] One valuable portion in this training book deals with the fact that there are a number of natural and strong barriers to conversion, a fact which is often ignored, which in turn results in budding evangelists and counselors becoming frustrated because people they witness to do not respond. People do not respond *naturally*, for, as *CLWC* reminds us "The god of this age has blinded the minds of unbelievers" (2Cor. 4:4).[24] Details of this problem are often lacking in similar publications.

The counseling booklet was the six page *My Commitment*. Page one gave space for indicating why the inquirer had come forward; the following pages were headed respectively: "How to know what I've done", "How to be sure that Christ has forgiven my sin", "How to come back to Christ", "How to find out more", and "How to receive Christ". The seemingly strange positions of the first and the last were, no doubt, to fit in with the Graham method of saying a pre-counseling commitment prayer, which therefore seems to assume an inquirer is converted before counseling starts. The phrase "How to know what *I've done*" is a highly questionable one, though consistent with invitation evangelism and some of the theology usually behind it. This phrase is supported by Billy Graham in his introduction in the follow-up booklet, *Growing as a Christian*, where he says, "becoming a Christian is the most important thing you will ever do."[25] Is one's conversion, primarily something one actually does? It can be said quite fairly that that phrase makes God seem secondary in salvation. Certainly, one believes and repents, though, as has been previously suggested, neither is possible without the regenerating power of the Holy Spirit, and surely the emphasis in salvation should be upon God.

It was noted above that the attendance at Festival '96 was less than half that of the 1968 Billy Graham Crusade in Brisbane. The probable reasons for this are: first, Franklin Graham is not as prominent an international figure as his father, secondly, this crusade was arranged in a shorter time frame than most similar events, and thirdly, a natural decline in crusades of this type, as demonstrated by Mavor's thesis, may still be continuing in Australia.

The Billy Graham Global Mission

The Billy Graham Global Mission was a new step in mass evangelism. On three nights in March 1995 Dr. Graham conducted a campaign in Puerto Rico, which was beamed, via satellite, to about 1700 venues around the world.[26] This represents an extension in the use of the altar call, as, theoretically, one person, with one invitation is asking people to come forward in hundreds of different venues, though as shall be seen this was usually done with the aid of local evangelists.

I attended the Mission at two different Brisbane venues, the Chandler complex and Gateway Baptist Church. Graham's sermons (interpreted into Spanish for the Puerto Rican listeners) were simple, biblical and relevant, portraying the character of God, the sinfulness of mankind, and the solution in Christ. At the end of each sermon Graham gave an invitation for public response. These invitations were low key, and, assuming we saw all that transpired in Puerto Rico, surprisingly brief. The longest of the appeals took six minutes from the time Billy said, "I am asking you to make that commitment tonight", till the beginning of the short address to those who had come forward in Puerto Rica. In both Australian venues the local hosts had great difficulty in coordinating their invitations with Graham's pauses, which were very brief, and thus the local invitation became rather confused. In neither venue I attended did anyone move forward other than the counselors as far as I could judge. (It was suggested in a training video for the Global Mission that counselors move forward after the appeal, to encourage non-Christians to do likewise.) It appears that at some Australian locations, particularly after the first night, the video was turned off immediately after Graham's appeal, and the local host took over to apply the invitation more directly. Graham's appeals in this campaign were shorter, less emotional and contained less pressure to respond than his appeals earlier in his career and the invitations of many other evangelists.

During one appeal Graham stated, "Nothing will happen until you start", which certainly gives the impression that the key factor in conversion is human decision, and, though probably unintentionally, seems to promote the idea that a public response to such an appeal is essential to salvation.

Summary

Both on the local church level and in the field of mass evangelism the altar call is still very widely used. In mass evangelism, however, there is some indication that its results have declined over the years. In both fields, particularly the local church, its modern usage has expanded to embrace moving forward for prayer about a wide range of issues including in some cases healing.

Notes

[1] Some parts of Billy Graham's ministry will be noted here, but there will not be a detailed account of his career and methods. W.O. Thompson has a lengthy chapter on Graham's methods, Thompson, "Public Invitation", 163-187, and there are numerous biographies of him, including his autobiography.

[2] Statistics are from *Reaching People: A Study of Witnessers and Non-witnessers: Pilot Study Phase,* H. Joe Denny, (Nashville: SBC, 1969), quoted by Thompson. I wrote to the Southern Baptist Convention on 18 Feb. 1997, inquiring whether a later survey of this type had been done. A reply was received from J. Clifford Tharp, Jr., of the Strategic Information Unit of the Sunday School Board of that convention, who stated that as far as he was aware no further studies of that nature had been conducted, letter 25 Feb. 1997.

[3] Thompson, "Public Invitation", 209-215 (see also 189-201).

[4] E-mail from Judson Poling of Willow Creek, 3 Mar, 1999; Lynne & Bill Hybels, *Rediscovering Church* (Grand Rapids: Zondervan, 1995), 41, 172-75.

[5] The Uniting Church is a recently established church that did not show 100% "Yes" response, but it has been excluded here as it was formed from three denominations, (Congregational, Methodist and Presbyterian), which existed prior to the nineteenth century.

[6] For example, one AOG pastor gave as his reason for inviting people forward only "at least once a month" (rather than the normal AOG response of "most services") as being because his church was "small".

[7] Stuart Piggin having examined the 1959 Billy Graham crusades even feels justified in stating that "a revival" took place in Australia at that time, see his "Billy Graham in Australia, 1959: Was it Revival?" *CSAC Working Paper* 4.1: 28. Piggins' view is supported by Jim Rawson, conversation (13 July 2000).

[8]   John E. Mavor "The Light Beneath the Cross Grew Dim. The Decline in Impact of the Billy Graham Crusades in Sydney between 1959 and 1979". (M.Litt, University of New England, 1995), 29-30. For an analysis of the 1959 figures, see Faith Alleyne & Harold Fallding, "Decisions at the Graham Crusade in Sydney: A Statistical Analysis". *Journal of Christian Education* 3: 1 (July 1960): 32-41.

[9]   Conversation with author, 13 July 2000.

[10]   I was present on March 16 and had the sermon and appeal privately recorded. I listened to the radio broadcast of the next day's meeting, and recorded the invitation.

[11]   *Summary of Attendance and Enquirers for Festival 96 with Franklin Graham: Brisbane* (Brisbane: Festival Office); Jim Rawson, who was in charge of counseling and follow-up, phone call, 28 Mar. 1996.

[12]   Jim Rawson, personal conversation, 13 July 2000.

[13]   According to Jim Rawson, in a personal conversation (10 Apl. 1996), over 2000 counselors were trained but not all were present on any one occasion. Viewing the counselor reports (each counselor had to fill in a report and return it to Dr. Rawson) showed that some counselors were only present once or twice.

[14]   "Festival '96 with Franklin Graham": Sermon and Invitation 16 Mar. 1996 and Invitation 17 Mar. 96, taped from Brisbane Family Radio; commentators Leanne McDougall and others.

[15]   This is not to accuse Franklin Graham, or anyone else involved in the festival, of believing that the moving forward is either necessary for salvation, nor assures it.

[16]   The final two comments are from the audio tape of Family Radio, "Festival '96 with Franklin Graham."

[17]   This is the commitment prayer and associated remarks of Sunday 17, taped from Brisbane Family Radio.

[18]   Audio tape of Family Radio, "Festival '96 with Franklin Graham." These two extracts are from the meeting on Sunday, March 17.

[19]   Jim Rawson, personal conversation 10 Apl. 1996.

[20]   Gleaned from the counselor reports.

[21]   Jim Rawson, personal conversation, 10 Apl. 1996.

[22]   Gleaned from the counselor reports.

[23]   *Christian Life and Witness Course* (Minneapolis: Billy Graham Evangelistic Assoc., 1995).

[24]   *CLWC*, 38-40.

[25]   *Growing as a Christian* (Minneapolis: Billy Graham Evangelistic Assoc., 1995), 2. This booklet was being used by Catholics and Anglo-Catholics for follow-up, but most other churches were using *Christianity Explained*, conversation with Jim Rawson, 10 Apl. 1996.

[26]   *Global Mission with Billy Graham Newsletter* No. 3; *New Life* 57: 37 (9 Mar. 1995): 5.

Chapter 11

What is the Rationale Behind the System?

The rationale behind the public invitation system falls into two main divisions: the Scriptural and the practical. First, the supposed Scriptural support for the system will be examined, then the practical.

What do the Scriptures Say?

What does the Bible say on the subject? Does it contain anything either by way of example or command that supports the giving of public invitations? Is there anything there that might prohibit its use?

Alan Streett is a major advocate of the system, whose book (based on his dissertation) seems to have been widely circulated, so his work will be used as the primary example of those who state that the Bible does support the use of the public invitation. Streett's arguments do run into some difficulties because he does not define what he means by "public invitation". In his section *The Public Invitation - Is It Biblical?* he repeatedly joins a gospel invitation with a convert's later taking "a public stand for Christ" and then seems to regard the hybrid as an invitation for a public response of the type earlier defined in this book. This is not the only problem with his biblical rationale for the system. Another example is his use of the parable of the two men praying in the Temple (Lk. 18:9-14). To Streett, the publican calling on God for mercy out loud is an example "of public response related to faith and salvation."[1] Now, that story is primarily related to pride, but even if it was related to salvation, there is not a hint in it of a public invitation to draw forth any response, and its use to support the invitation system is highly questionable.

The Old Testament

The problem with Streett's lack of definition appears right at the beginning of his section *Is It Biblical?* He describes the Lord God's question to Adam, "where are you?" (Gen. 3:9-10) as an "invitation" ("public invitation" in his thesis), in an effort, presumably, to extend the use of the practice to the very beginning of time.[2] To regard this as such an invitation makes any question asked by God, or on behalf of God, which seeks a reply before at least one witness, a public invitation, and reduces the debate to absurdity.

He is on stronger ground when he cites (as do Thompson and Whitesell) Moses and Joshua challenging the children of Israel.[3] After descending Mount Sinai, Moses challenges the people by saying, "'Whoever is for the Lord, come to me.' And all the Levites rallied to him" (Ex. 32:26). At Shechem Joshua said to the Israelites, "choose for yourselves this day whom you will serve...", and the people responded verbally in favor of Yahweh (Josh. 24:15-18).

The Joshua passage does not clearly contain every aspect of the public invitation as has been defined in this volume. Though Joshua challenges the people to make a decision about their religious allegiance (vv14-15), he does not urge a public response (whether he expected one is arguable), though this is certainly what he got (vv16-18). In the Moses incident, it is clear that a request for a public response is given and acted upon, and thus this occurrence has some similarity to a modern appeal. But there is nothing to correspond to counseling or the inquiry room (unless one counts Moses' instruction to slay those who had sinned!), which we regarded in our definition as a normal aspect of the public invitation. Significantly, Robert Coleman states that it is, in part, the addition of this after-response counseling which gives the modern invitation its newness and distinctiveness.[4]

Streett also cites the case of Elijah on Mount Carmel. Elijah challenged the people of Israel with the words, "How long will you waver between two opinions?" They needed to make a decision: "If the Lord is God, follow him; but if Baal is God, follow him." The narrator then continues, "But the people said nothing" (1 Kgs. 18:21), which probably, but not certainly, is to be seen as implying that an observable response was expected. Finally, in the face of the divine pyrotechnics, the people decided publicly for Yahweh (1 Kgs. 18:36-39). Elijah's "counseling" that followed, as with Moses, was to kill, this time the prophets of Baal. This is a very different picture from that of the modern-day evangelistic campaign.[5]

M.H. Woudstra is correct in stating that Joshua's challenge is to be seen within "the legal setting of covenant",[6] and all these incidents should be viewed in that way. It is questionable whether one can make a precise parallel between exhortations made to the covenant people of Israel, and appeals addressed to those outside the faith in our modern age, though a paradigmatic approach may be justified to some degree.

In addition, these incidents should be seen as occasional rather than a regular practice. They were specific and bold moves to deal with particular, dangerous or key situations. They alone cannot be used to justify the regular or frequent use of the modern altar call, because clearly they were not systematic.

Streett makes a dubious statement when he says that, "Only those who obeyed the command of Moses and publicly stepped forward received an atonement for their sins" (Ex. 32:30).[7] If one directly relates this to the modern invitation, as Streett does, then the implication is that coming forward automatically results in salvation.

R.T. Kendall uses the Old Testament Scriptures in a different way. He prefers the term "public pledge" to "invitation" or "appeal", which seems to throw the initiative on to the listener rather than the preacher. He sees this public pledge particularly evident in the life of Abraham and his response to God, but makes no claim that he was responding to a public invitation,[8] thus here he would seem to be arguing for what, as Nettles puts it, "no one argues against."[9]

The Gospels

When Streett turns to the New Testament, he once more begins badly. In his thesis Streett says that "The most obvious example[s] of a public invitation in the New Testament" were our Lord's calling of the Apostles, specifically the ones mentioned in John chapter one.[10] That is the two disciples of John the Baptist, one of whom was Andrew (v40), to whom Jesus said, "Come, and you will see" (v39), and Philip, whom He instructed, "Follow me" (v43). There are a number of problems with Streett's stand here. First, it is not clear if these invitations were public. With regard to the two men, they had moved away from John the Baptist and were walking behind Jesus (vv35-38), and it would seem quite possible that only Jesus and the two was present when Jesus addressed them. In the case of Philip, there is not the slightest indication whether he and Jesus were alone or not (v43). Indeed, it is not even clear where and when the meeting took place. Was it before Jesus left for Galilee, on the journey, or after His arrival there?[11] These calls were quite possibly not public, and even if they were, any particular significance in the calls was probably not evident to those who witnessed them. In this setting, the terms "Come, and you will see" and "Follow me" gain their importance through hindsight.

Secondly, there is the notoriously difficult problem of determining when the Apostles were actually converted. For example, R.T. France, says that God does not tell us at what stage Peter was "born again", and he suggests that "it would be a bold man who tried to fill the gap."[12] What is said of Peter can also be said of the others. Can an invitation to the house where Jesus was staying (vv38-39) really be equated with someone going forward at a Billy Graham crusade and being "converted", even if one allows for some form of recognition of Jesus' Messiahship soon after the encounter (v41)? Surely not! What was the significance of the words "Follow me", that our Lord spoke to Philip (v43)? Did He mean "Follow me to where I am staying?" or "Follow me and give your life totally to me?" or something else? It is not clear from the text, though Leon Morris argues that the present tense of the word *akolouthei* "has continuous force", and should be seen here "in its full sense of 'follow as a disciple'."[13] The passage certainly suggests that the gospel writer, if not the original witnesses, saw the term as significant. It later became obvious that these encounters were the start of something vitally important in the lives of these men, but a twentieth century conversion, even one through an evangelistic rally, can be preceded by several crucial encounters with different people. Thus it would seem unrealistic to parallel these New Testament meetings with the modern public invitation.

Strangely, Streett does not mention the accounts of the calling of the disciples in the Synoptic Gospels, though they could be considered better examples of public calls. For example, James and John appear to have been invited to follow Jesus in the presence of their father and the family servants (Mt. 4:21-22; Mk. 1:19-20) and possibly before Peter and Andrew (Mt. 4:18-22; Mk. 1:16-20). Thompson and Whitesell do cite these calls, the latter stating that they "clearly imply a call for action."[14] But even with these callings there is still the problem that they are quite different from someone responding to a modern-day appeal, for the reasons just outlined.

Hulse makes the interesting point that Jesus did not seem to use any form of public invitation when speaking to the vast crowds to which he ministered on such occasions as the feeding of the 5000 and the 4000, and the Sermon on the Mount.[15] In addition, our Lord's dealing with the rich young man (Mk. 10:17-22) seems the very antithesis of modern evangelistic method, a point both Walter Chantry and John MacArthur make in detail.[16] It would not be unfair to state that many modern public invitation counselors would have had that man "saved" very quickly, something Jesus "failed" to do. On another occasion, Jesus deals with an inquiring scribe (Mk. 12:28-34), but again makes no attempt to bring this man to a "decision". Nor did Jesus compromise his message to retain his disciples, as is particularly evidenced when many left him after he spoke of his followers eating his flesh and drinking his blood (Jn. 6:53-60). In some cases Jesus took people away from the crowds to deal with them privately (Mk. 7:32-36; 8:22-26),[17] rather than in a highly public situation.

The Acts of the Apostles

Probably the most important biblical passages to consider in regard to this issue are to be found in the Acts of the Apostles, and relate to the evangelistic practices of the New Testament church. Is there any justification for the use of the public invitation system in those practices?

The many passages in Acts which deal with evangelism, probably fit into three main categories as far as this study is concerned:

1/ Those where there is insufficient detail to have any real idea what occurred, e.g., Paul and Silas in Thessalonica (17:2-4), Paul and Silas in Berea (17:10-12).

2/ Those where a public declaration of faith is made soon after hearing the gospel, but not, as far as is recorded, in response to a specific invitation to make such a declaration. Here are included Paul and Barnabas in Pisidian Antioch (13:42-43) and the conversion of Lydia (16:13-15).

3/ Those references which give more detail and warrant close examination and comparison with this book's definition. These all end with people being baptized.

The first two categories will be set aside as not being relevant, but three passages in the third will be closely examined.

The first of these is Acts 2:36-41. If there is any biblical incident that supports the giving of a public invitation, this is it. Indeed, R.T. Kendall says that here "Peter was doing the very same thing as the modern public pledge, or public invitation",[18] but even in this story, important detail is lacking. Peter clearly and undeniably urges his hearers to "Repent, and be baptized", thus expecting the inner response of repentance[19] and the outer response of baptism. It is also hard to deny from the tone of the passage (N.B. vv38, 40) that Peter seemed to expect an immediate response, and in the circumstances this would have been hard to keep private. If the hearers were being urged to be baptized, then they had to make their desire known to someone, and though this could have been done privately, any immediate response amidst those crowds would most likely be public.

It is, perhaps, possible that the baptism of the 3000 (v41) did not take place until the following day, or even later. Luke's writing style often gives the impression of events taking place in a shorter time frame than was probably the case.[20] Yet, even this does not nullify the likelihood of Peter's expectation of an immediate response, and prospective converts stating their desire for baptism actually on the Day of Pentecost.

Streett draws attention to the Greek word *parakaleo* (v40), and spends over three pages of his book (five in the thesis) discussing its use in the New Testament.[21] He argues that because the parts of the word mean: *para* = "to the side" and *kaleo* = "to call", that this might well indicate that "Peter actually called for his listeners to respond publicly" to the gospel.[22] He seems even more positive about this when discussing the word's use in 2 Cor. 5:20, for he states that "Paul called for the people to *come forward* and be reconciled to God."[23]

Does this word justify this kind of interpretation? *Parakaleo* is a word of numerous meanings which include: "To call for", "to call upon", "to console", "to exhort", "to persuade" and "to admonish", even "invite to come",[24] or "to call to one's side".[25] Yet, though the NT has several of these meanings, and, as O. Schmitz says it receives its "main content from the NT event of salvation",[26] there appears to be no justification for Streett's stand. Some translations for the Acts 2:40 occurrence are: "exhorted" (RSV; NRSV), "exhorting" (NASB), "pleaded" (NIV; NEB), "urged" (NJB) and "beg" (CEV), varied in wording but reasonably consistent in meaning. H.K. Moulton lists the Acts 2:40 usage in his group of meanings "to call upon", "to exhort", "to admonish", and "to persuade",[27] while Joseph Thayer includes it in the section "to admonish" and "to exhort".[28] Schmitz, significantly, says that "the sense 'to call in' fades into the background in the NT", and that the meaning "exhortation" is used "both for missionary proclamation and pastoral admonition."[29] It is therefore concluded that Streett's understanding of the word is not justified in this context. Thompson also places some emphasis upon this word, but does not go as far as Streett.[30]

But even discounting Streett's interpretation of *parakaleo*, it cannot be denied that there appears to be some expectation of an immediate, public response to Peter's preaching in Luke's account of the Day of Pentecost.

The second passage to be examined closely is Acts 8:26-40, Philip's encounter with the Ethiopian eunuch. First, it must be noted that though no specific mention is made of others accompanying the eunuch, it is highly unlikely that such an important official was traveling alone, and the statement "he ordered the chariot to stop" (v38) confirms the presence of others, thus whatever happened should be considered to have taken place in public.

Clearly Luke's account is a heavily abridged edition of the actual event. Philip told the Ethiopian "the good news about Jesus" (v35). This suggests that not only did Philip name Jesus as the answer to the man's question about the identity of the suffering servant, but he widened the scope to tell him more about the Savior, and to relate Christ's death to the Ethiopian. Howard Marshall suggests that Philip spoke to him "along the lines of Peter's sermon in Acts 2",[31] which is supported by F.F. Bruce.[32]

Though it cannot be doubted that Philip made a presentation of the gospel, and most likely included something about baptism,[33] there is not enough detail to definitely assume that Philip's teaching included instruction for an immediate response in baptism. The initiative for baptism appears to have come from the eunuch. The words of Philip in verse 37 ("If you believe with all your heart ...") certainly seem to expect a spoken response, but this verse is generally regarded as a later addition,[34] and is omitted from most modern translations.

All considered, there is no clear evidence of a gospel presentation expecting an immediate public response in this passage, though it cannot be ruled out.

The third incident in Acts that will be investigated is that which describes Peter's visit to the home of Cornelius (Acts 10:34-48). Peter preaches to the Gentile Cornelius and his household, and before he finishes God comes down in power upon these foreigners. There is no evidence in the text that at this stage Peter had invited them to do anything, nor that the listeners had done anything on their own initiative. The initiative rested with God. He acted and came down upon them in power. The similarity between this and the altar call is only at the end when Peter "ordered that they be baptized in the name of Jesus Christ" (v48). Yet the correct understanding of the Greek here is uncertain. Did Peter order the new believers, themselves, to be baptized (and in that situation one would have expected it to have been immediately or almost immediately), or did he order his companions to baptize the new believers? The former is preferred by Bruce[35] and is given in the readings of NRSV, RSV, NEB, NASB and CEV. Marshall favors the latter.[36] The NJB and NIV prefer to reflect the passage's original ambiguity. If Peter's instruction was to Cornelius and his companions, then there is some justification in seeing it as similar to, say, Finney inviting some who had been converted earlier that day indicating so publicly at the next meeting.[37] If on the other hand the command was to Peter's companions, then no such comparison can be made.

After examining the three passages it should be concluded that little can be drawn from them to support the modern usage of the public invitation system. The Ethiopian almost certainly made a public response, but there is no clear indication that Philip invited him to do so. With Cornelius and his household, God clearly acted before the listeners had a chance to do so, and it is not clear whether the new converts were actually invited to be baptized, or baptized almost by command.

The account of the Day of Pentecost is kinder to those who are looking for biblical justification for the altar call. Peter urged his listeners to "Repent and be baptized" (Acts 2:38). That baptism was expected of them obviously indicates that those who repented had to make that fact known to the Apostles, and, if the 3000 were baptized the day they were converted, they must have made their desire known that day, and that, presumably, would have been Peter's expectation.

But even this does not justify the modern invitation *system*. First, it is similar, but not the same as the methods used today. Secondly, this incident is clearly unique in Christian history,[38] and it is questionable whether one should use a one off occurrence as a basis for a system of evangelism. Interestingly, some that favor the invitation system acknowledge that there is no biblical example of a public invitation of the type defined in these pages, and rather look for biblical principles to support its use.[39]

Baptism

In the three accounts considered in Acts, the public response participated in by the converts was baptism. It is not surprising that Streett[40] and Whitesell both see baptism as the NT equivalent of "coming forward and making an open declaration of faith,"[41] whilst R.T. Kendall says that "the Public Pledge", as he terms it, "temporarily takes the place of baptism."[42] Yet, as Hulse points out, NT baptisms were not always especially public.[43] The case of Paul comes to mind; the baptized and the baptizer seem to have been the only ones present (Acts 9:17-19), whilst the Philippian jailer and his family were seemingly baptized in the presence of only each other and Paul and

Silas (Acts 17:31-34).

Summary

When all these Scriptures are considered, the use of the public invitation in exceptional circumstances can be justified, but they do not support the systematic use of the practice.

The Practical Rationale

In his *Lectures on Revivals*, Finney said that "In preaching the gospel" it is necessary to adopt "some kind of measures",[44] an argument undeniable. But in addition, he stated that "The Bible", indeed, "God" had "established no particular system of measures to be employed ... in promoting the gospel", therefore preachers were at liberty to use those which worked.[45] Though that is in some respects true, there are limits. It surely can be gleaned from Scripture that brainwashing, for instance, is contrary both to the spirit of the gospel, and the practice of the Apostles. Tricking people into "believing", a practice perhaps more common than many would care to admit, is also contrary to biblical teaching on honesty. So if no precise methods are taught in Scripture, other than the preaching of the gospel (Acts 2:14-40; 3:12-26; etc.) and sensitive counseling (Mk. 10:17-22; Acts 8:29-39), there are still limits as to what the evangelist is at liberty to do.

Specific reasons

There are a number of practical reasons given for the use of the altar call, which have changed little over the years. The major ones will be stated here, with a variety of advocates for each named, then a brief critical comment will be made where appropriate. Chapter fourteen will examine what is probably the principle reason given for the use of the public invitation, i.e., the results it produces, which at times appear to be most remarkable.

One reason given for supporting the use of the altar call is that particular individuals would not have been saved without it. F.D. Whitesell doubts that he personally would ever "have been saved", if it had not been for a minister giving a very overt appeal, to which he responded as a thirteen year old.[46] R.T. Kendall quotes the experience of Rev. Arthur Thompson, General Superintendent of the Baptist

Church in London. Arthur Thompson says that he responded to a public invitation and that "if there had not been an appeal that night, I would probably have gone home and that would have been the end of it."[47] Similar claims arise in the literature and from what one hears from time to time. Whilst it is always very hard to argue with personal experience, the difficulty with this reasoning is that no one can really be sure what one would or would not do in the future, and, indeed, this is implied by Thompson's word "probably".

Another oft quoted reason for going forward is that it is a witness to one's need of, or new-found belief in Christ. Jacob Knapp, the American Baptist evangelist of the second quarter of the nineteenth century, claimed this, as have Finney, and more recently Kendall,[48] and many more today. This is probably the weakest of all justifications of the invitation, for no one really knows the reason why any individual is going forward. Over 2700 went forward in three days at Festival '96 with Franklin Graham, but less than half of these were for "salvation" or inquiry.[49] One counselor recorded that one who went forward "was a committed Christian and did not require counseling", and another spoke of two who had come out to encourage members of their youth group. Other examples could be given.[50] Anyone who has done regular counseling in major crusades, or even at evangelistic services at a local church, knows that the reasons people come forward are varied, whatever the terms stated by the preacher, therefore responding to a public invitation is not really a witness to belief in Christ, be it actual or desired.

A third reason given is that the sight of people responding visibly to the gospel is an encouragement to the church, particularly the minister.[51] There is no doubt that this is often the case. Public responses can have a dynamic impact upon those watching, which might last for days, even weeks, though when no one responds the result can be quite deadening to the congregation both individually and collectively. Hulse also suggests that it can be very discouraging later when a check is made of "those who persevere",[52] for, as shall be seen, the "falling away" rate with this type of evangelism is very high.

Colton, Kendall, Knapp, and Whitesell all state that the sight of people going forward makes others respond to Christ.[53] It can certainly be argued that the sight of some going forward encourages others to go forward. Sometimes counselors are told to move forward immediately the appeal is given so that this might happen.[54] Indeed, the sight of dozens of counselors going forward at a major rally can make it quite easy for others to do so too; oddly, it even gives the seeker a degree of anonymity amongst the moving crowd. The desire to conform with the behavior of those around us, which is probably more common than many believe,[55] would make this "copycat" moving forward a frequent occurrence. But as going forward cannot be equated with conversion, this argument is on shaky grounds. Missionary W.T. Grenfell, however, seems to state that his conversion (not just his own public response) was triggered by a young sailor standing alone in response to a public appeal.[56]

Harkey, Kendall, Streett, and Whitesell all argue that the public invitation is a good, practical way of dealing with someone's spiritual needs while the issue is hot.[57] This point has some merit. People can be strongly convicted of their sin and powerfully convinced of their need of Christ under the work of the Holy Spirit, and personal counseling, though not by any means always necessary, can be of help to many in that situation. The public invitation does, to some degree at least, segregate those with that need. But an offer of private counseling without the need of a public response can surely do the job just as well in most circumstances. Hulse warns that the public invitation can create "an urgency not necessarily attributable to the work of the Holy Spirit" and thus press "people into a premature confession."[58] Lloyd-Jones argues similarly, stating that such appeals tend "to produce a superficial conviction of sin, if any at all",[59] so what may appear at first to be the work of the Holy Spirit might just prove to be the product of the system.

Other reasons include: though it doesn't save, it can be a blessing;[60] going forward makes it harder to backslide;[61] and the method can originate or promote a revival.[62] All three of these arguments are unconvincing, and in the case of the second the evidence usually seems to point the other way, as will be noted in chapter fourteen.

Summary

When all the arguments supporting the use of the altar call are taken collectively they still remain far from convincing, but there is one other argument for the method, which, if correct, could win the day, and thus needs detailed consideration. The main reason usually given to justify the use of the public invitation system is that it works. Finney is supposed to have responded to critics, "The results justify my methods",[63] and certainly many more have claimed that the many converted through the altar call justify its use. This will be dealt with separately in chapter fourteen.

Notes

[1]   Streett, *Effective Invitation*, 61 (62). Streett later says, *"Each* of these case studies lends biblical support to the modern-day concept of the public invitation", 62 (63) (emphasis added). "These case studies" include this parable.

[2]   Streett, *Effective Invitation*, 55-56 (56-57); Kendall and Thompson also quote these verses, but do not make the claims for them that Streett makes, Kendall, *Stand Up*, 37-38; Thompson, *Public Invitation*, 5.

[3]   Streett, *Effective Invitation*, 56-57 (57-58); Thompson, "Public Invitation", 5-6; Whitesell, *65 Ways*, 12-13.

[4]   Coleman, "Altar Call": 19.

[5]   See Hulse's comments, Hulse, *Great Invitation*, 118.

[6]   M.H. Woudstra, *The Book of Joshua* (NICOT; Grand Rapids: Eerdmans, 1981), 350-51.

[7]   Streett, *Effective Invitation*, 56 (57).

[8]   Kendall, *Stand Up*, 13, 36-41. Kendall sees it primarily as a "public confession of Christ rather than a public receiving of Christ", 73-78.

[9]   Nettles, *Grace & Glory*, 422.

[10]   Streett, "Public Invitation", 60 (the wording has been changed in Streett's book to, "Jesus publicly called to Himself...", Streett, *Effective Invitation*, 59).

[11]   Leon Morris, *The Gospel According to John* (NICNT; Grand Rapids: Eerdmans, 1971), 162; Barclay M. Newman & Eugene A. Nida, *A Translator's Handbook of the Gospel of John* (NY: UBS, 1980), 47.

[12]   R.T. France, "Conversion in the Bible", *The Evangelical Quarterly* 65: 4 (Oct. 1993): 301-2. One such "bold man" is Richard Peace, who, basing his argument on Mark's Gospel, puts a good case for the conversion of the Twelve being a gradual process that did not reach its final stage until after the death and resurrection of Jesus. Richard V. Peace, *Conversion in the New Testament: Paul and the Twelve* (Grand Rapids: Eerdmans, 1999), 12-13, 106, 216, 242. However, that argument is weakened when one takes into account the other Gospels.

[13]   Morris, *John,* 162. C.K. Barrett suggests that both meanings stated above are intended, C.K. Barrett, *The Gospel According to St. John* (London: SPCK, 1978), 180.

[14]   Thompson, "Public Invitation", 6; Whitesell, *65 Ways,* 15.

[15]   Hulse, *Great Invitation,* 112-13.

[16]   Walter Chantry, *Today's Gospel: Authentic or Synthetic?* (Edinburgh: Banner of Truth, 1970), 19-92; John F. MacArthur, Jr. *The Gospel According to Jesus* (Grand Rapids: Zondervan, 1994), 84-95.

[17]   Hulse, *Great Invitation,* 115.

[18]   Kendall, *Stand Up,* 27.

[19]   It is accepted here that repentance means changing one's direction, which could fairly be considered, at least in part, an outward act, but there first must be a change of attitude.

[20] Examples of this are his accounts of the conversion of Zacchaeus (Lk. 19:1-10), the resurrection of Jesus (Lk. 24), and, possibly, Paul's stay in Damascus (Acts 9:18b-25).

[21] Streett, *Effective Invitation*, 62-65 (63-68).

[22] Streett, *Effective Invitation*, 63 (64-65).

[23] Streett, "Public Invitation", 66 (emphasis added). This has been changed in the book to "Although Paul did the calling, it was as if God Himself gave the invitation", Streett, *Effective Invitation*, 64.

[24] H.K. Moulton, (ed.) *The Analytical Greek Lexicon Revised* (Grand Rapids: Zondervan, 1978), 303.

[25] Joseph H. Thayer, *A Greek-English Lexicon of the NT* (4th. ed. Grand Rapids: Baker, [1901] 1977), 482.

[26] Schmitz's discussion is on the two words *parakaleo* and *paraklesis*, G. Kittel and G. Friedrich, *Theological Dictionary of the NT* (abr. G.W. Bromiley, Grand Rapids: Eerdmans, 1985), 781.

[27] Moulton, *Greek Lexicon*, 303.

[28] Thayer, *Greek Lexicon*, 482.

[29] Kittel, *Dictionary of NT*, 782.

[30] Thompson, "Public Invitation", 8.

[31] I. Howard Marshall, *The Acts of the Apostles* (TNTC; Leicester: IVP, 1980), 165.

[32] F.F. Bruce, *The Acts of the Apostles* (3rd. ed. Grand Rapids: Eerdmans, 1990), 229.

[33] Bruce says that the Ethiopian may have already known something about baptism from his time in Jerusalem, Bruce, *Acts*, 229.

[34] Bruce, *Acts*, 229; Marshall, *Acts*, 165; Bruce M. Metzger, *A Textual Commentary on the Greek NT* (3rd. ed. London: UBS, 1975), 359-360.

[35] Bruce, *Acts*, 265.

[36] Marshall, *Acts*, 194-95.

[37] Finney, *Memoirs*, 161-62.

[38] Nettles, *Grace & Glory*, 421.

[39] Thompson, "Public Invitation", 4; Whitesell, *65 Ways*, 12.

[40] Streett, "Public Invitation", 80-85.

[41] Whitesell, *65 Ways*, 14-15.

[42] Kendall, *Stand Up*, 15, 45, 123.

[43] Hulse, *Great Invitation*, 112.

[44] Finney, *Lectures on Revivals*, 239.

[45] Finney, *Lectures on Revivals*, 173, 238. Finney's view is supported by, amongst others, Simeon Harkey, *Best State*, 14-15.

[46] Whitesell, *65 Ways*, 44-45.

[47] Kendall, *Stand Up*, 26.

[48] Hervey, *Manual of Revivals*, 79; Finney, *Memoirs*, 306; Kendall, *Stand Up*, 22-25, 123, 125.

[49] *Summary of Attendance and Enquirers for Festival 96 with Franklin Graham*: Brisbane (Brisbane: Festival '96 Office); Jim Rawson, telephone conversation, 28 Mar. 1996. It is true, however, that when large numbers are

moving forward it is most likely that at least a few of them are genuine converts, or soon to become such.

[50] Counselor reports for Festival '96 with Franklin Graham.

[51] Colton, *American Revivals,* 73, 94; Harkey, *Best State,* 153; Kendall, *Stand Up,* 126; McLendon, "Mourner's Bench", 90; Streett, "Public Invitation", 168-69,171-72.

[52] Hulse, *Great Invitation,* 175.

[53] Colton, *American Revivals,* 97; Kendall, *Stand Up,* 125-26; Jacob Knapp, *Autobiography of Elder Jacob Knapp* (NY: Sheldon, 1868), 215; Whitesell, *65 Ways,* 19.

[54] This instruction was given in the first counselor training classes I ever attended. This was in 1961 in London, to where a Billy Graham Crusade was being relayed from Manchester. It was also an instruction given on the Australian training video for the Billy Graham Global Mission in 1995.

[55] In his chapter entitled "Conformity", Em Griffin relates some experiments and gives other examples showing how frequently, and remarkably, people conform to group example and pressure in certain circumstances, even to the extent of going against sound judgment, see Em Griffin, *The Mind Changers* (Wheaton: Tyndale, 1976), 193-212.

[56] Kerr & Mulder, *Conversions,* 166.

[57] Harkey, *Best State,* 153; Kendall, *Stand Up,* 124-25; Streett, *Effective Invitation,* 143 (163-64); Whitesell, *65 Ways,* 16-18.

[58] Hulse, *Great Invitation,* 173.

[59] Lloyd-Jones, *Preaching,* 275.

[60] McLendon, "Mourner's Bench", 81.

[61] Streett, "Public Invitation", 167-68.

[62] Colton, *American Revivals,* 98 (Colton believed in two types of revival: that brought in solely by God and that brought about by a combination of God and human measures, see Colton, 2-9. The latter is meant here).

[63] Franks, *Conquerors,* 23.

Chapter 12

Counseling and Follow Up

This chapter will primarily examine the counseling techniques usually associated with the altar call, and follow up only very briefly. It will commence by examining the counseling manual published by the Southern Baptists of the USA, and then look at a similar training technique in action.

The Southern Baptist Counseling Manual

As was noted in chapter ten, the altar call is widely used among the Southern Baptist churches in America. It is, therefore, useful to examine the *Commitment Counseling Manual* (*CCM*) produced by the Southern Baptist Convention (SBC),[1] particularly as American materials and methods, not infrequently with SBC origins or influence, are used to train counselors not only in America but also in other countries.[2]

The subtitle of the *CCM* gives us a clue to its approach: *A Strategy for Decision Counseling*. Its whole rationale is to bring people to one spiritual decision or another, and so conversion is seen in this booklet as primarily a human decision.

The manual recommends a five stage counseling procedure. First come the formalities: i.e., introductions and recording the inquirer's name and address on a *Personal Commitment Card*.[3] Secondly, the counselor is urged to *"Discern the person's decision"*, yet to "Deal with each person as though he or she were coming for salvation until otherwise indicated". This allows for the fact that some that come forward may not be able to express their situation adequately.[4] Counselors are urged in CCM not to "'lead' or manipulate the counselee into a decision he or she is not ready to make." It is sad that this wise piece of advice is not always stressed or even given in counselor training,[5] and some counselors do not always mix zeal with wisdom. (One recent incident drawn to my attention concerned a woman who signed the commitment page in the counseling booklet *Steps to Peace with God* just to keep her rather persistent counselor "happy", rather than for any reasons of religious concern or experience.)[6]

Once the reason for the counselee's coming forward is determined the next (third) step is to use the *Personal Commitment Guide (PCG)*, a counseling booklet with a wider scope than most similar booklets. That is, it includes outlines for counseling in areas such as "Assurance", "Baptism", "Rededication", and "Commitment to Church Vocation", in addition to "Salvation".[7]

Fourthly, the remainder of the *Personal Commitment Card* is filled in, that is, recording the nature of that individual's decision. The filling in of this card is done primarily that "follow up", the fifth stage, might be carried out.

In one portion of the *CCM* the *PCG* appears on the right hand pages, with, on the left hand pages opposite, instructions for its use.[8] The "Salvation" section of the guide is divided into several parts: "God's purpose" ("God loves us and has a purpose for our lives"); "Our need" ("our sinful nature keeps us from fulfilling" that purpose); God's provision" (the life, death and resurrection of Jesus); "Our response" ("receive", "repent", and "place our faith in Jesus"); and "Commitment" ("to confess Jesus publicly and follow Him in baptism and church membership"). This is then followed by two prayers. The first, a "Prayer of Commitment", runs (in its entirety):

> Dear Lord Jesus ... I believe You are the Son of God ... and died to forgive me of my sins ... I know I have sinned ... I ask You to forgive me ... I turn from my sins and I receive You as my Lord and Savior ... Thank You for saving me. Amen.

The second, "My Commitment", is a prayer of thanks to God and a commitment to follow him always. Thus the guide seems to assume that the praying of the first prayer will automatically bring salvation.

Counselor Training

As was seen previously, in March 1995 Billy Graham conducted a campaign in Puerto Rico, which was beamed via satellite to about 1700 venues around the world.[9] The counselor training for this in Australia was done in four sessions, using a video hosted by Kel Richards and the *Christian Life and Witness Course Training Manual,*[10] and led by a local minister. The training focused on the use of the *2 Ways to Live (2WTL)*[11] counseling tract and method. An integral part of this involves the counselor drawing a number of simple diagrams, pictured in the booklet, to illustrate six points:

1/ "God is the loving ruler of the world. He made the world ..."
2/ "We all reject the ruler - God - by trying to run life our own way without him ..."
3/ "God won't let us rebel forever. God's punishment for rebellion is death and judgment."
4/ "Because of his love, God sent his son into the world: the man Jesus Christ ... by dying in our place he took our punishment and brought forgiveness."
5/ "God raised Jesus to life again ..."
6/ Here was presented a choice of "2 ways to live": "Reject the Ruler - God ..." or "Submit to Jesus as our ruler ..."

Each section included an appropriate Scripture passage. The booklet concluded with: "What must I do?" To which the threefold answer was: "Pray ... Submit to Jesus ... Rely on Jesus ..." Then followed a prayer, similar to the one in *PCG*, for those wishing to respond to Christ.

Broadly speaking, this booklet takes the same counseling approach as many other such booklets, including *PCG*, but its primary difference from most of the others was that it was not intended that the counselor use the booklet in the presence of the inquirer. Rather it was preferred that during the counseling session the counselor just use the method outlined in it from memory, drawing the diagrams on paper to illustrate the points. Whilst acknowledging that drawings can assist people in understanding abstract concepts, this would seem to be a rather dubious method, in that most people do not draw well, nor usually use such a method when explaining other concepts to people. I gave the method a number of trial runs and found that I was concentrating more on getting the method right, than on genuinely presenting the gospel, though it must be admitted that greater familiarity with that presentation would have lessened, though almost certainly not eliminated, that difficulty. Previously drawn diagrams would seem to be a better option. Leading

194   *The Altar Call*

from that was another problem, in that too much time was spent in the sessions on getting the method right, including the drawing, and insufficient time spent on explaining such things as the theology of conversion, problems that might be encountered, and troubleshooting.

Other counseling booklets include *Steps to Peace with God, Four Spiritual Laws*, and *Guide to Life*,[12] which are very similar to each other and are used both in personal evangelism and in public invitation evangelism. The approach of all these is similar to *2WTL*, though with some differences. All make use of diagrams. The theology behind them is very similar; the three booklets just mentioned, for example, all start with some form of the concept that God has a plan for each individual's life, which we noted was also the way *PCG* started. Whilst *2WTL* does not have this clearly stated, it does seem implicit in its early pages. They all have a strong emphasis on the human role in the conversion process, teaching that one must "receive" Christ,[13] and all contain commitment prayers similar to *PCG*. The *My Commitment* booklet used at Festival '96 also adopts this general approach. One danger with booklets of this type is that, unless they are used with great care, they lead to a mechanical kind of counseling. Indeed, they are probably produced with that in mind, for it is easier to train people in that approach. This counseling often, perhaps most often, fails to adequately establish the precise spiritual condition of the counselee. People do not just fit neatly into "decision" categories - the experiences, needs and spiritual condition of each are unique. This method tends to treat all inquirers in the same, or at least very similar, manner. It also usually presents vital matters inadequately, in particular the nature of God, sin, salvation, and repentance.

Even though Kel Richards in the Global Mission training video insisted that counselors should make sure that inquirers have clearly understood the *2WTL* presentation, one has to ask does the basic presentation go anything like far enough for an inquirer who is, say, completely new to biblical and Christian concepts? Though the key issues are generally explained in the booklets, the presentation is very brief, resulting in the character of God being displayed very narrowly, the problem of sin very lightly, and becoming a Christian appears as a simple human decision. Such a presentation might be adequate for those reared on the Bible and with a reasonable knowledge of its teaching, but does it go far enough for those to whom the Christian message is completely new, or nearly so, even allowing for a clear presentation of the gospel from the pulpit? If counseling such as this is expected to be done in fifteen minutes, as in Festival '96,[14] the problems are further compounded.

Watching two trial "counseling sessions" on the Global Mission video,[15] it seemed so logical for the counselee to decide for Christ, i.e., the way of life that presented the best options. It all seemed so sensible that one could not help but feel that no one in their right mind would say no to the gospel. Yet, isn't Christ crucified "a stumbling block to Jews and foolishness to Gentiles" (1Cor. 1:22)? Surely Christian conversion is more than just choosing a lifestyle?

A further problem with the method taught in the video was that it encouraged counselors to teach assurance of salvation to those who had only just made a "decision",[16] and this has been the usual practice in all similar programs that I have attended both in Australia and England. (Whitesell also clearly advocates making sure that the counselees have "assurance of salvation" before they leave the counseling session.)[17] John MacArthur relates that in some evangelism training seminars he has attended it has even been stated that for anyone to have doubt about their salvation is satanic, therefore assurance must be stressed.[18] This surely is both presumptuous and dangerous. Determining that another person has become a Christian is not something that can be done quickly (and can probably never be done with certainty), and evidence of a changed life is needed before this should be done. If a counselor declares an individual "saved", when unbeknown to the counselor the "convert" is as far from God as he or she ever was before, the "convert" is being led into a fool's paradise, and the door could be closed to any future response to Christ. How can anyone know for sure that God has really been working in that person's life? Just because someone has come forward does not mean that God has been touching that person. Some just go forward out of curiosity. Can counselors be sure that such "converts" really understand the gospel they supposedly have embraced? Were their prayers for salvation genuine responses to the Holy Spirit's workings, or just intended as a method of accepting the way of life with better prospects?

This problem is further highlighted by the fact that in the fourth session of the video Philip Jensen mentions that the first two studies in the follow up material major on assurance. This is because it is acknowledged that some who have come through the system to the point of follow up may not be converted, and these two studies are deemed a good way of establishing that. According to that video, the Billy Graham organization believes that 2% of converts through its campaigns become Christians during the sermon, 48% in a counseling session and 50% during follow up,[19] which itself is an argument against teaching assurance prematurely.

All this presents a stark contrast with the counseling methods of

Edwards, Wesley and Whitefield, detailed in chapter one. They saw their role as presenting the gospel clearly and powerfully, whether it was in pulpit, field or counseling room, but they were then quite prepared to withdraw to let God do his work. None of them used the modern practice of pressing an inquirer into making a "decision".

The Selection of Counselors

In the eighteenth century and before, there was usually reluctance about letting the laity counsel inquirers, and that task was normally the province of the clergy.[20] It had become more common for the laity to do such counseling in the nineteenth century, perhaps, partly under the influence of the camp-meetings, where lay exhorters were common.[21] It would seem to have been Moody at the end of that century who set the seal on the laity's widespread use in this specific ministry with his Chicago (Moody) Bible Institute, which was founded primarily to train lay people for this purpose.[22] Whilst the greater use of the laity is to be applauded, it is not without its problems. In our desire to use lay people there is, perhaps, today too great a tendency to use those with a limited understanding of the doctrine of conversion and the various problems likely to be encountered in such ministry.[23] The efforts of such people may well do more harm than good.

We do well to note a comment of an American minister Charles McIlvaine in 1832. He said, "Let care be used as to who shall be put to the work of conversing with inquirers."[24] Are we in today's evangelical churches being careful enough?

Follow Up

As previously indicated, follow up will only be examined briefly. Colin Marshall defines follow up as, "A one to one meeting with a new Christian to establish them in Christ."[25] It is probably true to say that it is, in the strictest sense, a recent innovation. True the early Methodist class meetings provided a form of teaching and support for new converts (and even those still seeking), but it was not usually the one on one, post-counseling teaching defined above. In the mid-nineteenth century, James Caughey, for example, could speak of 40 new converts after one of his meetings having their names and addresses "carefully recorded", so that they might all receive a ticket to admit them to a class.[26]

Perhaps oddly, before the introduction of the invitation system, much of what we call follow up was done prior to conversion in what has traditionally been called catechizing. It is interesting to note that J.W. Nevin who strongly opposed the altar call, firmly advocated catechizing as its alternative.[27]

Towards the end of the nineteenth century, evangelists such as Moody, A.B.Earle, E.P. Hammand and B.F. Mills were all having their inquirers fill in decision cards. In some cases these cards, or a portion of them, were given to the inquirer, while a record was kept for follow up purposes; in other cases the cards were just kept by the counselors and passed on to local ministers.[28] In the next century, Billy Sunday was another that used decision cards, which were handed over to the appropriate local ministers.[29] Follow up has been common with altar call mass evangelism since that time.

The use of follow up by the Billy Graham organization has been most notable. In 1948 Billy Graham and his associates held a mission in Modesto, California, during which they drew up what became known as the Modesto Manifesto. The fourth and final point of this was the "Systematic follow-up of new believers".[30] Since then the Graham organization has always made preparations for follow up to be carried out by local churches.

The follow up material used at the Australian end of the Global Mission was a series of seven Bible studies, entitled, *Just for Starters*.[31] Significantly, Philip Jensen, the author, stated that the first two studies were specifically intended to highlight the issue of assurance, because it was quite common for the inquirer still not to be converted at the commencement of follow up (a point which has already been noted in this chapter), and the matter in those two studies was developed so that the candidate's spiritual condition might be clearly determined. The seven studies deal with: salvation, faith, Christian living, the Bible, prayer, the church, and how to relate to those outside the faith.

As Festival '96 was supported by a wide range of denominations, including the Roman Catholic Church, two basic follow up methods were used. The official Festival '96 follow up material (produced by the Billy Graham Evangelistic Association) was used by the Catholics (along with some of their own material) and the Anglo-Catholics. Other churches used *Christianity Explained*, which had been already widely used in Australian churches, many people having previously been trained in its use.[32] An individual's follow up was generally to be conducted by the counselor who conducted the interview, though the help of local churches was also enlisted. An examination of the counselor reports just a little over three weeks after the festival indicated that many counselors had made further contact with the person(s) they had counseled, either by a visit, letter or phone call. The responses of those contacted varied considerably from very cooperative to "not interested".[33]

It has often been said that the reason many people fall away after crusades is because of bad follow up. Yet, is this the real reason? Erroll Hulse says that of the 26 people he and his wife counseled at the Billy Graham meetings at Wembley in 1955 "not one came to anything".[34] In personal correspondence, Hulse elaborated that "there was no conviction of sin and no idea of the meaning of the gospel in any that we counselled" at those meetings.[35] Whilst not denying for one moment the great importance of adequate follow up, when one encounters claims like that, one must ask whether lack of, or poor, follow up is the real reason that many fall away? Or is it something more basic than that: the method of evangelism?

Summary

Counseling for altar call evangelism usually uses various but similar counseling booklets, which teach a decision-type conversion process, the culmination of which is the inquirer praying a prayer to receive Christ. However, if becoming a Christian cannot be biblically defined as simply making a decision, nor even primarily so, then this method is faulty at its root. Though the method is fairly simple to use, it does not seem to go far enough in establishing an individual's spiritual condition, nor does it teach adequately the doctrines of the nature of God, sin and salvation, particularly in the case of those unfamiliar with biblical concepts. Most counselors nowadays are trained lay people, yet some of them seem to have limited understanding of essential doctrine and knowledge of the problems likely to be faced in counseling. The practice of following up those who made decisions in mass evangelism was developed during the last sixty years of the nineteenth century, and now is a common.

Notes

[1] *Commitment Counseling Manual: A Strategy for Decision Counseling* (Nashville: SBC, 1985).

[2] I have been trained in evangelistic counseling techniques in both England and Australia usually using American materials or books and booklets adapted from American ones. Also the material used for Festival '96 was produced by the Billy Graham Evangelistic Association.

[3] Printed in *CCM*, 13.

[4] *CCM*, 14-15.

[5] It did not, as far as I can recall, feature in a counseling course for a local church-based mission in Brisbane I attended, but in the second session on the *Christian Life and Witness Course: The Time is Now Video*, (St. Matthias Press & Billy Graham Evangelistic Assoc., 1995), used for training counselors for the Billy Graham Global Mission, counselors were urged not to "trick, bully or coerce" inquirers.

[6] Raymond Bickerstaff (a Brisbane Christian layman), personal conversation, 10 Apl. 1997.

[7] *Personal Commitment Guide* (Atlanta: Home Mission Board SBC, 1985).

[8] *CCM*, 19-33.

[9] *Global Mission with Billy Graham Newsletter* 3; *New Life* 57: 37 (9 Mar. 1995).

[10] The *Time is Now Video*; *Christian Life and Witness Course Training Manual* (Kingsford: St Matthias, 1994). This is a different book from the one of similar name used in Festival '96. I attended the counselor training classes for this "Global Mission" held at a Uniting Church in Brisbane. I had a second look at the video privately at a later date.

[11] Philip Jensen, *2 Ways to Live* (Sydney: AIO, 1989).

[12] *Steps to Peace With God* (Minneapolis: Billy Graham Evangelistic Association); *Four Spiritual Laws* (Campus Crusade for Christ, 1965); *Guide to Life* (Australian Baptist Publishing House, 1973).

[13] *2WTL* lacks the idea of receiving Christ, but the others have it, and *Four Spiritual Laws* and *Steps to Peace with God* emphasize it.

[14] Jim Rawson, conversation, 10 Apl. 1996.

[15] *Time is Now Video*, sessions three and four.

[16] This was clearly stated by Colin Marshall, *Time is Now Video*, session four.

[17] Whitesell, *65 Ways*, 46.

[18] MacArthur, Jr. *Gospel*, 29.

[19] *Time is Now Video*, session four.

[20] In times of revival it was not uncommon for the clergy to spend many hours in this pursuit. George Whitefield recorded that on one day he counseled inquirers from 7 a.m. to midnight, Whitefield, *Journals*, 84-85.

[21] Conkin, *Cane Ridge*, 94-95.

[22] Pollock, *Moody*, 226-232. This is probably an example of the Brethren's influence on Moody.

[23] Some of the clergy may also be lacking in these areas.

[24] Letter from Charles P. McIlvaine (6 Apl.1832) in Sprague, *Lectures on Revivals*, 94.

[25] *Time is Now Video*, session four.

[26] Caughey, *Earnest Christianity*, 106.

[27] Nevin, *Anxious Bench*, 110-133.

[28] Daniels, *Moody*, 257; Streett, *Effective Invitation*, 97-98 (107-8); Thompson, "Public Invitation", 122-23.

[29] Thompson, "Public Invitation", 153.
[30] Mavor, "Light Grew Dim", 15.
[31] Phillip Jensen, *Just for Starters* (Kingsford: St Matthias, 1992).
[32] Jim Rawson, conversations, 10 Apl. 1996, 13 July 2000.
[33] Counselor reports for Festival '96 with Franklin Graham.
[34] Hulse, *Great Invitation*, 10.
[35] Letter from Erroll Hulse, 17 May 1994.

Chapter 13

Christian Conversion[1]

Introduction

Is Christian conversion mainly about human persuasion and decision, or is it primarily about the movement of the Spirit of God in an individual's life? The answer to this question will go a long way in determining one's evangelistic method. This chapter will investigate the nature of Christian conversion, focusing primarily on whether conversion can be biblically and theologically thought of mainly as a human decision, and in doing so note the tension between the sovereignty of God and human responsibility.

Probably the term most commonly used to describe a conversion in evangelical churches today, particularly in casual conversation, is the expression he or she "made a decision" (or variations). "Made a commitment" is a similar and commonly used phrase to describe it. Christian publications frequently use these terms or their variants.[2] Also, the concept is commonly portrayed in public invitations given by preachers. For example, the word "choice" (or variations) appeared frequently in Franklin Graham's appeal on 16 March at Festival '96.[3] In addition, as has already been seen, the materials used in public invitation counseling seem to assume that conversion is mainly a human decision. Few evangelicals, if any, would view it purely as a human decision, and it would generally be regarded that God is involved in the process in some way or ways. But one could be excused for believing that many evangelicals see Christian conversion primarily as a human decision, that is a simple decision of the human will, at least, if the popular terminology is anything to go by.

As Martyn Lloyd-Jones said, "There has been so much emphasis upon 'decision', 'receiving', 'yielding', 'being willing', and 'giving ourselves' that salvation is regarded almost exclusively in terms of" human activity. Yet "the emphasis in Scripture is always on the other side, the God-ward side."[4] R.T. France says that the New Testament writers would have been "horrified" at the idea that conversion was "simply a matter of human decision and persuasion."[5]

Without doubt the influence of Finney is to be seen in this modern concept of conversion by decision. R.E. Davies says that Finney's methods, both in his time and since, have produced "great numbers of temporary converts". He sees evangelistic methods descended from Finney's views and practices as producing "a method of evangelistic persuasion which is basically calculated to convince people *against their will* to accept Christ", with a resulting frequent falling away.[6] Though this certainly cannot be said to be true in every case, nor even, perhaps, in the majority, the system often seems to lead to this situation.

In addition, many modern evangelists and evangelistic publications undervalue repentance. Confession is often emphasized it is true, but repentance is much more than that. It is a turning right around. An example of this lack of stress on repentance is the multi-million-selling *Four Spiritual Laws*, which barely contains the concept and certainly does not emphasize it. Also it is common to reject the quite appropriate place of emotion in conversion. Modern evangelists often stress that one should not trust one's feelings, emphasizing that the Bible says we are saved because we have "believed", and even if we do not "feel" saved that does not matter. Once more *Four Spiritual Laws* is an example of this. It has a page headed, "Do Not Depend Upon Feelings", which states: "the promise of God's Word, not our feelings, is our authority".[7] It was noted earlier that these tendencies might go back to the teaching of some Brethren teachers and evangelists.

Conversions in the New Testament

To try to establish the nature of Christian conversion the pages of the New Testament will first be examined. As has already been suggested in chapter eleven, determining when the Twelve Apostles were actually converted is not an easy matter, and using them as models for Christian conversion has its limitations. Richard Peace argues, using the Gospel of Mark as his basis, that one can trace the conversion of the Twelve as a process throughout that Gospel. He says that their conversion has the same core characteristics as that of Paul ("insight", "turning" and "change"), but over a different, longer time frame.[8] But, whilst recognizing that their conversion was either a lengthy process or was sudden but preceded by a process of some duration, it is still difficult to determine when they were actually converted, particularly when one considers the other Gospels, which do not record the steps in the same order as Mark. John's first chapter, for example, gives some of the disciples a much earlier awareness of whom Jesus was than does Mark.

Furthermore, if one looks at the stories of such as Zacchaeus (Lk. 19:1-10) crucial detail is lacking, which also makes them hard to use as examples. With Zacchaeus, what happened between verses seven and eight? We simply just do not know. So in this section instead of looking at the Gospels, attention will be paid to various conversions in Acts, where sufficient detail is available to give us clues as to their nature, recognizing that no one of Luke's accounts necessarily gives us all the components of a specific Christian conversion. Those passages looked at in chapter eleven, with one exception, will also be omitted.

First, Paul's conversion (Acts 9:1-19; 22:4-21; 26:9-23) will be investigated. This conversion should be considered an excellent example for, as Michael Green points out, though Paul's conversion is often considered exceptional, the fact that Luke records it three times suggests that apart from its "external trappings" it was considered "normative for all Christians everywhere".[9] Saul was on a mission to Damascus to round up any he found "who belonged to the Way". He may have had some doubts about his mission at this stage, and he may have been influenced by the noble death of Stephen a little while before, as has often been suggested (Acts 22:20 may be a hint of that). But his "breathing out murderous threats against the Lord's disciples" (Acts 9:1) does suggest he was very focused on the persecution of Christians. Suddenly, he has an encounter with the resurrected Christ, and his life is completely turned around. From the data Luke provides Paul's conversion is portrayed as something that happened to him; there is not a hint of Paul making a decision to change. True, Paul says that he "was not disobedient to the vision from heaven" (26:19), which suggests some form of decision, but this seems to have more to do with post-conversion action. Indeed, Ananias had a vision, which he relayed to Paul, indicating that Paul had been "chosen" by God to have that specific conversion experience (22:14) and to fulfill a certain ministry (9:15-16; 22:15), which loudly proclaims a divine initiative in his conversion. Yet, no doubt, Paul's "mind", "conscience", "emotions" and "will" were all involved in the experience.[10] This is evidenced by his conversation with the risen Christ.

As mentioned above, Peace sees three elements in Paul's conversion that are to be considered normative: "seeing" (insight), "turning" from evil to the way of God, and "transformation", and these are, indeed, evident in Paul's life and words. In addition, Peace asserts that the phrase "pleased to reveal his son *in* me" (Gal. 1:15-16) indicates that "it was not just Paul's mind that was touched but his whole being at its depth",[11] and this certainly seems to have been Paul's experience. A genuine Christian conversion touches the whole person.

The conversion of the 3000 on the day of Pentecost also speaks of the emotional component in conversion. At the end of Peter's address the listeners "were cut to the heart", and cried out in desperation, "Brothers, what shall we do?" (2:37). From the human perspective these conversions were not just a matter of the intellect, they also involved the emotions.

If Acts 13 does speak of the conversion of Sergius Paulus, and presumably "he believed" in verse 12 means that, then clearly his conversion resulted, at least in part, from a reasoning process (Paul's God is stronger than the magic of Elymas, therefore worthy of attention) and thus, presumably, at least an element of decision would be involved.[12]

Acts 13:48 tells us that "all" of the Gentiles of Pisidian Antioch "who were appointed for eternal life believed". This suggests that conversion is primarily an act outside human endeavor, though resulting from the proclamation of the Word for that response came through the preaching of Paul and Barnabas.

In the case of Lydia (16:13-15) we are told that "The Lord opened her heart ("mind" - Howard Marshall)[13] to respond to Paul's message." This, with its subsequent result (the baptism of Lydia and her household), does indicate a human response, which no doubt did include some form of a decision, but this is clearly preceded by a positive divine operation upon the heart. It was not just the Holy Spirit *persuading* hearers to believe they were sinners and to believe in Christ, *a la* Finney, God seems to have actually made it possible for Lydia to respond positively.

In Thessalonica, some of Paul's hearers were persuaded to join the Christian way, at least in part, it would seem, by Paul's arguments (17:1-4), and in Berea conversions resulted from a dual process of hearing the message and examining the Scriptures (17:10-12). Both of these instances indicate that the conversions resulted from a reasoning process, culminating presumably in some form of a decision.

In Corinth Paul argued and tried "to persuade" his hearers of the truths of the gospel from the Old Testament Scriptures (18:1-4) and many believed (18:8). In the closing chapter of Acts, Paul tries "to convince" his hearers "about Jesus" through a detailed exposition of the law and the prophets, and whilst some "would not believe" others were "convinced" (28: 23-24). "Convinced" here is in opposition to "would not believe" so presumably equals believe.

Though these accounts are not very detailed, taken collectively the indications are that though a human reasoning process resulting in some form of decision is a part of conversion, human activity is useless without the prior action of the Holy Spirit on a specific individual. The emotions are also involved in the process.

A Theological Perspective

Conversion as Decision

The concept of conversion as primarily decision would seem to be a fairly recent phenomenon, probably emerging at the end of the eighteenth and the beginning of the nineteenth centuries. No example of the specific terms "decision" or "decide" in a conversion context has been discovered in the course of this study prior to 1832, when Calvin Colton described conversion as "a plain, common sense, practical business, intelligible to all. It is a decision in mind and heart..."[14] in the 1840s James Caughey urged his listeners to "Decide now",[15] and J.W. Nevin criticized preachers using the terms "decision" and "decision acts" in this context, which to him spoke of decisions "that decided nothing".[16]

A form of the concept, however, if not the term, appear earlier in a hymn by Philip Doddridge (died 1751), which commences:

> O happy day, that fixed my choice
> on Thee, my Saviour and my God![17]

That this refers to a conversion experience cannot be doubted because he goes on in verse two to speak of his vows being sealed, and in verse three he states:

> 'Tis done, the great transaction's done!
> I am my Lord's, and He is mine.

Yet later in that verse Doddridge seems to state that this "choice" is dependent on being drawn by Christ.

Sin and the Human Will

It is true to say that in the centuries from the Reformation to the beginning of the nineteenth century, most Protestant teachers saw sin as having a much more powerful hold over humanity than is commonly taught today. This was seen in chapter five, where various theological changes were examined, and it certainly was the view held by Edwards, John Wesley and Whitefield. A man or woman could not simply "decide for Christ" because the power of sin had placed restrictions upon the individual's free will. Sinful human beings were incapable of making such a decision.

There are a number of passages of Scripture that emphasize this hold that sin has over humanity. Just a few of these will now be examined. The issue of original sin as such will not be looked at here, but it is here accepted that the traditional view or something close to it lies behind the problem of sin. [18]

When Jesus was addressing some Jews, he made the shocking statement that "everyone who sins is a slave to sin",[19] and then He contrasted that slavery with sonship, and, significantly for our purposes, freedom. He then goes on to state that it is only the Son, Jesus, who can make anyone really "free" (Jn. 8:34-60). The idea seems to be that humanity cannot naturally move from the slavery of sin to the freedom of sonship; Jesus the Son is the only one who can free us. This concept is also found in Rom. 6:6-11, 19; and Gal. 4:1-7, with slight variations of thought.

In addition, the Apostle Paul tells us that people are naturally blind to the gospel, for "the God of this world has blinded the minds of the unbelievers" (2 Cor. 4:4). It does not matter how well, how clearly, how persuasively the gospel is presented, no one is capable of "seeing" it unaided by the Spirit of God, for it is God who has shone in the hearts of Christians "to give us the light of the knowledge of the glory of God ..." (2 Cor. 4:6).

Finally, Paul states that naturally human beings are "dead" in their "transgressions and sins in which" they once lived (Eph. 2:1-2, 5), and can only be made "alive" by the grace of God (Eph. 2:5-10). As Bruce emphasizes, this condition of spiritual death is caused by "trespasses and sins".[20] A similar idea can be found in Jn. 5:19-24. Deliberately or otherwise, both passages echo the Genesis account of the Fall (Gen. 2:17; 3:1-19).

Slavery, blindness, and particularly death are powerful metaphors describing humanity's natural, sinful condition, and when linked with the solutions that only God can free, give light, and make alive, present powerful arguments in favor of our inability to believe the gospel without the Holy Spirit's direct action.

These and other such arguments have been commonly used to indicate human inability to believe the gospel. Martin Luther, for example, when considering the verse "The Spirit gives life. The flesh profits nothing" (Jn. 6:63), from the perspective of what human beings could contribute to their regeneration, stated that "that 'nothing' is not a 'little something'",[21] clearly indicating his position. Even Arminius could state that:

> the free will of man towards the true good is not only wounded, maimed, infirm, bent, and weakened, but is also imprisoned, destroyed and lost ... it has no powers whatever except such as are excited by divine grace.[22]

We have also seen that John Wesley, another arminian, also held this view, thus this is not necessarily an argument between calvinists and arminians, for traditionally both parties were in broad agreement on this issue. However, it does need to be noted that many modern arminians would not agree with Arminius and Wesley on this issue.[23]

The Pietists, whose influence was considerable, considered that sin made it impossible for one to believe in Christ without divine aid, indeed, as natural birth was a "passive act", so was the new birth, with the newborn incapable of conceiving or birthing themselves, for these things were the work of God.[24] To John Wesley, one of those influenced by Pietism, human beings had no "natural power to choose anything that is truly good" because of the Fall,[25] for "sin is mightier than" human beings.[26] Thus, to him, it is certain that we could not naturally choose Christ. Yet though "every man has a measure of free will restored to him" it is only by God's grace.[27] Indeed, "the very first motion of good is from above, as well as the power which conducts it to the end".[28]

To Martyn Lloyd-Jones "The amazing thing is not that most people do not believe; what is astounding is that anyone believes. For we all born natural men at 'enmity against God'",[29] entrapped by sin, which is "the greatest power next to God Himself."[30] We are "incapable" of believing and being saved without the direct intervention of God.[31] Others describe humanity as being naturally "in bondage to sin", with both will and reason "captive to his flesh",[32] and, because of the power of sin, having no natural ability "to know, please or seek after the true God."[33] Donald Westblade says that according to Romans 7, "Apart from God" sin so reigns in our lives that "its effect is to leave us no more able to choose what is good than a corpse can."[34]

Regeneration

If salvation is by grace alone, and represents no merit in the one to whom it is granted, then the first move in the regeneration of any individual must be by God. For if the first move is by the human being then grace ceases to be grace, for God would then be responding to something worthy in the sinner. John Calvin expressed it this way: "For any mixture of the power of free will that men strive to mingle with God's grace is nothing but the corruption of grace".[35]

Nettles emphasizes that "God's quickening power comes upon the sinner *while* he is dead."[36] Even the faith that saves is a gift of that grace. Wesley believed that Eph. 2: 4-10 indicated that not only was salvation the result of God's grace, but the faith that led to it too.[37] To John Piper this "Faith is so radical it cannot be self-generated," indeed, it is rather "the evidence that we have" already been born of God, for "We do not make ourselves born again by deciding to believe."[38] If that is the case, faith must be dependent upon the prior regenerating influence of the Spirit of God.

This saving faith is also much more than an intellectual assent to basic Christian truths, necessary though that is. As James reminds us even the demons believe basic Christian doctrine, but it does them no good, indeed, they "shudder" (Jam. 2:19). For faith in Christ also means a personal knowledge of him and his Father, a relationship with God the Son and God the Father, not just a knowledge about certain facts. As Jesus said in his great prayer just before his arrest, "Now this is eternal life, that they may know you, the only true God, and Jesus Christ whom you have sent" (Jn. 17:3).

Repentance should also be seen as a result of this grace, not something we simply decide to do. Indeed, it is "tails" to the "heads" of faith on the coin of salvation. The two though different are inseparably linked. As Charles Hodge put it, "Repentance (which 'is a turning from sin unto God') is the act of a believer; and faith is the act of a penitent. So that whoever believes repents; and whoever repents believes."[39]

Yet, no one is ever "saved against his will", for the Spirit enlightens and persuades "so that we desire the things of God. He puts a new principle, a new disposition into us, and then we desire these things."[40] Our minds, our wills and our emotions are very much involved in the process. With regard to our feelings, a dramatic change in them is certainly not to be regarded as a sure sign of conversion. But our feelings do have a legitimate place in the experience, because God's

Spirit converts our entire being, and such emotions as joy, peace and relief may well play a significant part in what happens. What is to be avoided in evangelism is emotionalism, not the genuine touching of the heart through the mind.

The encounter between Jesus and Nicodemus (Jn. 3:1-10) resulted in the declaration that for one to "see the kingdom of God" one must be *gennethe anothen*, "born from above" or "born again".[41] Now, does this idea (indeed, ideas) convey just the concept of making a new start with some help from God, or is something more radical intended? In normal human birth the child has no say in being born, so does this mean that human beings have absolutely no input into their "new birth", or is this reading too much into our Lord's parallel of the two births?

John mentions this concept of the new birth in other places, and does throw some light upon these questions. In John 1:12-13 he states that "children" resulting from such a birth are born "not of natural descent, nor of human decision or a husband's will, but born of God." And in his first letter John speaks of the "children of God" (3:1) and "everyone who loves" (4:7) as actually being "born of God" (3:9; 4:7). In these verses the emphasis is upon God's action in this birth. This also seem to be the emphasis in other Scriptures which mention this concept, such as Titus 3:5; Jam. 1:18; 1Pet. 1:3-5, 23. It is a new start, but it is so much more than that. It is a radical new beginning, commenced and empowered by the Spirit of God.

Leon Morris sees the words of Jesus to Nicodemus as speaking of a "rebirth brought about by the very Spirit of God." For "Entry into the kingdom is not by way of human striving, but by that re-birth which only God can effect."[42] Peter Toon says that,

> There is no question here of Jesus' telling people that they must go ahead and do something in their own power and by their own volition. Rather the opposite is being stated: there is no way other than rebirth from heaven through the direct action of the Holy Spirit.[43]

He also says that in John 1:12 God is "being presented as the sole cause of the origin of life".[44] As there is every likelihood that the meaning of *gennao* in these contexts is "begotten" rather than "born",[45] this even more strongly places the initiative with God.

With that in mind, it is strange that Billy Graham could write a book entitled *How to be Born Again*, which even in its title implies that the new birth is dependent upon its potential human subject.[46] It is probably not unfair to say that Graham's view represents the majority understanding of regeneration today amongst evangelists and other evangelical preachers. Yet, Christ's words, "You must be born again", though highlighting a necessity, were not a command.[47] We cannot be born again of our own volition.

Ian Hawley says that many of the NT words that relate to conversion (e.g. "turn to", "repent", "believe", etc.) "describe something which a person does, or is required to do", and therefore in effect require "a decision to be made." Yet, though he acknowledges that such a decision is "entirely due to God", in his summary of the NT teaching on conversion he is surprisingly silent on the biblical terms which emphasize God's role in this process, for example, "born again" is omitted.[48] This is another example of the fact that though God's role in conversion is generally acknowledged in Christian circles today, it is usually understated and rarely given the biblical emphasis.

This regeneration is a radical work initiated by God, which changes every aspect of the being of the one worked upon. Paul said, "if anyone is in Christ, he is a new creation; the old has gone, the new has come!" (2 Cor. 5:17).[49] True, those changes may be more marked in some than others, for example, one brought up in the church, and for the most part already largely practicing Christian behavior, is less likely to exhibit dramatic change than, say, an alcoholic. But Christian conversion changes all that experience it into new creations after the pattern of Christ.

Receiving

We cannot ignore the passage which gives rise to the modern teaching on "receiving Christ" being perceived as conversion, or at least a crucial part of it. John 1:11-12 says, "his own did not receive him. Yet to all who received him, to those who believed in his name, he gave the right to become children of God..." This passage is rooted in an historical situation: the majority of the Jewish people of that time did not accept him, though some did, yet its application goes beyond that situation and states eternal principles, and involves two issues relevant to our purposes here: 1/ what comes first, the receiving or the giving of power? and 2/ what is meant by receiving Christ?

What, then, comes first, the receiving of Christ or the giving of power? Whilst C.K. Barrett in his commentary on John states that "the birth is conditional upon receiving" and "believing",[50] William Hendriksen argues that as both the Greek verbs here, *elabon* ("received") and *edoken* ("gave"), are in the aorist tense they should be viewed as happening simultaneously.[51]

Many modern evangelicals see this receiving as a decisive human act in conversion, as we have noted, but what does this "receiving Christ" mean? When placed besides the not accepting in the previous verse, this receiving is most likely meant to be taken, to some degree, in an active sense. Leon Morris sees receiving and believing as "different ways of looking at the same spiritual change, wherein a man ceases to rely on his own merits ... and puts his trust in Christ instead."[52] Yet, though these concepts imply something that one must do, that action must be subordinate to what follows in verse thirteen, which clearly states that this new birth is not the result "of human decision", rather it is "of God". It has been said that though "Human beings choose to believe ... they make that choice only because divine grace opens ... blind eyes".[53] In whatever sense conversion is a decision, then that decision is totally subordinate to the grace of God.

Progress towards conversion

James Engel lists eight graded categories through which an unconverted person might progress to become a Christian. They are:

-8 Awareness of a Supreme Being
-7 Some Knowledge of Gospel
-6 Knowledge of Fundamentals of the Gospel
-5 Grasp of Personal Implications of Gospel
-4 Positive Attitude Toward Act of becoming a Christian
-3 Problem Recognition and Intention to Act
-2 Decision to Act
-1 Repentance and Faith in Christ.[54]

This is a useful listing, though, as no doubt Engel would concede, the various categories are not watertight. He rightly recognizes that people are at varied levels of understanding the Christian faith and have different attitudes to it, which may change or develop. Expressing a similar idea, Peter Corney states that it is unlikely that one will be able to "take someone from neo-paganism to conversion to Christ in one short step,"[55] and this needs to be recognized. Peace says that "Understanding (the gospel) is the key to conversion", without it one cannot "turn" to God, and often acquiring that understanding is a lengthy process. He, too, though different from Engel, details steps within that process.[56]

Some people are at a stage where immediate conversion is unlikely or even impossible, making praying a commitment prayer highly inappropriate.

While it is not intended here to work out a detailed *ordo salutis*, it needs to be clearly stated that however much of a human role there is in "receiving", "believing" and "repenting", even "deciding", none of this is possible until the Holy Spirit has regenerated an individual's life. Thus the initiative in conversion is with God not humanity, so no one can "decide" for Christ at any time considered convenient.

"The Sinner's Prayer"

As has been seen it is commonly believed that one can "receive" Christ through praying a prayer of commitment, or "sinner's prayer." Whilst not rejecting the principle entirely, Engel says that to pray such a prayer does not automatically make one a Christian. Indeed, in his view,

> People can be induced to pray such a prayer for many reasons - as an act of courtesy, as an act of desperation to get rid of us, as a desire to curry our favor and gain some advantage through this means and so on.[57]

As an example of this, Engel mentions a door-to-door evangelistic campaign conducted in Japan in which it was believed "thousands ... had accepted Christ". Engel says that "'Accepted Christ' ... was defined as having prayed a prayer to invite 'Christ into one's heart.'" He attended a later meeting held by the pastors conducting this evangelism and the vast majority of those who were thought to have been converted later showed no evidence of it. He assumes that many prayed that prayer just out of courtesy, or perhaps as an expression of interest in Christianity, but nothing more definite.[58] Though we would seem to have here an example of a system developed in one culture, being used and probably misunderstood in another, it does give an example of the dangers of the method.[59]

It is often said that if such a prayer is prayed "sincerely", then God will certainly answer it. But it is quite possible to pray such a prayer sincerely, and yet have little or no awareness of the Christian Gospel or what one is doing. Nor is there necessarily any genuine work of grace going on in the individual's life. Whilst not saying that a thorough knowledge of theology is necessary before conversion, a seeker must surely be made very conversant with such basics as the nature of God and Christ, the sinfulness of humanity and their own sinfulness, and the way to God through Christ through faith. Though it is possible that an inquirer might understand all this adequately after one sermon and one fifteen minute counseling session, the probability would seem to be that most will not. To expect someone in Engel's stage minus seven, with, say, little more knowledge of the Gospel than the existence of Christ and a vague idea that He is somehow the Savior of the world, to recite such a prayer is highly unlikely to result in a genuine conversion.

It is also essential that God is working in the individual's life. Yet there is no guarantee that because a person has found themselves in church or at a crusade and moved forward after the altar call that the Holy Spirit is actually working in their lives. Even when the Spirit does begin to work upon a human soul, the process leading up to conversion often still takes weeks, months, or even years.

Summary

With the conversions we have examined in Acts, it is evident that in most cases, if not all, some time had previously been spent examining the Old Testament Scriptures, and relating them to the claims of Jesus Christ, so though the conversions may have been sudden, they had been preceded by a process, which in some cases may have been quite lengthy. In other words, the converts had reasoned matters through over a period. Though clearly reasoning, then, is an essential human component in the conversion process, and the emotions will often quite properly be moved, its successful outcome is totally dependent upon divine intervention. This divine work goes beyond conviction of sin and persuasion and includes the Spirit's action upon the human being that triggers human response and radically changes that individual through a "new birth" into a "new creation". This is particularly evident in the cases of Paul and Lydia, and also the household of Cornelius (examined in chapter eleven). Though it must be stated that for someone to believe and repent does require some form of human decision, this is impossible without the prior positive activity of the Holy Spirit. Therefore, the prime mover in a Christian conversion is God, not the convert. To think of conversion as mainly (or perhaps even totally) a human decision or resulting from the reciting of a formula prayer flies in the face of biblical teaching. It is therefore ill advised to counsel in a way suggesting that someone can make such a decision at almost any time they choose.

The paradox of God's sovereignty and human responsibility are clearly apparent in all this. Though this presents a problem to our minds, the Scriptures teach both concepts, and therefore we are bound to believe both.

Notes

[1] The definition of Conversion used in this book is found on page xvi.

[2] Arn & Arn, "Closing the Evangelistic Back Door", 25-26 (though the Arns go well beyond this); *Decision* 37/6 (June 1996), 6-11, 23n (the name of this magazine, itself, is a significant example of this); *New Life* 59/4 (27 June 1996), 1; 59/5 (4 July 1996), 1; Bill Newman, *Called to Proclaim* (Brisbane: BNC, 1986), 72-74.

[3] "Festival '96 with Franklin Graham", taped from Brisbane Family Radio.

[4] D. Martyn Lloyd-Jones, *Romans: An Exposition of Chapter 8: 17-39 The Final Perseverance of the Saints* (Edinburgh: Banner of Truth, 1975), 337.

[5] France, "Conversion in the Bible", 304.

[6] Davies, *My Spirit*, 247 (emphasis in the original).

[7] *Four Spiritual Laws*, 12.

[8] Peace, *Conversion*, 280-81.

[9] Michael Green, *Evangelism in the Early Church* (Crowborough: Highland, 1984), 193. Hugh Kerr and John Mulder express a similar viewpoint, Kerr & Mulder, *Famous Conversions* 1.

[10] Green, *Early Church* 193-94.

[11] Peace, *Conversion*, 24-27, 85.

[12] Bruce says that whether Sergius Paulus was actually converted at this point is debated by some, Bruce, *Acts*, 299. Howard Marshall suggests that the proconsul's conversion might have been short-lived, on the basis that Luke makes no further mention of one who would have been a significant addition to the church. Marshall, *Acts*, 219-220. This is possible, but Luke often omits information we would have expected him to have included.

[13] Marshall, *Acts* 267.

[14] Colton, *American Revivals*, 218-19.

[15] Carwardine, *Transatlantic* 119.

[16] Nevin, *Anxious Bench* 54, 80-81

[17] *The Methodist Hymn Book* (London: Methodist Conference, 1933), Hymn 744. All wording quoted from this hymn corresponds with all other hymn books checked, though there are slight, insignificant changes in punctuation. *Sacred Songs & Solos* (*Sankey's*) omits verse two. The Methodist and Sankey versions do have an added chorus, but this has not been quoted.

[18] For a brief, modern examination of original sin see David Parker, "Original Sin: A Study in Evangelical Theory" *The Evangelical Quarterly* LXI/1 (Jan. 1989) 51-69.

[19] Some New Testament manuscripts omit the words "to sin", but even if they were not in the original, they are implied here. It also needs to be noted that in this context the Greek word *doulos* seems to have the full force of "slave", rather than servant.

[20] F.F. Bruce, *The Epistles to the Colossians, to Philemon, and to the Ephesians* (NICNT, Grand Rapids: Eerdmans, 1984) 280, 284.

[21] A comment echoed by R.C. Sproul who cites it, R.C. Sproul, *The Mystery of the Holy Spirit* (Wheaton: Tyndale, 1990), 95-96.

[22] Charles M. Cameron, "Arminius - Hero or Heretic?" *The Evangelical Quarterly* 64:3 (July 1992) 216, quoting Arminius, *Works* 1:526-29.

[23] See Clark H. Pinnock (ed), *The Grace of God and the Will of Man* (Minneapolis: Bethany, 1995).

[24] Gary Sattler, "Moving on Many Fronts" *Christian History*, 5:2, 20; C. John Weborg, "Reborn in Order to Renew" *Christian History*, 5:2, 17-18.

[25] *Some Remarks on "A Defence of the Preface to the Edinburgh Edition of Aspasio Vindicated."* Wesley, *Works*, 10:350.

[26] Sermon on "The Spirit of Bondage and of Adoption", Wesley, *44 Sermons*, 103.

[27] *Some Remarks on Mr. Hill's "Review of all the Doctrines Taught by Mr. John Wesley."* Wesley, *Works*, 10:392.

[28] Sermon *"On Working out our own Salvation."* Wesley, *Works*, 6:509.

[29] Lloyd-Jones *Romans: The Final Perseverance* 246.

[30] D. Martyn Lloyd-Jones, *Romans: An Exposition of Chapters 7.1-8.4 The Law: Its Functions and Limits* (Edinburgh: Banner of Truth, 1973) 79.

[31] D.Martyn Lloyd-Jones, *Romans: An Exposition of Chapter 5 Assurance* (Edinburgh: Banner of Truth, 1971), 347.

[32] Nettles, *Grace & Glory*, 292.

[33] Thomas Schreiner & Bruce A. Ware (eds.) *The Grace of God, the Bondage of the Will* (2 vols.; Grand Rapids: Baker, 1995), 1:11.

[34] Westblade, in Schreiner & Ware, *Grace of God* 1:66. Others teaching this inability include: R.B. Kuiper, *God Centred Evangelism* (Grand Rapids: Baker, 1961), 164; Nevin, *Anxious Bench* 111-12; J.I. Packer, *Evangelism and the Sovereignty of God* (Downers Grove: IVP, 1991), 106-9. This concept has a very ancient history being taught by Augustine and the Reformers such as Luther and Calvin; see John H. Gerstner, in Schreiner & Ware, *Grace of God*, 2:279-290.

[35] John Calvin, *Institutes of the Christian Religion* (ed. T. McNeill, trans. F.L. Battles; 2 vols. LCC 20; Philadelphia: Westminster, 1960), 1:335.

[36] Nettles, *Grace & Glory*, 290 (emphasis in original).

[37] Sermon on *"Salvation by Faith"* Wesley, *44 Sermons*, 7.

[38] John Piper, *Future Grace* (Sisters: Multnomah, 1995) 215, 161; see also Green, *Early Church* 384n47; Packer, *Evangelism*, 27; C. Samuel Storms, in Schreiner & Ware, *Grace of God* 1:221-22.

[39] Charles Hodge, *The Way of Life: A Handbook of Christian Belief and Practice* (Grand Rapids: Baker, 1977) 219.

[40] D. Martyn Lloyd-Jones, *Romans: An Exposition of Chapter 8:5-17 The Sons of God* (Edinburgh: Banner of Truth, 1974), 167.

[41] The Greek word *anothen* can mean either, and in this context is probably intended to convey both meanings, see Morris, *John* 212-3. Toon's paraphrase of this passage contains both concepts, Toon, *Born Again* 14.

[42] Morris, *John* 212n12, 213. See also Edmund P. Clowney, Schreiner & Ware, *Grace of God* 1:239.

[43] Toon, *Born Again* 28.

[44] Toon, *Born Again* 25.

[45] Morris, *John* 101, 213n14; Toon, *Born Again* 25, 27.

[46] Billy Graham, *How to be Born Again* (Waco: Word, 1977).

[47] Toon gives some examples of books and other materials which take the Graham view, Toon, *Born Again* 179-182. The writer of this book has heard John 3:3 preached from that perspective, and in the distant past has done so himself!

[48] Hawley, *Conversion*, 9-12.

[49] Other Scriptures which speak of this change include: Lk. 19:1-9; Acts 9:1-22; Gal. 5:16-21; and Eph. 2:1-10.

[50] C.K. Barrett, *The Gospel According to St. John* (London: SPCK, 1978), 164.

[51] William Hendriksen, *The Gospel of John* (London: Banner of Truth, 1959), 81.

[52] Morris, *John* 99.

[53] Schreiner & Ware, *Grace of God* 1:13.

[54] James F. Engel, *Contemporary Christian Communications: Its Theory and Practice* (Nashville: Nelson, 1979) 80.

[55] Peter Corney, "Have you got the right address? Post Modernism & the Gospel" *Grid* (Spring, 1995): 2.

[56] Peace, *Conversion*, 216, 297-303, 309-329.

[57] Engel, *Christian Communications* 214.

[58] Engel, *Christian Communications* 63-64.

[59] Ethel Caddy mentions a similar misunderstanding when a colleague was ministering to a group of Australian Aborigines. After preaching to them this eager missionary asked, "Will you put up your hand if you want to accept Jesus as your Saviour?" They all raised their hands. The missionary was delighted, but later discovered that to these people a question was the same as a command, thus from their perspective they were doing no more than obeying his instruction, Ethel Caddy, *Dindarlee: The Life and Work of Wes Caddy* (Lawson: Mission Publications, 1993), 138-39.

Chapter 14

Results Examined

Introduction

As was suggested at the end of chapter eleven, the main justification claimed for the use of the public invitation system is that it is highly successful. Finney, Billy Graham (more often his associates than Graham himself), Streett, Whitesell[1] and many more point to the seemingly remarkable results produced by the method, and from those results argue that this not only justifies the use of this system, but also that it is the best method of evangelism, and it is a mistake not to use it. This chapter will examine the claimed results of public invitation evangelism, and see whether it is as successful as is claimed. It has been said that one million people came to Christ through the preaching of D.L. Moody,[2] and another million responded through the preaching of Billy Sunday. (Though Sunday did not appear in the historical survey in this book - most of his ministry being early in the twentieth century, which is outside the period covered - a look at some statistics in relation to his work is instructive.)[3] Both Moody and Sunday gave public invitations. When one examines a non-public invitation preacher such as Asahel Nettleton, there are just 25 000 converts claimed.[4] Even if one allows for the facts that the population of the USA in Nettleton's time was much smaller than when the later two evangelists were preaching, and that he did not travel as much, receive as much publicity, or preach to such large crowds as the other two, one is still left with a vast difference. Surely this proves the superiority of evangelism which uses the altar call over that which does not employ it. But how accurate are the claims?

Claims and Counterclaims

There are many claims made about conversions through altar call evangelism, both concerning individual cases[5] and also in the form of statistics. It is readily acknowledged at this point that many people are converted through this form of evangelism, and some most remarkably. Specific conversions will not be examined in this study, but some of the statistics will be.

One of the most staggering claims of converts from an evangelistic endeavor encountered in the course of this study was not actually of a public invitation, but because of its close relationship to it this event demands attention. In 1991, American evangelist Bill Bright went to Russia. He writes that

> On Easter Sunday ... I preached on the resurrection of Jesus in the Palace of Congress ... from 50 to 80 percent of the 5,000 people present responded to the invitation to receive Christ. The message was carried on nationwide television ... It is believed that a minimum of 100 million viewed the program and that *many millions received Christ as their Savior* via television that day.[6]

On 10 May 1994, I wrote to Bill Bright, stating my doubts about his claim, and asking him to justify it. As Dr. Bright was traveling in the period immediately following the receipt of my letter, his assistant, Jim Bramlett, replied in his stead. Bramlett admitted that "no individual recording" of converts had been possible after the TV presentation, so the method used was to estimate "based on experiences of similar presentations and audiences when accurate counts are possible."[7] So, as 50 to 80 percent had responded actually at the Palace of Congress and at some similar presentations in Russia, it was assumed that a similar percentage had done so from the TV broadcast. Instead of "many millions" being converted through that TV program, it is possible that not a single person was converted, certainly Bramlett gives no concrete evidence of even one conversion.

The problems with the claims in Bright's book and their justification in the letter are numerous, but we will just deal with the ones relevant to our subject.[8] First, Bright seems to confuse a public response with conversion. At the Palace of Congress 50 to 80 percent "responded to the invitation to *receive Christ.*" Then, based on that percentage, he assumes that "many millions *received Christ as their Savior* via television on that day."[9] Linked to that, Bramlett speaks of the "'many millions' of estimated *decisions*" as being "probably very accurate", being based "on the percentages of "*responses*" previously experienced.[10] Thus we have "responses" equal "decisions", and most often in evangelical jargon "decisions" equal conversions. True, evangelical jargon does also include the phrase "second-time decisions". These do not normally seem to be regarded as conversions, but as a recommitment. But the terms "made a decision" or "he or she decided for Christ" usually refer to a "first-time" decision, and thus presumably an assumed conversion.

When one examines other evidence concerning Bright's claim, one's doubts grow. In 1997 Beverly Nickles stated that though there were about 3000 evangelical churches in Russia at that time, and it would seem that they have only about one and a half million members.[11] If one allows that some that may have been converted through Bright's broadcast may have ended up in non-evangelical churches, it would still seem that Bright's estimate of conversions is a gross exaggeration.[12]

It is, perhaps, not surprising that Hawley could say, citing a 1978 study produced by the Institute for American Church Growth, that Bright's organization, Campus Crusade for Christ, has "registered hundreds of thousands of 'decisions'," but "only 3% of the persons responding were ever incorporated into a local congregation."[13]

We have a similar situation with Billy Graham's major apologist, Robert Ferm. Ferm stated in 1988 that at Billy Graham Crusades "more than two million have *come forward to register decisions for Christ*," apparently referring to the number that have gone forward at Billy Graham meetings up until that time.[14] Once more we have an apparent assumption that "inquirers" equals "decisions". Though the Graham organization records different types of decisions (not all are claimed to be conversions), with the common evangelical concept that "decision" equals conversion, the impression is given that over two million people have been converted through Billy Graham. The number is almost certainly far less.

In Roger Palms' report on Festival '96, which appeared in *Decision*, several times he states that a particular percentage of the attendees "responded to the invitation to accept Christ" (or similar phrase), quoting statistics which seem to refer to all those who came forward.[15] Without precisely saying so, the impression is once again given that response equals conversion.

Elijah Brown estimated that, up to the time he was writing (1914), Billy Sunday had preached to about 2 130 000 "*different* people, of which 568 000 (27 %) had become "converts", and "converts" is the word Brown uses.[16] This would again seem to be confusing response with conversion, as the second estimate would presumably include those who went forward for reasons other than a conversion experience, and almost certainly includes those who went forward on several occasions.

This book has pointed previously to this frequent confusion between public response and conversion, and the material just mentioned indicates that this is common. Even Billy Graham, himself, could speak about "scores of people walking down the aisles from every direction accepting Christ as personal Savior when the invitation was given" in one of his early crusades,[17] apparently confusing going forward with conversion. One frequently hears in casual conversation such comments as, "200 (or five) made a decision last night", apparently meaning 200 (or five) were converted. Whilst probably nobody believes that going forward or raising one's hand in response to an evangelistic invitation actually saves, that impression is frequently given, and is often apparent in reports of evangelistic crusades. Is it any wonder that Erroll Hulse can observe that "All too often the term 'enquirers' is changed by enthusiasts to 'converts'"?[18] His criticism is totally justified.

Evidence of a related area of confusion was apparent in Festival '96 with Franklin Graham. At the end of Graham's appeals, as has previously been seen, he prayed a prayer of acceptance on behalf of the inquirers, as his father has so often done. Then when the inquirers went for counseling they were immediately confronted with page six in the counseling booklet, headed "How to Receive Christ",[19] which concluded with another prayer of commitment. Festival officials released statistics before any widespread follow up had been conducted which suggested that 43 percent of those coming forward had been converted, and less than 4 percent were still inquiring (the remainder had come forward for such matters as assurance and rededication). Yet the Billy Graham Association estimates state that of converts made through Billy Graham crusades over the years, 2 percent occur during the sermon, 48 percent during counseling, and the remaining 50 percent through follow up. On two counts this data suggests confusion: first, is the repeated commitment prayer; and secondly, the Festival '96 figures seem to be so totally different from those of Billy Graham, one wonders whether a substantial portion of the 43 percent "saved" at Festival' 96, were not brought to Christ until the follow up sessions, and some, perhaps many, were not even converted then. When this is allied with the fact that many did not get as far as follow up classes (see below), one is entitled to wonder about the validity of the statistics produced, and the quality of the counseling.

There is a disturbing number of those going forward who never seem to end up in a church, or do so only for a brief while. The official *Commitment Counseling Manual* of the Southern Baptist Convention quotes an estimate that 50 percent or more of "those making decisions" later "'drop out' of the church and Christian community".[20] This horrifying statistic alone suggests that something serious is wrong with our evangelistic method, and not just the inadequate training of counselors and the poor follow up blamed by the manual.

David Wells mentions a 1990s Gallup poll which indicated that 32% of Americans responded "Yes!" to the question "Are you born again?" In 1993 a study was done which asked that and other questions, such as "Do you go to church with some regularity?" "Do you pray with some regularity?" and "Do you have some minimal structure of formal Christian belief?" When those questions were added the "yeses" faction declined to 8%.[21] Thus three-quarters of those originally claiming to be "born again" were showing little evidence of it. In another study, Gallup states that "church attendance, it appears, makes little difference in people's ethical views and behaviors."[22] The regular churchgoer in America, it would seem, behaves no better than those who do not attend. Whilst this rather disturbing state of affairs cannot be laid at the door of the altar call alone, it would be surprising if it were not a major component in the creation of this unsatisfactory situation, as it remains the major form of evangelism.

One problem is that many who have gone forward resist all invitations by those who visit them to go to church or follow-up sessions. From my own church, one minister visited seven, who had been referred after Festival '96. Two of these were already in attendance at our church and seem to be showing some evidence of Christian conversion. Another had belonged to a sect, and has now been through *Christianity Explained*, and regularly attends our church. None of the others, as far as we know, have attached themselves to a church, and certainly not ours. One man, who had also gone forward in response to an invitation at another local church a couple of years before, does attend church pretty regularly, though he "gets around a bit". One or two of the others appear to have had past church experiences that have left a negative imprint and have seemed reluctant or unable to return to church life. Another woman laughed in the visitor's face, and said, "Don't worry about it", and closed the door.[23] It is difficult from all this to ascertain what proportion of the seven were genuinely converted or had another type of genuine religious experience at Festival '96, but it seems probable that one of the seven did not, plus possibly two or three of the others. If one allows that such crusades do good (and it is not being argued that they don't), it does justify our questioning the validity of the statistics usually presented at their conclusion.

But let us just look at Billy Sunday for a moment and consider whether the estimate of a million converts at his meetings is realistic. First, according to Weisberger, more than half of those who signed decision cards at Sunday's campaigns "rarely showed up on succeeding Sabbath mornings" in the local churches.[24] He also states that between one third and a half of all Sunday's decision cards had the "Reconsecration" section ticked.[25] If these figures are accurate, this reduces the figure of actual converts to probably less than 300 000, perhaps much less. It could be argued that those who ticked "Reconsecration" were more likely to later attend church regularly than those who had made some form of first-time decision. If this is so, it could be that considerably less than half of Sunday's "new converts" attended church regularly after their "decisions", e.g. say 50% of respondents went to church; if 75% of those ticked "Reconsecration", and the remaining 25% were assumed "new converts", this would be 12.5% of the original million, or just 125 000 new converts attending church. (It is acknowledged here that church attendance does not prove conversion, and non-attendance does not necessarily prove non-conversion. But genuine converts are much more likely to attend church regularly than non-converts.)

Lyle Dorsett says that "if as little as five percent" of those who went forward at Sunday's meetings "were truly transformed" then he "was reaching more people" than any contemporary American preacher.[26] Now, whilst Dorsett is not suggesting that only one in twenty of Sunday's converts were genuine, he does seem to be hinting that he believes that the reality falls well short of claims being made. Ironically, five percent of one million is 50 000, which is not far above Nettleton's 25 000, and Sunday had a large machine to back him, a sensational approach, and much larger congregations. In truth there is no way of knowing for certain how many were converted through Sunday's campaigns, but the true figure is likely to be well below a million.

Significantly, Bill Bright, whose claim of converts through Russian TV was criticized earlier, said in 1966, "It is estimated that approximately ninety-five percent of all Christians are living defeated, fruitless, carnal lives."[27] He does not give reasons for his particular estimate of "ninety-five percent". But, perhaps, Bright's hammer has missed the nail. The probability is that many of these "defeated, fruitless, carnal" "Christians" are not Christians at all, for without doubt there are very many in evangelical churches in the western world, some who only appear for a time, who show little evidence of having actually experienced the saving grace of God.[28] Indeed, some call these people "carnal Christians", that is Christians with "self on the throne" instead of Christ, but this concept is alien to the New Testament. Those genuinely converted by the Spirit of Christ seek to please him. They are not indifferent to his commands. Luke 13:3; 1 Cor. 6:9-11; Heb. 12:14 are just a handful of the many verses and passages which demonstrate this. This issue will not be dealt with here, but those wishing to follow it through should read John F. MacArthur Jr.'s *The Gospel According to Jesus*, which deals with it in detail.

Though it is hard to prove, it would seem probable that false conversions produced through the public invitation system are a major reason for the decadence often evident in the lives of those claiming to be Christian. Public invitations often steer people into the hands of the church, without bringing them into the arms of Christ, and such people are normally assumed converted, both by themselves and others. Often these people cease to seek for Christ, because they have been told that they have found Him.

Many of those who go forward, though, do not attach themselves to a church, and others do so only for a short while. At the Billy Graham Crusade at Wembley in 1955, Erroll Hulse says that he and his wife "joined in whole-heartedly and without reservations of any kind", working as counselors every night. As noted above, of the 26 inquirers they counseled, in Hulse's words, "not one came to anything."[29] I wrote to Hulse requesting more details about this claim, and in his reply he said that, "there was no conviction of sin and no idea of the meaning of the gospel in any that we counseled."[30] This experience of the Hulses is remarkable and disturbing, but one suspects is not isolated. One can only guess how many others of the 23 806 who went forward at Wembley also did not "come to anything".

Hulse states that the crusade in Haringay, the previous year, was believed to have been more successful with regard to genuine conversions.[31] John Pollock says of Haringay that "more than half of the converts described themselves as of no *regular* church connection".[32] Interestingly, a much smaller percentage of attendees went forward at Haringay in 1954 than did at Wembley the next year.[33] The reasons for this are not clear, though Wembley being a much larger stadium than Haringay, the shortness of the Wembley programme (one week as against twelve), and the increasing familiarity with the practice of going forward (which does not seem to have been common in post-war Britain), may have all been factors. But there is some justification, with the Wembley crusade at least, of regarding the public invitation as used by Billy Graham and many other evangelists as producing an abundance of false conversions.

Questions related to the apparently high falling away rate of "converts" at major crusades using the altar call, usually meet the response that some of Jesus' disciples fell away too, so what is unusual about it,[34] or a recitation of the parable of the sower. Whilst not ignoring the validity of those biblical examples, and readily accepting that all evangelists in all ages have had those who have fallen away, they are inadequate to explain the situation.

I have heard dozens, perhaps even hundreds, of testimonies over the years. It has often amazed me how so many of them follow a similar pattern. It is probable that over half of them can be summarized in the following four stages:

> 1/ The individual makes a decision (frequently through some form of the public invitation).
> 2/ It has little or no impact.
> 3/ There is a later religious experience (sometimes through the public invitation).
> 4/ This results in a changed lifestyle.[35]

Is it possible that the real conversion of most, perhaps the vast majority, of those people was at stage three, not stage one? Does it matter? It probably matters little for those who reach stage three and four (the ones we usually hear give testimonies), but it matters a great deal for those who never go beyond stage two (the ones we do not usually hear give testimonies). If true conversion is most commonly at stage three in this scenario, then many people assumed to be Christians are not genuinely converted. How many are there who make a "decision" for Christ and it results in nothing, or nothing lasting?

Win and Charles Arn state that, "Research is now demonstrating that the process by which people arrive at a point of Christian decision is a key factor in whether they become responsible members or drop out."[36] And though the Arns may not agree, it is being argued in this volume that the altar call is not the best way to arrive at such a point.

Summary

It is impossible to establish what percentage of public invitation "converts" are genuine, but it is almost certainly much less than is generally thought. "Decision" statistics given by evangelistic organizations on occasions do give the impression that all who come forward become converted at that time, though closer examination of those claims usually indicate that less than half of those are actually considered new converts, while others respond for other reasons. In addition, as many of those who are claimed to be "converts" later show no evidence of being truly changed, genuine converts as a percentage of those going forward is probably less than twenty-five percent, and could be considerably less. It is not being suggested here that there is any intention to deceive people with the statistics produced, but the nature of the public invitation seems to create confusion over "results" and makes some degree of accidental deception inevitable.

Notes

[1] Robert O. Ferm, *Persuaded to Live* (Westwood: Revell, 1958) (this is a collection of testimonies by people converted through Billy Graham Crusades, written, in part at least, to answer arguments that converts through Graham's meetings don't last); John Pollock, *Crusades: 20 Years with Billy Graham* (Minneapolis: World Wide, 1969), 59, 71, 73, 137-38, 143-46, 158, 180, 190, 194, 200; Streett, *Effective Invitation*, 129-130 (147) (this principle seems to underlie much of Streett's book, note especially his chapters "Extending a Public Invitation - The Reasons Why" and "How to Prepare and Deliver a Public Invitation", 139-168 (158-195); Whitesell, *65 Ways*, 18-20.

[2] "When brother Moody preached, the city and the world listened", *Chicago Tribune* (3 Aug. 1987); Moody himself refused to count converts, Gundry, *Love Them*, 82-83.

[3] Lyle Dorsett, *Billy Sunday and the Redemption of Urban America* (Grand Rapids: Eerdmans, 1991), 93, 146; Streett, "Public Invitation", 103 (114), quoting Homer Rodeheaver, *Twenty Years With Billy Sunday* (Winona Lake: Rodeheaver, 1936), 127.

[4] Thornbury, *Revival*, 233.

[5] See Robert O. Ferm, *Billy Graham: Do the Conversions Last?* (Minneapolis: World Wide, 1988), 140-42; Ferm, *Persuaded to Live.*

[6] Bill Bright, *A Man Without Equal* (San Bernardino: New Life 2000, 1992), 12-13 (emphasis added).

[7] Jim Bramlett (assistant to Bill Bright of Campus Crusade for Christ International), letter, 11 July 1994.

[8] One of the non-relevant problems is that Bright and Bramlett appear to expect that if the response is 50-80 percent when preaching to a more-or-less captive audience at a rally or crusade, then it must be the same from a TV presentation. This is surely unrealistic. James Engel has a chart with comments comparing the likely results of "Interpersonal communication" and "Mass communication", which indicates that the latter is less likely to result in conversion, Engel, *Christian Communications*, 44-45.

---

⁹ Bright, *Without Equal*, 12-13 (emphasis added).

¹⁰ Jim Bramlett, letter, 11 July 1994 (emphasis added).

¹¹ Beverly Nickles, "Training Shortfall May Imperil Growth" *Christianity Today* 41: 4 (7 Apl. 1997): 54.

¹² Another remarkable claim is made concerning two Luis Palau crusades in Romania and Bulgaria in 1990. According to Keith Hardman, "31 percent" of attendees "made commitments to Christ" in Romania and "36 percent" in Bulgaria, Hardman, *Seasons*, 268-69. I am unaware of any testing of these figures.

¹³ Hawley, *Christian Conversion*, 23.

¹⁴ Ferm, *Do Conversions Last*, 127 (emphasis added).

¹⁵ Roger C. Palms, "Reaching Four Cities in Australia with Good News", *Decision* 37/6 (June 1996): 7-9.

¹⁶ Elijah P Brown, *The Real Billy Sunday* (NY: Revell, 1914), 207 (emphasis added).

¹⁷ Pollock, *Crusades*, 59.

¹⁸ Hulse, *Great Invitation*, 10.

¹⁹ This was the method recommended to counselors, according to the festival's organizer of counseling and follow-up, Jim Rawson, personal conversation 10 Apl.1996.

²⁰ *Commitment Counseling Manual*, 6, quoting from Delos Miles, *Introduction to Evangelism* (Nashville: Broadman, 1983), 355-56.

²¹ David F. Wells, *The Bleeding of the Evangelical Church* (Edinburgh: Banner of Truth, 1995), 7. See also MacArthur, *Gospel*, xxi.

²² William D. Hendricks. *Exit Interviews* (Chicago: Moody, 1993), 250.

²³ Rev. David McDougall, conversation, 16 July 96; above details later read and confirmed by him.

²⁴ Weisberger, *Gathered*, 260.

²⁵ Weisberger, *Gathered*, 254.

²⁶ Dorsett, *Sunday*, 108-9.

²⁷ Carl F.H. Henry, & W. Stanley (ed.) *One Race, One Gospel, One Task* (2 vols. Minneapolis: World Wide, 1967), 2:370.

²⁸ Observations of this nature are made by, amongst others, R.K. Hughes, *Are Evangelicals Born Again* (Wheaton: Crossway, 1995), 9-19; Bill Hull, "Is the Church Growth Movement Really Working" in Michael Scott Horton (ed.) *Power Religion: The Selling Out of the Evangelical Church?* (Chicago: Moody, 1992), 144; Ernest C. Reisinger, *What should we think of "The Carnal Christian"?* (Edinburgh: Banner of Truth, n.d.), 1.

²⁹ Hulse, *Great Invitation*, 10.

³⁰ Erroll Hulse, letter, 17 May 1994.

³¹ Hulse, *Great Invitation*, 10.

³² Pollock, *Crusades*, 133, emphasis in the original. His use of the term "converts" here one suspects is another example of inquirer equals convert.

³³ Frank Colquhoun, *Harringay Story: A Detailed Account of the Greater London Crusade, 1954* (London: Hodder, 1955), 231-33; Pollock, *Crusades*, 158.

34 Ferm, *Do Conversions Last?* 130-31.

35 I have kept no record of this, but I believe that something like 60% can be so summarized. This may be because most of my Christian experience has been in Methodist and Baptist churches, where the altar call and this type of spoken testimony have been common. Printed testimonies come from a wider denominational range, and seem to follow this pattern less often. E. Stanley Jones account of his own conversion, however, is one that does follow this outline, Kerr & Mulder, *Famous Conversions,* 181-83.

36 Arn & Arn "Closing the Evangelistic Back Door": 25.

Chapter 15

Problems with the System

There are a number of problems with the public invitation system, several of which have already been mentioned during the course of this study. We will now have a critical look at these.

Criticisms of the System

Going Forward is Equivalent to Conversion

Even when the invitation system is functioning at its best, there are some undeniable problems. First, as noted several times in this book, the impression is often given by evangelists, pastors, reporters and writers that going forward is equivalent to conversion. This impression is given so often and in such a variety of circumstances, that it almost seems that the normal conduct of the public invitation inevitably gives rise to that understanding. It seems to be a Pavlov-like situation where two distinct things are associated, and the two become confused as one in the observer's mind. One of Nevin's criticisms of the system in the 1840s was that it was virtually impossible to conduct the method without giving the impression that moving forward equated to conversion.[1] A decade earlier Englishmen Andrew Reed and James Matheson also noted the confusing of the outward act with the inward reality in the altar call.[2] Thornbury suggests that both by lecture and practice Finney gave that impression,[3] and the situation still seems the same at the commencement of the twenty-first century.[4] Based on the practices of several evangelists, Olive states, without criticism, that "the 'coming forward' of an individual has come to be thought of as synonymous with the conversion experience", and "To walk forward ... was synonymous with having accepted Jesus Christ as personal Savior."[5] So in his view in the 1950s, responding to an invitation was commonly confused with conversion.

Some have observed that the public invitation has become like a kind of new sacrament, that is that it almost seems to be believed by its practitioners that grace is bestowed through the observance of the practice. Nevin suggested this, without actually naming it such,[6] and in our own times, Hulse asks whether it has become "A new evangelical sacrament".[7] W.O. Thompson said that going forward at a Billy Sunday meeting "became sacramental for some Christians", because of Sunday's seeming confusion of the method with conversion itself.[8] Nettles regards the counseling methods usually used with the altar call as "resembling Roman Catholic sacramental regenerationism."[9] If people believe that coming forward or reciting a formula prayer equals conversion, or even if that impression is given, as has just been suggested is common, then this criticism is justified.

Ironically, it has also been feared in some Baptist circles that the altar call can also nullify the point of baptism. G. Beasley-Murray puts it this way: "badly handled, and with a low view of baptism, it could render baptism superfluous".[10]

If justification is by grace alone through faith alone, not by works or a combination of faith and works, then the act of moving forward cannot equal conversion or earn, or even assist in earning, salvation.

False Conversions

Secondly, some go forward who are not experiencing a genuine work of the Holy Spirit. One old American preacher was probably not strong enough when he said that some who go forward "feel very little".[11] There would seem to be many who go forward with no true religious awareness at all. Hulse puts it this way: the public invitation "calls people to a profession of faith irrespective of whether the hearers have been truly brought face to face with God."[12] Probably the major reason why so many fall away after making "a decision" after a public invitation is because the Holy Spirit is not working in their lives, or, at least, not in the way assumed by those who counsel them.

It has been argued that the problem here is not with the system itself, but abuses of the system.[13] However, though abuses certainly make the situation worse, this evangelistic method does naturally promote the idea that if one goes forward it is expected that the issue of one's salvation will be quickly settled, irrespective of one's current spiritual state.

False Conversions Weaken the Church

It would seem, then, that many who go forward are not genuinely converted. Some of these, though, do find themselves attached to a church. This is good in one sense, in that there should be further opportunity for them to hear the gospel, but it is also bad in that if there are many people in churches who are not converted, but thought to be so, this can cause various problems. They could, for example, be active in the decision-making process of the church, perhaps, with disastrous results. Their behavior might also be well below what one should reasonably expect of Christians, which can give the church a bad name, and deter others from seeking Christ. W.B. Sprague was right when he said that such would bring the "spirit of the world" into the church, and that if the church received many unconverted people, it would find its most "formidable foes" would be within its "own household".[14]

Charles G. Trumbull of the Victorious Life movement said in 1916 that many Christians were "monstrosities" who had not grown spiritually during their entire Christian experience.[15] It is quite likely, though, that Trumbull was wrong. Perhaps the majority of his "monstrosities" were people thought to be Christian but were not, perhaps deceived by an altar call experience, and possibly bringing discredit and weakness upon the church by their behavior. The public invitation being the most common form of evangelism in America during the fifty years or so preceding Trumbull's comment, it is not wrong to assume that many of these, probably most, would have been "converted" through that system.

In 1984 George Gallup said that in America "There is very little difference in the behavior of the churched and the unchurched on a wide range" of ethical issues. Whereas one would expect noticeably higher standards of morality from people in the church, according to Gallup, this is far from the case.[16] There is, then, here an indication that all who claim to be converted are not converted, and with resulting discredit upon the church.

It Promotes a Reliance on Means rather than God

God uses human means to bring about his purposes. All would agree with that, except, perhaps, the most extreme hyper-calvinist. But what means should be used, and to what extent? Preaching is a biblical method of presenting Christian truth, demonstrated by Jesus and the Apostles. Speaking with individuals was also a means used in the New Testament. But there are no precise methods taught in Scripture. The means we use, though, need to be true to the principles of Scripture, i.e., no tricks, no strong psychological pressure, no promotion of confusion etc., and central always must be dependence upon God rather than the means employed.

One can only wonder if the emphasis on human means is going too far when people strongly urge, for example, the creation of the "right atmosphere" in the evangelistic setting. According to one writer, it is vital to have an atmosphere which is "warm, spiritual, bright" and "living", for only in this can one seriously expect "positive results". Indeed, *"The message is not as important as the atmosphere"*.[17] Here it is assumed that God is unable or unlikely to work unless a particular "atmosphere" has been created, primarily, or at least significantly, it would appear, by human means. The preaching of the word of God (the means clearly advocated by Scripture for the salvation of men and women) is here relegated to a secondary position.

Certainly the emphasis upon specific means is very strong in much of today's evangelism, following, as it so often does, the public invitation pattern. Sometimes, people who question the validity of the public appeal, are asked, "Aren't you interested in evangelism then?" Such a reaction seems to indicate that some think that one cannot evangelize if invitation system formulas are not followed. As an example of this, Martyn Lloyd-Jones says that he was often criticized for not using the public invitation, and some even told him that he was sinning because of that omission.[18] But whatever the validity of the altar call, God is not dependent upon particular human methods of evangelism. He surely can work just as effectively, perhaps more so, outside the methods many evangelists insist on.

John Wimber is critical of what he calls "programmatic evangelism", that is, in his terms, a presentation of the gospel relying upon "rational arguments" and "an appeal to emotions", with an emphasis upon "organization and technique", but lacking spiritual power. Included in Wimber's "programmatic evangelism" seems to be much of today's public invitation evangelism.[19] Even without going the whole way with Wimber's "Power Evangelism", he definitely has a point, for the emphasis in much of evangelism today seems to be on method rather than the power and influence of the Spirit of God. True altar call evangelistic meetings are backed by prayer, enlisting God's aid, but so strong is the emphasis on method that the impression is usually given that God cannot work outside the invitation system formulas.

Even early in the twentieth century Reuben Torrey, an evangelist who used the public invitation, and friend and successor to D.L. Moody, could complain that

> Many of the evangelists are being ruined by commercialism that has entered in evangelistic work. A good deal of commercialism has been creeping into our work, and more and more machinery and I fear, less dependence upon God."[20]

The world of evangelism seems to have moved further down that road since Torrey's time, matching the inroads of materialism into society at large.

It Attracts those who like to be the Center of Attention

As far back as 1832, the Rev. Archibald Alexander complained that the altar call had a tendency to encourage those who liked to be the center of attention to display themselves publicly, and as such was an encouragement to pride.[21] Though this may not be a major problem, it could be a reason why some go forward frequently, particularly in our own age, when there is such an emphasis on public display, particularly by the media.

It Puts some off Christianity

It is difficult to establish how many people are put off Christianity by the use of the public invitation, because such people are usually outside the church, and thus their opinions are largely unheard by those inside. However, some have done research into the reasons people leave the church. One of these, an American author, William Hendricks, conducted a number of interviews with people who had left the church, some of which are included in his book *Exit Interviews*. He states that "Altar calls and missionary calls fared poorly" amongst those he interviewed.[22] This is only evident at a couple of points in his book, but as he has conducted other interviews which do not appear in this volume,[23] this view presumably also features in some of the other interviews. There is also criticism of the "faith-fact-feeling" concept that lies behind much of public invitation counseling, in which human emotion is relegated to a matter of little, or even no importance.[24]

I placed a letter in a secular Brisbane newspaper (*The South-East Advertiser*), immediately after Festival '96 (thus while Christian evangelism was in the news), asking people with "negative experiences" of the public invitation to contact me.[25] The only response received was from a young man who had attended an evangelical church for six years in which public invitations were given at "most evening services" and at "some" held in the morning. He often responded to those appeals. He no longer has anything directly to do with any church, and now regards himself as an agnostic. He was very critical of prolonged appeals, and considered such invitations, particularly when backed by music, "hypnotic" and "manipulative". The altar call as practiced in his local fellowship was one of the reasons he left the church.[26]

My respondent's case is not unique. B.H. Carroll, a senior pastor of the Southern Baptists in America during the second half of the nineteenth century, also rejected Christianity for some years in his late teens and early twenties because of an unfortunate experience with a public invitation. It would appear that Carroll responded to an appeal and was assured by counselors that he had thus become a genuine Christian. But Carroll, painfully aware of his own heart, knew he was not. His response was, if that is "religion", then it "was not worth having."[27] Ironically, he did go forward at a public invitation some years later, and though he was not converted during that act, he was converted later that night through listening to a group of women singing after that meeting had concluded.[28]

It would seem, then, that some people do react against the system, but this may be mainly because of abuses in the system rather than the system itself. When people reject the method it is probable that many of them will also reject the gospel, with which it seems inseparably linked. Indeed, it needs to be stressed here that the *initial* rejection may not be of the gospel, but the method.

Abuses of the System

Prolonged and Excessively Emotional Appeals

It is common to hear evangelists and other preachers give prolonged appeals, that is a repeated appeal, sometimes repeated more than once, which may be sandwiched between the various verses of a hymn. One often hears complaints about this practice along the lines: "We sang ten (or twenty - depending on who is doing the exaggerating) verses of 'Just as I am', so the preacher could keep offering invitations."[29] Though the advocates of prolonged appeals argue for it on the basis that "Some people only become Christians at the end of an extended appeal, and may never have done so otherwise" (a point that has already been suggested is impossible to prove or disprove), it is without any question a great source of irritation to many in the pews. It is certainly the main criticism I have heard of the altar call at local church level. It can also be fairly argued that extended appeals, often couched in highly persuasive language, exert undue psychological pressure on the hearers.

Allied with this is the excessive emotional content of many public invitations. True, the emotions should be engaged in a public presentation of the gospel, but when one has a choir or congregation singing touching songs, with the preacher telling sentimental stories and making plaintive pleas with arms outstretched, Christ-like, then it comes as no surprise when some who go forward seem to have had no more than an emotional experience. Em Griffin of Wheaton College calls this approach emotional "rape".[30]

Strangely, some public invitations are cold and clinical (often like the sermons that preceded them), and are made with little or no discernible emotion, which is probably an over reaction to this criticism. The emotions should be roused in preaching, but not excessively, and not at the expense of reason, indeed, they should be approached through the mind.

Dishonest Appeals

Another problem arises when an evangelist asks, say, "Those who wish to give their hearts to Jesus, please raise your hands. All eyes will be closed, so no one will see except me." The preacher's repeated "Thank you, sir!" and "Thank you, madam!" indicate the responses. Then after this the preacher asks, "All those who raised their hands, please come to the front", and this is expected, usually, in full view of everyone. That final, hidden punch is most unfair, and turns what those raising their hands expected to be a more or less private matter into a very public one. Whitesell even advises preachers to adopt something of this nature in his book. The passage reads:

while all have their heads bowed in prayer ... ask Christians who wish prayer for their unsaved loved ones in the audience to raise their hands. Before you pray for the unsaved loved ones, request those unsaved loved ones to lift their hands to receive Christ now. Press the matter upon the unsaved. Pray for the lost, and if any have raised their hands to accept Christ, invite them to come to the front after the benediction.[31]

While Whitesell makes no definite mention of the initial stages of this being carried out in complete privacy (he elsewhere suggests "workers" should be stationed at strategic points to be on the lookout for such responses,[32] a strategy which might be known to all in the congregation), the "heads bowed in prayer" would seem to suggest it.
Preachers, above everyone, must be transparently honest, and consistent in their dealings with people, and this approach falls short on both counts.

Confused Appeals

Olive, an advocate of the public invitation, criticizes the lack of clarity in some invitations, which often lead to confusion in the mind of seekers.[33] Some preachers give broad-based appeals that are either so all-embracing that the whole congregation should respond, or that are so confused that it is unclear for what purpose(s) people are expected to move forward.

Aggressive and Manipulative Counseling

Hulse mentions one person who had gone forward at a crusade but "had no concept of repentance or faith." The counselor endeavored to explain their meaning and significance, but the counseling supervisor got impatient with the counselor, and took over.

"You don't want to go to hell, do you?" the supervisor asked the inquirer.
"No!"
"You do want to go to heaven, don't you?"
"Yes, I do!"
"You believe that Christ died for sinners, don't you?"
"Yes, I do!"
"Then let's give thanks that he died for you and has given you salvation."

The supervisor then prayed, "Lord I thank you for giving this soul eternal life. Thank you, Lord, Amen," and then assured the "convert" that they did have eternal life.[34]

Now, this may be an extreme example of heavy-handed counseling, but such methods are only encouraged by books and other materials which advocate the adoption of very persuasive methods. Nettles quotes a passage from L.R. Scarborough's *A Search for Souls*, in which the author encourages his readers to use highly persuasive, though in this case, not aggressive, methods. For example, Scarborough suggests using such phrases as "Turn him (Christ) not away. Would you turn away a friend? Would you turn away your mother? Then do not turn Christ away."[35] This is a very strong appeal to the emotions (after all, few would turn away their mother), and could be fairly considered a manipulative approach.

Summary

Abuses such as prolonged and highly persuasive appeals, dishonest invitations, and aggressive counseling are not part and parcel of the public invitation system, and can and should be removed from it. But even when they are removed, it can still be seen that there are a number of problems remaining in altar call evangelism, the chief of which are the seemingly inevitable equating of the outward act of moving forward with the inward work of conversion, the production of many "false converts", and the apparent elevation of human means above the power of God.

Notes

[1] Nevin, *Anxious Bench,* 68-72.
[2] Bruce, *Hallelujah,* 78, quoting Andrew Reed and James Matheson, *A Narrative of the Visit to the American Churches* (2vols. NY: Harper, 1835), 2: 34.
[3] Thornbury, *Revival,* 201-2.
[4] Murray gives examples from Billy Graham's ministry, Iain Murray, *The Invitation System* (Edinburgh: Banner of Truth, 1967), 3-8, and this was also noted in chapter ten of *The Altar Call.*
[5] Olive, "Evangelistic Invitation", 52, 54.
[6] Nevin, *Anxious Bench,* 68, 86.
[7] Hulse, *Great Invitation,* 104-9.

8 Thompson, "Public Invitation", 159.

9 Nettles, *Southern Baptists*, 14. See also Nettles, *Grace & Glory,* 413-14, 418.

10 Beasley-Murray, *Baptism*, 86.

11 Ashbel Green, letter, 10 Apl. 1832, in Sprague, *Revivals,* 139.

12 Hulse, *Great Invitation,* 138.

13 McLendon, "Mourner's Bench", 110. It is not quite clear here what McLendon means by "abuses", but it would seem to include over persuasive appealing, McLendon, "Mourner's Bench", 110.

14 Sprague, *Revivals,* 253-54.

15 Frank, *Conquerors,* 116, quoting *Victory in Christ: A Report of Princeton Conference, 1916* (Philadelphia: Board of Managers of Princeton Conference, 1916).

16 John Wimber, *Power Evangelism* (London: Hodder, 1985), 48, quoting George Gallup's report *1984 Religion in America*. In addition, it could be fairly argued that this not only weakens the church but society too.

17 Nettles, *Grace & Glory,* 412, quoting from *Proclaim* (Jan-Mar. 1977): 40 (emphasis in the original article).

18 Lloyd-Jones, *Preaching,* 269. I have also heard statements of that nature in the local church scene.

19 Wimber, *Power Evangelism,* 56-57.

20 Hardman, *Seasons,* 221; Weisberger, *Gathered,* 221, quoting one of Torrey's letters.

21 Archibald Alexander, letter 9 Mar.1832, Sprague, *Revivals* (Appendix) 7.

22 Hendricks, *Exit,* 260.

23 Hendricks, *Exit,* 169-170; 216-17, 291.

24 Hendricks, *Exit*, 184-85, 268.

25 I also tried to have the same letter placed in the *Courier-Mail*, the paper with the largest daily circulation in Queensland, but it was rejected.

26 "Bill" (real name withheld by request), telephone conversation, 14 May 1996.

27 Nettles, *Grace & Glory,* 223-24.

28 Whitesell, *65 Ways,* 83-85, quoting J.B. Cranfill, *Sermons and Life Sketch of B.H. Carroll* (Philadelphia: American Bapt. Publ. Soc., 1895), 13-23.

29 Nevin mentions the practice of repeated appeals sandwiched by verses of a hymn, but in his day, the 1840s, it was "Come, humble sinner", Nevin, *Anxious Bench*, 41.

30 Griffin, *Mind Changers*, 36.

31 Whitesell, *65 Ways,* 53.

32 Whitesell, *65 Ways,* 52. See also 85-86, where he does make an effort to discourage such deception, though it could be argued that this method rather lends itself to deception.

33 Olive, "Evangelistic Invitation", 65.

34 Hulse, *Great Invitation,* 109.

35 Nettles, *Grace & Glory,* 263, quoting L.R. Scarborough, *A Search for Souls* (Nashville: Southern Baptist Convention, 1925), 122-134.

Chapter 16

Recommendations

Whatever one's views of the public invitation system, it is clear that it is a major part of the evangelistic system in the evangelical church generally, and it is unlikely to vanish in the foreseeable future. Yet, there are also many evangelical preachers who do not use it. It is only fitting, therefore, that recommendations are made here both for those using the system as well as for those choosing not to.

The recommendations are under five headings.

1/ All preachers and counselors should engage in a thorough study of the Bible's teachings on conversion.
2/ Preaching devoid of the public invitation should be tried.
3/ Greater dependence needs to be placed upon the Spirit of God and less on human method.
4/ For those still wishing to use the altar call, every attempt should be made to minimize the effects of the problems in the system.
5/ Continued attempts should be made to present Christian truth to the general public.

The Bible on Conversion

There has never been and never will be entire agreement upon what constitutes a Christian conversion, and as those conversions have always been varied that situation is probably inevitable. However, many of today's views, particularly at the coal face of church life, are very different from those held two hundred years ago by both calvinists and arminians, different from the definition of conversion used in this book, and are very difficult to square with Scripture. The dominant modern views are also different from the understanding of many scholars and other thoughtful Christians today. No one engaged in evangelistic ministry should assume that what they have been taught from within a particular tradition is correct; it is imperative that all go back to the Bible to re-examine its teachings on the nature of God, the condition of humanity, the nature of sin, and the way of salvation through Christ, and, where necessary, adjust their beliefs and methods.[1]

Preaching Evangelism

Herbert Arrowsmith said, "Exposition is the best evangelism. It is still true that the Spirit of God takes the Word of God to make a child of God."[2] Preaching, supported by prayer, is the primary biblical method of evangelism, and should be carried out in church, chapel, large venue,[3] or wherever practicable. Appropriate Biblical truths, presented in a clear and interesting manner and applied by the Spirit of God can win men and women into the Kingdom of God without recourse to the public invitation. The doctrines of God, humanity, sin and the way of salvation through Christ need to be understood by prospective converts, so it is therefore necessary for preachers to make such teachings a central and regular part of their normal pulpit ministry.[4] It is also necessary not to leave these teachings "hanging" as apparently irrelevant theories, but to apply them in a way that shows their importance and relevancy, and stresses the urgent need of response. Sinners should be pointed to Christ and urged to believe in Him.

J.I. Packer has a point when he calls "really silly" the expectation that people will be converted after hearing just one evangelistic sermon.[5] Peter Corney takes that a step further by stating that in this post-modern age "People will need to hear the Gospel multiple times" before conversion can be expected,[6] at least in the vast majority of cases. Indeed, this may have been by far the more common situation in times past, too. So, then, persistence in preaching the gospel is necessary.

With the lack of awareness of Christian doctrine, even amongst many in the churches, sermons full of anecdote and short on teaching (which may have helped a more biblically literate generation in Moody's day) will not do. Preaching must have both cutting edge and depth.

Personal counseling is often helpful and opportunity should be given for seekers to avail themselves of such ministry, but privately not publicly. Steps should also be taken by the counselor to thoroughly understand the spiritual condition and comprehension of those being counseled. It should not be taken for granted that because someone presents himself or herself for counseling that they are necessarily near to closing with Christ. It needs to be recognized that all conversions do not happen in the same time frame, as Peace reminds us. Some happen suddenly, some gradually. Our preaching and discipling must take that into consideration.[7]

Preachers such as John Wesley, Whitefield, Jonathan Edwards and Nettleton saw both revival and many people converted through their ministry without using the altar call. In recent times D. Martyn Lloyd-Jones has been the dominant figure amongst those who have evangelized without using it. Lloyd-Jones usually preached an evangelistic sermon in the evening services at Westminster Chapel, and many became Christians through them, though, as there was no attempt to keep records, the number is unknown.[8] John Blanchard is a present day evangelist who does not use it.[9]

With regard to the content of our preaching, John Wesley's recommendation to his preachers is still a valuable guideline for us today. Wesley said that every sermon should "in some measure" "invite", "convince", "offer Christ" and "build up".[10] Whilst it must be acknowledge that the world of today is a very different one from that in which John Wesley lived, and we must respond to those differences, for example, a necessary reaction to post-modernism will often influence the precise content of our sermons, John Wesley's words are still most relevant.

The conversion of people, even many people, is not dependent upon any system. Preachers faithfully proclaiming the Word of God and trusting God to bring people to himself will normally see results.

Dependence upon God not Method

This study has repeatedly touched upon the subject of revival, and it has been evident that at times of awakening many more people are converted than at other times, often without any changes of evangelistic method or any greater emphasis upon external practices. God is not dependent upon particular human methods, though preaching is a biblical method often greatly used. The invitation system is at best an expendable human-made appendage to preaching. It is worth being reminded at this point, that Finney's ministry experienced many of its greatest blessings before he made regular use of public invitations.

Lloyd-Jones tells of the seventeenth century Scot, John Livingstone, who exercised a useful but, for the most part, rather undramatic ministry. Yet, on one day, the Spirit of God came down upon him in such power during his preaching at a united Communion season that about 500 were added to the church. There was no change in his method or preaching style, just God moving far beyond human endeavor. Lloyd-Jones also mentions other similar incidents.[11]

One hundred years later William M'Culloch, a Scottish minister, experienced revival at Cambuslang. Though scholarly, he was not a good preacher. The locals dubbed him a "yill or Ale-minister", because it was said that when he rose to preach many of the congregation left to go for a drink in the public house. Yet, the Spirit of God overruled his speaking limitations and many came to Christ through him.[12] The key issue in his work was not human ability, nor even specific means, but the power of God.

"Not by might, nor by power but by my Spirit says the Lord" (Zech. 4:6) is often quoted in the context of depending upon God rather than our own efforts in Christian work, including evangelism, but it could be fairly said that in evangelism it is a text more often heard than heeded. Public invitation procedures are followed so slavishly in some circles that the impression is given that God cannot work outside them, or at least not work as well if they are not used. An example of this is that public invitations have been given at every meeting of every major crusade that I have ever attended.[13] It would be a valuable exercise at some meetings in a crusade to refrain from giving public invitations, to see if God is as good as his word and can work outside the "might" and "power" of public invitation method.

The Public Invitation System

The Invitation Itself

For those wishing to use, or continue to use, the public invitation it is recommended:

1/ That preachers teach widely and thoroughly the doctrines concerning the nature of God, the state of humanity and the way of salvation.
2/ That a public invitation never be given except where a clear

presentation of the gospel has been made.

3/ That preachers make it clear *every time* that moving forward does not save.

4/ That the parameters of the appeal be clearly spelled out, i.e., if the invitation is for "salvation" or "rededication", or for some other reason, state it clearly. If it is a multi-purpose appeal, make that clear.

5/ That preachers be not dependent upon the method, for God can work outside it.

6/ That prolonged and highly emotive appeals be avoided, and anything that might even appear to be trickery be rejected.

Counseling

One of the areas which most needs reform in the invitation system is the method of counseling inquirers. The booklet counseling method, though it may work in some instances, is it would seem more likely to produce non-converts than converts. The main problem with the method is that it assumes that everybody is at about the same stage in their spiritual quest, which is manifestly untrue, and is thus bound to lead to confusion and false results.

American pastor, Richard Halverson writes that

The one completely safe and dependable manual on personal evangelism and witness is the New Testament; yet the more one studies the New Testament, the less one can deduce from it a system of personal evangelistic methods. Jesus employed a different approach with each person.

He then goes on to quote Christ's dealings with Nicodemus, the woman at the well, the rich young ruler and others to demonstrate his point.[14]

People inquiring about the Christian faith can be at very different stages in their awareness of Christian truth,[15] and, indeed, different people at any stage may require a quite different approach from one another because of their specific nature and life experiences. Flexibility is the key, and the usual public invitation counseling method allows very little room for it.

The counseling approach of such evangelists as Edwards, Wesley, and Whitefield is worth noting at this point. Though they counseled people faithfully and at length they did not push the counselee into making a decision. They rather let the Holy Spirit of God do the work which only He can do.

The selection of counselors needs to be done with greater care than is evident at the moment. No one should be allowed to counsel inquirers regularly who does not clearly understand the relevant doctrines, and have a sound understanding of the various stages that a person can move through in the journey towards Christ. Nor should people who thrive on the domination of others be allowed anywhere near those inquiring about Christ. Some can, and do, push their views forcibly upon others with, at times, devastating results.

Communicating Christian Truth in a Secular Society

To present Christian truth widely and thoroughly in most modern western societies is very difficult, but attempts must be made to do so. In most western countries today many people are unaware of the basics of the Christian message. In earlier generations, through Sunday School, catechizing, or other means, people were generally aware of the more popular Bible stories and the Bible's basic teachings, even if they had not experienced a relationship with Christ. This is not to say that all outside the churches today have little or no Christian knowledge, but when using any form of evangelism today, it needs to be recognized that many are ignorant of biblical teaching.

What needs to be communicated? Engel's listing of the minimum knowledge needed for one (on his terms) "to make a valid and lasting decision for Christ" is a reasonable answer to the question. Engel states that one needs to know about:

1/ The existence of the one Creator God.
2/ Humanity's "self-seeking existence" and the impossibility of "restoring communication with God" by its own action.
3/ That the death and resurrection of Jesus Christ has provided the only means by which "fellowship with God" can be restored.
4/ The validity of the Bible.
5/ That we must "accept God's free gift on the terms that God has provided."[16]

Many in our society would not only not believe these things, but would be largely unaware of the concepts, and, though possible, it is unlikely that one or two sermons and a counseling session at a crusade are going to correct the matter sufficiently with any particular individual. Teaching is necessary. But how can this be done? In most cases people are not likely to become Christian until after receiving considerable exposure to the Christian message, and the best way to do this is through the regular ministries of the local church.

But, of course, many do not attend church, nor are they usually exposed to its ministries. What can be done to remedy this? There are no easy solutions, but there are some methods that can help.

Radio and, particularly, TV are good ways to present Christian truth, though they need to be used well and, especially in the case of TV, they are expensive. Some people would be more likely to listen to a Christian message when alone at home than when surrounded by their friends. Whilst such programs are unlikely to attract large non-Christian audiences, they are at least on popular media which the curious and channel/station switchers can stumble upon. TV and radio, however, are also open to embarrassing abuse.

The Internet is a new way of presenting the Christian message, the use of which is rapidly escalating. Perhaps even more than with TV and Radio, information presented on this medium can be stumbled upon by the dedicated "surfer", which most often no doubt would be ignored, but at other times might commence and continue a quest. Again an individual can consult the available sources (and there are many - good and bad) in privacy and without embarrassment.

Holding seminars which are open to the general public on issues such as marriage and the family or unemployment can show that the Christian message is relevant to modern life, and be a stepping stone to people coming to Christ. This is especially so if they are backed up by counseling and support in these areas.

Another method is a series of leaflet drops in a church's neighborhood. Here it is important that the leaflets do more than invite people to church and they should present a short, easily digested Christian message, which contains some elementary doctrinal content. Articles and letters in the print media also have value, particularly if one can contribute in a regular column.

It is also important that individual Christians make regular contact with people outside the Christian faith. There is a tendency for Christians to succumb to the ghetto mentality, and it is vital that at work and at play we have contact with those outside the church. Opportunities to make formal presentations of Christian truth may be rare in such circumstances, but they do come. They never come, if that contact is not made and maintained.

"While we must always remember that it is our responsibility to proclaim salvation, we must never forget that it is God who saves" (Packer).[17]

Notes

[1] W.O. Thompson suggests at the end of his dissertation that those using the public invitation should "study afresh the doctrine of God, the doctrine of man, the doctrine of soteriology", Thompson, "Public Invitation", 206.

[2] Herbert Arrowsmith, in Henry & Mooneyham *One Race,* 2: 15.

[3] No criticism of mass evangelism *per se* has been made in this book, nor is such criticism intended.

[4] J.I. Packer's chapter "What is the Evangelistic Message?" is both concise and thorough in presenting the essential content of evangelistic preaching, Packer, *Evangelism,* 57-73.

[5] Packer, *Evangelism,* 120.

[6] Peter Comey, "Have you got the right address? Post Modernism & the Gospel" *Grid* (Spring, 1995): 2.

[7] Peace gives some excellent suggestions for what he calls "process evangelism"; see Peace, *Conversion,* 330-345.

[8] Tony Sargent, *The Sacred Anointing: The Preaching of Dr. Martyn Lloyd-Jones* (Wheaton: Crossway, 1994), 76. See also Hulse, *Great Invitation,* 152-57.

[9] John Blanchard, personal letter stating that he has not used the public invitation since adopting a Reformed theological viewpoint over twenty years before, 3 July 1997; Hulse, *Great Invitation,* 9.

[10] Wesley, "Conversations", in *Works,* 8:317.

[11] Lloyd-Jones, *Preaching,* 316-324. See also Fawcett, *Cambuslang,* 5, 54.

[12] Fawcett, *Cambuslang,* 38-39, 104-112.

[13] This includes meetings featuring Billy and Franklin Graham, Bill Newman, Stephen Olford, Tom Rees and Jim Wilson, a mixture of American, Australian and British evangelists.

[14] Richard C. Halverson, "Methods of Personal Evangelism" *Christianity Today* 11: 2 (Oct. 28, 1966): 28. See also Engel, *Christian Communications,* 71, 78.

[15] Engel's scale is one listing of the different stages people pass through on their journey to Christ, Engel, *Christian Communications,* 80.

[16] Engel, *Christian Communications,* 184.

[17] Packer, *Evangelism,* 27.

Chapter 17

Conclusions

The public invitation system seems to have emerged from the eighteenth century practice of counseling inquirers after church services, and from occasional, impromptu public invitations, the first of which appears to have been in America in 1741. It is possible that it first developed into a system in some Separate Baptist churches in the USA in the final quarter of that century, but it is more likely that it became systematized in the first two decades of the nineteenth century through the American camp-meetings, which were operated mainly by the Methodists. Later, Charles Finney, by example and in lecture and book, probably did more than anyone else to establish and popularize the system and to build a rationale for its use.

There were two main devices associated with the public invitation in this period, namely the "mourner's bench" or "anxious seat" and the "altar" (an enclosure with seats). These were usually at the front of the evangelistic setting, and inquirers were expected to move forward to occupy them.

This evangelistic method did not emerge from a social vacuum, but was born in an age of great changes in society, politics and theology.

Its use in the British Isles followed that in America, and the first definite instance of it there was by the American preacher, Lorenzo Dow, at the very end of the eighteenth century. However, two English Methodist ministers may have used it before him, though this is not certain. One of those two certainly used it by 1817. Both of these Methodists were subject to American influence, direct in one case and indirect in the other, so it does not seem that the system developed independently in Britain. The usage in Britain in the first half of the nineteenth century seems to have been mainly by the Methodists. However, it then spread to other denominations mainly through the influence of itinerant evangelists from both America and Britain.

It was first used in Australia in the mid-1830s by the English Methodist, Joseph Orton. Following that it was used almost exclusively by the various branches of Methodism until the advent of numerous overseas evangelists in the late-1870s and 1880s, when it spread to other denominations.

The American D.L. Moody further developed the system by encouraging the use of soloists to supplement his preaching, and the training of lay workers to act as counselors.

The system is still used widely, both in major crusades and in the local church Most major Protestant denominations use it; it being very common in some but rare in others. Its scope has widened over the years. Where originally it was used almost exclusively with regard to conversion, then later for such issues as seeking holiness and the reclamation of backsliders, it is now also used with regard to healing and requests for prayer for a whole range of issues.

There is no clear teaching in the Bible to support the use of this method of evangelism, and such scriptural teaching which speaks against it deals more with its abuses than the system itself. However, the repeated, and seemingly inevitable, confusion of the outward act of responding by moving forward or raising a hand with the inward act of conversion almost gives the act a sacramental standing, and thus comes close to denying the core Protestant teaching of salvation by grace through faith alone.

The counseling methods commonly used with the public invitation system are poor, and at times dangerously misleading, in that it seems to be usually assumed that those who come forward can be fitted neatly into a decision group and dealt with by a particular rehearsed method. People and their needs are far too varied for this type of mechanical approach. In addition counselors are not always well selected, some having little knowledge of a basic theology of conversion and scant awareness of the types of problems likely to be encountered in such ministry. The training and materials given to them are also usually inadequate and to some degree inappropriate.

It has been difficult to assess the statistics produced with regard to the altar call. It is certain that they are frequently exaggerated, but more by misunderstanding than intentional deception. This is partly because many in evangelical circles have a cloudy theology of conversion, which means that many declared to be "converted" probably are not. This exaggeration is also due to the repeated confusion of the outward act of moving forward with the inward act of conversion, so that if ten people go forward after a sermon, it is frequently assumed that ten people have "decided" for Christ and are therefore converted. It is clear that a substantial number who respond to public invitations later show little or no sign of genuine conversion. It is probable that less than 25% of those who respond to this form of evangelism are actually converted on the occasion of that response, and it could be considerably less. Such figures suggest that those engaged in evangelism need to review both their theology and their method.

Select Bibliography

Because of the vast number of sources used in research for this book, it has been decided to include just a select bibliography. Details of all sources quoted are in the endnotes.

Books

Airhart, Phyllis D. *Serving the Present Age: Revivalism, Progressivism, and the Methodist Tradition in Canada.* Montreal & Kingston: McGill-Queen's Uni. Press, 1992.

Asbury, Francis. *The Journal and Letters of Francis Asbury.* 3 vols. ed. Elmer T. Clark *et al.* London: Epworth, 1958.

Bangs, Nathan. *A History of the Methodist Episcopal Church.* 2 vols. NY: Mason & Lane, 1839, 1840.

Baylis, Robert. *My People: The Story of those People Sometimes Called Plymouth Brethren.* Wheaton: Shaw, 1995.

Boles, John B. *The Great Revival, 1787-1805.* Lexington: Uni. Press of Kentucky, 1972.

Bourne, Hugh. *History of the Primitive Methodists.* 2nd. ed. Bemersley: Primitive Methodist, 1835.

Bright, Bill. *A Man Without Equal.* San Bernardino: New Life 2000, 1992.

Brown, Elijah P. *The Real Billy Sunday.* NY: Revell, 1914.

Bruce, Dickson D. Jr. *And They All Sang Hallelujah.* Knoxville: Univ. Tennessee Press, 1974.

Burtner, Robert W. & Robert E. Chiles (eds.) *A Compend of Wesley's Theology.* Nashville: Abingdon, 1954.

Cartwright, Peter. *The Backwoods Preacher: An Autobiography of Peter Cartwright.* London: Hall, Virtue, 1859.

Carwardine, Richard. *Transatlantic Revivalism.* Westport: Greenwood. 1978.

Church, Thomas. *A History of the Primitive Methodists.* 3rd. ed. London: Bemrose, 1869.

Coad, Roy. *A History of the Brethren Movement.* Exeter: Paternoster, 1976.

Colton, Calvin. *History and Character of American Revivals.* London: Westley & Davis, 1832.

Colwell, James. *Illustrated History of Methodism: Australia: 1812-1855, NSW and Polynesia:1856-1902.* Sydney: Brooks, 1904.

Conkin, Paul K. *Cane Ridge: America's Pentecost.* Madison, Uni. Wisconsin Press, 1990.

Cross, Whitney R. *The Burned-Over District.* Ithaca: Cornell UP, 1982.

Dallimore, Arnold. *George Whitefield.* 2 vols. Edinburgh: Banner of Truth, 1970, 1979.

Daniels, W.H. *D.L. Moody and His Work.* London: Hodder, 1875.

Devin, R.I. *History of Grassy Creek Baptist Church.* Raleigh: Edwards, Broughton & Co., 1880; (photocopied from a copy in Southwestern Baptist Theo. Seminary, Fort Worth).

Dorsett, Lyle W. *Billy Sunday and the Redemption of Urban America.* Grand Rapids: Eerdmans, 1991.

Doughty, W.L. *John Wesley: Preacher.* London: Epworth, 1955.

Dow, Lorenzo & Peggy, *History of Cosmopolite, Polemic Writings & The Journey of Life.* Cincinnati: Martin & Robertson, 1849.

Edwards, Jonathan. *Religious Affections.* ed. John E. Smith, Works of Jonathan Edwards; New Haven: Yale UP, 1959, vol. 2.

Edwards, Jonathan. *The Works of Jonathan Edwards.* 2 vols. Edinburgh: Banner of Truth, [1834] 1974.

Engel, James F. *Contemporary Christian Communications: Its Theory and Practice.* Nashville: Nelson, 1979.

Fawcett, Arthur. *The Cambuslang Revival : The Scottish Evangelical Revival of the Eighteenth Century.* Edinburgh: Banner of Truth, 1971.

Finney, Charles G. *Lectures on Revivals of Religion.* NY: Revell, 1868.

Finney, Charles G. *The Memoirs of Charles G Finney.* ed. Garth M. Rosell & Richard A.G. Dupuis, Grand Rapids: Zondervan, 1989.

Frank, Douglas. W. *Less Than Conquerors.* Grand Rapids: Eerdmans, 1986.

Gewehr, Wesley M. *The Great Awakening in Virginia, 1740-1790.* Gloucester: Smith, [1930] 1965.

Gillies, John. *Historical Collections of Accounts of Revival.* Edinburgh: Banner of Truth, 1981.

Goen, C.C. *Revivalism and Separatism in New England, 1740-1800.* New Haven: Yale, 1962.

Griffin, Em. *The Mind Changers.* Wheaton: Tyndale, 1976.

Gundry, Stanley N. *Love Them In.* Chicago: Moody, 1976.

Hambrick-Stowe, Charles E. *Charles G. Finney and the Spirit of American Evangelicalism.* Grand Rapids: Eerdmans, 1996.

Hardman, Keith J. *Charles Grandison Finney, 1792-1875.* Darlington: Evangelical, 1990.

Hardman, Keith J. (ed.) *Issues in American Christianity.* Grand Rapids: Baker, 1993.

Hardman, Keith J. *Seasons of Refreshing: Evangelism and Revivals in America* Grand Rapids: Baker, 1994.

Harris, Thomas, *A Memoir of the Rev. William Bramwell.* London: Kelly, c.1900.

Hulse, Erroll. *The Great Invitation.* Welwyn: Evangelical, 1986.

Hutchinson, Mark. & Edmund Campion. (eds.) *Re-Visioning Australian Colonial Christianity: New Essays in the Australian Christian Experience 1788-1900.* Sydney: CSAC, 1994.

Hutchinson, Mark, Edmund Campion, & Stuart Piggin. (eds.) *Reviving Australia: Essays on the History and Experience of Revival and Revivalism in Australian Christianity.* Sydney: CSAC, 1994.

Johnson, Charles A. *The Frontier Camp Meeting.* 2nd. ed. Dallas: Southern Methodist UP, 1985.

Kendall, H.B. *The Origin and History of the Primitive Methodist Church.* 2 vols. London: Dalton, c.1906.

Kendall, R.T. *Stand Up and Be Counted.* Grand Rapids: Zondervan, 1984.

Kent, John. *Holding the Fort.* London: Epworth, 1978.

Kerr, Hugh T. & John M. Mulder. (eds.) *Famous Conversions.* Grand Rapids: Eerdmans, 1994.

Lambert, Frank. *"Pedlar In Divinity" George Whitefield and the Transatlantic Revivals.* Princeton: Princeton Uni., 1994.

Lloyd-Jones, D. Martyn. *Preaching and Preachers.* London: Hodder, 1971.

Lumpkin, William L. *Baptist Foundations in the South.* Nashville: Broadman, 1961.

MacFarlan, D. *The Revivals of the Eighteenth Century, Particularly at Cambuslang.* Wheaton: Roberts, [1847] 1980.

McLoughlin, William G. *Modern Revivalism: Charles Grandison Finney to Billy Graham.* NY: Ronald Press, 1959.

McLoughlin, William G. *Revivals, Awakenings and Reform.* Chicago: Uni. Chicago, 1978.

M'Nemar, Richard. *The Kentucky Revival; Or, A Short History of the Late Extraordinary Outpouring of the Spirit of God in the Western States of America; With a Brief Account of Shakerism Among the Subjects of the Late Revival in Ohio and Kentucky.* NY: Jenkins, [1807] 1846, (photocopy).

Miller, Perry. *Jonathan Edwards.* New York: Meridian, 1959.

Muller, George. *A Narrative of Some of the Lord's Dealings with George Muller.* London: Nisbet, 1845.

Murray, Iain. *Australian Christian Life From 1788: An Introduction and an Anthology.* Edinburgh: Banner of Truth, 1988.

Murray, Iain. *The Invitation System.* Edinburgh: Banner of Truth, 1967.

Murray, Iain. *Jonathan Edwards.* Edinburgh: Banner of Truth, 1987.

Murray, Iain. *Revival and Revivalism.* Edinburgh: Banner of Truth, 1994.

Nettles, Tom. *By His Grace and for His Glory.* Grand Rapids: Baker, 1986.

Nevin, John W. *The Anxious Bench.* Reading: Miller, [1844] 1892.

Packer, J.I. *Evangelism & the Sovereignty of God.* Downers Grove: IVP, 1961.

Peace, Richard V. *Conversion in the New Testament: Paul and the Twelve* Grand Rapids: Eerdmans, 1999.

Petty, John. *The History of the Primitive Methodist Connexion.* London: R. Davies, 1864.

Pollock, John. *Moody Without Sankey*. London: Hodder, 1963.

Ritson, Joseph. *The Romance of Primitive Methodism*. London: Dalton, 1909.

Robinson, J. Campbell. *The Free Presbyterian Church of Australia*.

Rowdon, Harold H. *The Origins of the Brethren: 1825-1850*. London: Pickering & Inglis, 1967.

Sell, Allan. *The Great Debate*. Worthing: Walter, 1982.

Sellars, Charles. C. *Lorenzo Dow: The Bearer of the Word*. NY: Minton, 1928.

Sigston, James. *Memoir of the Life and Ministry of William Bramwell*. NY: Hunt & Eaton, 1820.

Stout, Harry S. *The Divine Dramatist*. Grand Rapid: Eerdmans, 1991.

Streett, R. Alan. *The Effective Invitation*. Old Tappan: Revell, 1984.

Taylor, W.G. *The Life-Story of an Australian Evangelist*. London: Epworth, 1920.

Telford, John. *The Life of John Wesley*. London: Hodder, 1886.

Templeton, C.B. *Evangelism for Tomorrow*. NY: Harper, 1957; (photocopy of relevant pages).

Thrift, Minton (ed.) *Memoir of the Rev. Jesse Lee with Extracts from his Journals*. NY: Arno, [1823] 1969.

Toon, Peter. *Born Again*. Grand Rapids: Baker, 1987.

Torbet, Robert G. *A History of the Baptists*. Valley Forge: Judson, 1963.

Tracy, Joseph. *The Great Awakening*. Edinburgh: Banner of Truth, [1842] 1976.

Tyerman, Luke. *The Life and Times of the Rev. John Wesley*. 3 vols. London: Hodder, 1880.

Tyler, Bennet. *New England Revivals*. Wheaton: Roberts, [1846] 1980.

Tyler, Bennet & Andrew Bonar. *Asahel Nettleton: Life and Labours*. Edinburgh: Banner of Truth, [1854] 1975.

Vedder, Henry C. *A Short History of the Baptists*. Valley Forge: Judson, 1907.

Watsford, John. *Glorious Gospel Triumphs*. London: Kelly, 1900.

Weisberger, Bernard A. *They Gathered at the River*. Boston: Little, Brown & Co, 1958.

Weremchuk, Max S. *John Nelson Darby*. Neptune: Loizeaux, 1992.

Wesley, John. *The Journal of the Rev. John Wesley*. 8 vols. ed. Nehemiah Curnock, London: Epworth, 1938.

Wesley, John. *The Letters of the Rev. John Wesley*. 8 vols. ed. John Telford, London: Epworth, 1931.

Wesley, John. *The Works of John Wesley*. 14 vols. 3rd. ed. Thomas Jackson, Grand Rapids: Baker, [1831] 1991.

Whitefield, George. *George Whitefield's Journals*. London: Banner of Truth, 1960.

Whitefield, George. *Select Sermons of George Whitefield: With and account of his life by J.C. Ryle*. Edinburgh: Banner of Truth, 1958.

Whitesell, F.D. *65 Ways to Give Evangelistic Invitations*. Grand Rapids: Kregel, 1984.

Williams Colin W. *John Wesley's Theology Today*. London: Epworth, 1960.

Wood, A. Skevington. *The Burning Heart*. Exeter: Paternoster, 1967.

Journals

Airhart, Phyllis D. "'What Must I Do To Be Saved?' Two Paths to Evangelical Conversion in Late Victorian Canada". *Church History* 59: 3 (Sept. 1990): 372-385.

Bennett, David M. "How Arminian was John Wesley?" *Evangelical Quarterly* 72: 3 (July, 2000), 237-248.

Bennett, David M. "John Wesley, George Whitefield and Jonathan Edwards: Their Evangelistic Methods in Relation to the Invitation System". *Lucas* 25 & 26 (1999).

Carwardine, Richard. "The Evangelist System: Charles Roe, Thomas Pulford and the Baptist Home Missionary Society". *Baptist Quarterly* 28: 5 (Jan. 1980): 209-225.

Coleman, Robert E. "The Origin of the Altar Call in American Methodism". *The Asbury Seminarian* (Winter, 1958): 19-26.

Galli, Mark et al. "Camp Meetings and Circuit Riders". *Christian History* 14: 1 (Issue 45).

Gerstner, John H. & Jonathan Neil Gerstner. "Edwardsean Preparation for Salvation". *Westminster Theological Journal* 42 (Fall 1979), 5-71.

Johnson, James E. et al. "Charles Grandison Finney: 19th Century Giant of American Revivalism (1792-1875)". *Christian History* 7: 4 (Issue 20).

Lambert, Frank. "The Great Awakening in Artifact: George Whitefield and the Construction of Intercolonial Revival 1739-1745". *Church History* 60 (June 1991, No 2), 223-246.

Methodist Magazine, The 23-31, 33-34 (1800-1808, 1810-1811); 3rd. Series 10-21 (1831-1842).

More, Robert Jr. "The Historical Origins of 'The Altar Call.'" *Banner of Truth* 75 (Dec.1969): 25-31.

Orton, Trish. "Reverend Joseph Orton: The Wesleyan Methodist Missionary known as 'The John Wesley of Australia'". *Understanding our Christian Heritage* 2 (1989): 90-101.

Piggin, Stuart. "Billy Graham in Australia, 1959: Was it Revival?" *CSAC Working Papers* 1:4. (1992).

Dissertations

McLendon, H.R. "The Mourner's Bench". (D.Th.) Southern Baptist Theological Seminary, 1902.

Olive, H.G. "The Development of the Evangelistic Invitation". (M.Th.) Southern Baptist Theological Seminary, 1958.

Streett, R. Alan. "The Public Invitation: Its Nature, Biblical Validity and Practicability". (Ph.D.) California Graduate School of Theology, 1982.

Thompson, W.O. Jr. "The Public Invitation as a Method of Evangelism: Its Origin and Development". (Ph.D.) Southwestern Baptist Theological Seminary, 1979.

Miscellaneous Documents

Counselor reports for Festival '96 with Franklin Graham.
Summary of Attendance and Enquirers for Festival '96 with Franklin Graham:
   Brisbane. (Brisbane: Festival '96 Office).

Counseling and Follow Up Aids

Christian Life and Witness Course. Minneapolis: Billy Graham Evangelistic
   Assoc., 1995.
Christian Life and Witness Course Training Manual. Sydney: St Matthias
   Press, 1994.
Commitment Counseling Manual. Nashville: Southern Baptist, 1985.
Four Spiritual Laws. Campus Crusade for Christ, 1965.
Guide to Life. Australian Baptist Publ. House, 1973.
Just for Starters. Kingsford: St Matthias Press, 1992.
My Commitment. Minneapolis: Billy Graham Evangelistic Assoc., 1995.
Personal Commitment Guide. Atlanta: Home Mission Board SBC, 1985.
Steps to Peace with God. Minneapolis: Billy Graham Evangelistic Assoc.
2 Ways to Live. Sydney: AIO, 1989.

INDEX

Graham, Billy xiii, 163, 168, 174-75, 180, 193, 195, 197, 198, 209-210, 217, 219, 220, 223-24

Graham, Franklin 163, 168-174, 186, 202, 220

Granade, J.A. 40

Great Awakening, The xv, 30-36, 57

Green, Michael 203

Grenfell, W.T. 187

Griffin, Em 235

Groves, A.N. 137

Guinness, Grattan 157

Gundry, Stanley 140

Hall, David 87

Hallock, Jeremiah 44

Halverson, Richard C. 243

Hambrick-Stowe, Charles 103

Hammand, E.P. 197

Hardman, Keith 105

Harkey, Simeon 57, 187

Harper, Miles 39, 70

Harris, Howell 58

Hatch, Nathan 57

Haw, James 40-41

Hawley, Ian 64, 113, 210, 219

Heath, William 70-71, 110-11

Hempstead, Joshua 32

Hendricks, William 233

Hendriksen, William 210-11

Henry, Parson 34

Hinton, John Howard 96

Hodge, Charles 208

Hodge, William 68

Hooper, Johnson J. xv

Hulse, Erroll 109, 180, 184, 186 187, 198, 220, 223, 230, 236

Hunt, Aaron 71

Hunt, Arnold 155, 157

Huntingtom, Catherine 107

James, John Angel 126

Jarratt, Deveraux 37-38

Jefferson, Thomas 56-57

Jensen, Philip 195, 197

Jenson, Robert W. 17, 18

Johnson, Charles 65, 66, 69, 74-75, 79

Johnson, J.E. 56, 111

Johnson, Richard 149

Keillor, Steven 59, 73

Kendall, H.B. 75

Kendall, R.T. 179, 181, 184, 185-86, 187

Kent, John 120, 122

Key, Robert 121

Kirk, Edward 124

Kirk, John 126

Knapp, Joseph 186

Knox, John 73

Lambert, Frank 58

Lee, Jesse 38-40, 63

Leigh, Samuel 149-150

Leland, John 57, 91

Livingstone, John 242

Lloyd-Jones, D. Martyn 17-18, 187, 202, 207, 232, 242

Lord's Supper, the 45-46, 65, 73, 75, 155

Lumpkin, William 35-36

Luther, Martin 207

Lutheran Church 164, 165-68

Lyman, Elijah 44

MacArthur, John, Jr. 180, 195, 223

McBeth, Leon 36, 112

M'Cullough, William 242

McDougall, Leanne 171

McGee, John 65, 68

McGee, William 65, 68

McIlvaine, Charles 196.

McLendon, H.R. 37, 40

McLoughlin, William 92, 139

M'Nemar, Richard 68, 74, 96

Marsden, Joshua 121

Marshall, Colin 196

Marshall, I. Howard 183, 204

Marshall, Robert 95

Matheson, James 229

Mavor, John 168, 174

Mead, A.P. 79

Mead, S.E. 92